LEGENDARY LOCALS

OF

CHATTANOOGA

TENNESSEE

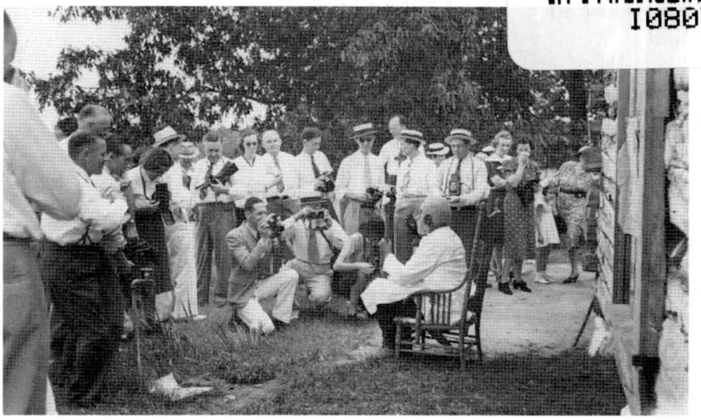

Page 1: See page 30 for more information about this image. (Courtesy Chattanooga History Center.)

LEGENDARY LOCALS

OF

CHATTANOOGA

TENNESSEE

WILLIAM F. HULL

LEGENDARY LOCALS

ISBN 978-1-4671-0028-1

Legendary Locals is an imprint of Arcadia Publishing
Charleston, South Carolina

Printed in the United States of America

Library of Congress Control Number: 2012934810

For all general information, please contact Arcadia Publishing:
Telephone 843-853-2070
Fax 843-853-0044
E-mail sales@arcadiapublishing.com
For customer service and orders:
Toll-Free 1-888-313-2665

Visit us on the Internet at www.arcadiapublishing.com

On the Cover: From left to right:
(TOP ROW) Adolph Ochs, publisher (Chattanooga Public Library, see page 80), Anna Safely Houston, collector (Chattanooga Public Library, see page 118), Charles Coolidge, soldier (Chattanooga Public Library, see page 90), Emma Bell Miles, writer (University of Chattanooga at Tennessee/Special Collections, see page 113), Estes Kefauver, US congressman and senator (Author's collection, see page 84).
(MIDDLE ROW) John Franklin, city commissioner (Chattanooga Public Library, see page 89), John Ross, Cherokee leader (Chattanooga Public Library, see page 10), Bessie Smith, blues singer (Chattanooga Public Library, see page 114), Jack Lupton, businessman and entrepreneur (Chattanooga Public Library, see page 39), Reggie White, professional football player (University of Tennessee, see page 110).
(BOTTOM ROW) Scrappy Moore, football coach (University of Chattanooga at Tennessee, Special Collections, see page 105), Roland Hayes, singer (University of Chattanooga at Tennessee, Special Collections, see page 112), Roland Carter, composer (Courtesy Dr. Roland Carter, see page 122), Ruth Holmberg, publisher (Ruth Holmberg, see page 81), Luther Masingill, radio personality (Chattanooga Public Library, see page 120).

CONTENTS

ACKNOWLEDGMENTS

I wish to thank the following individuals for their assistance: Rich Bailey, Rosalie Jean Basten, Karen P. Brown, Marie Bourassa, Steve Cox, Jennifer Crutchfield, Billy Faires, Barbara Kennedy, Tracy Knauss, Barry Parker, Jim Reece, Rachel Schulson, and Ellen Simak.

INTRODUCTION

From its early days, Chattanooga was a river town. It first took shape by the river, thrived on trade from the river, and today, it has returned to the river. That water was the dividing line between the Cherokee Nation and the European Americans looking for more land. The Cherokee had settled in small towns up and down the Tennessee waterways probably in the 1600s. This land belonged to them, and to a certain extent, they allowed some white settlers to live in the Chattanooga valley with them. By 1800, the two cultures certainly had frequent contact, as represented by the great leader of the Cherokee, John Ross, who was only one-eighth Cherokee but who chose his native relatives as his own. Ross was a man of many talents—both a negotiator and a savvy merchant—the leader of the Cherokee, who led the clans westward under federal armed guard on the Trail of Tears in 1838, the result of the Indian Removal Act.

With the valley land wide open, new occupants like John Long gathered to choose a name for the city in the "Little Log Cabin" and hired a surveyor to establish a grid of streets. The town of Chattanooga was born, recognized by the state of Tennessee, and looking for business. In December 1849, the railroad arrived near the present-day Read House, the end of the line of the Western and Atlantic Railroad that had taken years to make its way from Atlanta. By the time of the Civil War, Chattanooga was a major rail center so much so that the Union army deemed it a critical objective to conquer. The town of about 2,500 people found itself in the crosshairs of the great conflict when, in 1863, Union soldiers marching south diverted to Chickamauga, south of town, and in a bloody confrontation, were routed by the Confederate army. Seeking shelter in Chattanooga, they occupied the town, only to find themselves surrounded by tens of thousands of Southern troops on the high ground. With Ulysses S. Grant in command, the army engineers put up buildings for commissaries and supplies, essentially improving the town and laying the foundation for the future. Grant and William T. Sherman laid out a strategy to force their way out of Chattanooga, and in three days, in November 1863, they decisively defeated Braxton Bragg's troops, setting the stage for the final march to Georgia and the sundering of the South. As the Confederates faded into Georgia, the town became a giant supply depot for the Union, and citizens like T. Hooke McCallie lived cautiously in an armed camp.

Like many parts of the Southland, Chattanooga took a full generation to recover. By the 1880s, its iron manufacturing had grown substantially, led by carpetbaggers, many of whom had seen the city in a blue uniform. And African Americans, many of whom came to the city as refugees during the war, became business owners and office holders. Citizens escaping the summer heat—and the random threat of disease—sought higher ground on Lookout Mountain, and soon, a rail line ran up its slopes hourly. In 1882, a line of 26 electric lights was switched on, lighting up the night on Market Street. Ten years later, the town ferry became a thing of the past when a steel span, the Walnut Street Bridge, crossed the river and opened up the north side of the river for homes and schools. By 1900, the "Dynamo of Dixie" was taking shape. With iron casting, steel making, glass production, and rail shipping burgeoning, the town had a distinct working-class aura. What farming existed in the area at large was really done on a smaller scale. The town had a bona fide newspaper in the *Chattanooga Times*, run by the enterprising Adolph Ochs, who would go on to purchase the *New York Times*. And the negotiating skill of Benjamin Franklin Thomas brought the city one of the great, early American franchise success stories when the Chattanooga Coca-Cola Bottling Company got under way in 1899.

In the early 20th century, the Dixie Highway came through Chattanooga, weaving its way around the river. Charles James constructed a 13-mile trolley line up Signal Mountain to his hotel in a bid to rival the prestige of old Lookout. The presence of the old South lingered, and the memories of the "Recent Unpleasantness" were preserved in the first national battlefield, the Chickamauga and Chattanooga National Military Park, dedicated in 1895. Old Southern sympathies arose as well, affecting African Americans with a slow constriction of their rights and opportunities, culminating in a 1905 black boycott of the bus system when segregated seating was enforced. A bustling downtown demanded a new bridge, the John

Ross Bridge, at the steep cost of $1 million in 1917. And a tasty little marshmallow sandwich called the Moon Pie, favored by workers for a lunch box treat, got its start the same year.

Downtown began to have an urban flare by the 1920s. The city's first skyscraper, the James Building, built in 1906, was joined by the Maclellan Building on the same block and the beautiful Tivoli Theater in 1921, with its Italianate flourishes. For summertime entertainment, Lake Winnepesaukah opened south of town in 1925 with boat rides, bumper cars, games, and plenty of fun in the sun. Professional baseball came to town in the person of Joe Engel, known as the "Barnum of the Bushes" for his clever promotions and the classic baseball stadium he built that bears his name. Pastimes such as these took some of the onus away from the Great Depression, a particularly hard time in the southern mountain regions. When President Roosevelt proposed the Chickamauga Dam, many local men received good-paying, government jobs during the four years that saw the concrete rise over the troublesome Tennessee River. Nonetheless, resentments remained in many families who were moved off their lands by the great federal project.

When World War II broke out, Chattanooga mobilized its industry and its manpower. Men like Charles Coolidge distinguished themselves in battle, and the home front effort was stalwart as well. The years that followed offered expanded opportunities. In 1948, Dupont opened an enormous operation near the Chickamauga Dam spinning out reams of a new fabric, nylon, and employing hundreds of workers around the clock. The prosperity that was sweeping America in the 1950s touched Chattanooga, and the idea of a brand-new automobile or a modern ranch house became a reality for many, though much of the town in southern Appalachia still faced the reality of poverty. The town's new mayor, P.R. Olgiati, made use of a recent state law that made annexation simple and expanded the city limits quickly. Eisenhower's dream of a national interstate highway system plowed through downtown, consuming an inordinate amount of minority housing. The historic homes on Cameron Hill were demolished; over 100 feet came off the top of the rise simply to serve as fill dirt for the new highway.

As the decade wore on, racial changes were in the works. That tireless Atlanta Civil Rights voice Ralph Abernathy came to town in 1956 and was loudly applauded when he told his audience that "it's great to be arrested." By the early 1960s sit-ins by young African Americans—especially high school students—brought the message home that Chattanooga had to change. The demonstrations were tense but brief, and desegregation in schools and public places was surprisingly quick and peaceful. But if the city was able to come to a racial reconciliation of sorts, there was no way to escape the serious pollution of a century of smokestacks. One night in 1969, on the evening news, respected broadcaster Walter Cronkite termed Chattanooga "the dirtiest city in America," much to the Scenic City's deep embarrassment. Smoggy air inversions, befouled water, and unpleasant urban odors were all too common; downtown businessmen often came home at lunchtime to change into a clean, white shirt because of the brown atmosphere. But Chattanooga responded to the problem, and in a few short years, enforced stricter standards of air quality and laid the groundwork for the green-consciousness that would flourish at the end of the century.

Unfortunately, the next 20 years were tough ones. Local industry shrunk, and jobs disappeared. But in the early 1980s, a few citizens began to organize as Chattanooga Venture and envision what the city could become in 20 years. Citizen-based and city-backed, local leaders—some elected and some selected, like Mai Bell Hurley, Gene Roberts, Rick Montague, and many others—held endless meetings, mulling over obstacles, gathering ideas, and searching for a new vision for their town. Out of this process came a series of proposals for a rebuilding of Chattanooga, centered around the riverfront and emphasizing the valley's natural heritage. The Tennessee Aquarium, the first manifestation of this long process, opened in 1992 to an enthusiastic welcome. Just blocks to the east, the work of the Portera family changed a sliver of a turn-of-the-century neighborhood into a welcoming hilltop of delicious dining and tasteful art called the Bluffview Art District. The Walnut Street Bridge reopened and reawakened a sense of community. Beneath the bridge, Coolidge Park came to life in old Hill City in 1999. Six years later, the 21st Century Waterfront Project breathed more life into the river town, adding a unique, glowing pedestrian pier and a captivating passageway that honors the Native American history of Chattanooga. City leaders were able to leverage the city's industrial past and talent by luring a green-conscious, state-of-the-art manufacturing facility when the auto giant Volkswagen chose Chattanooga for its new North American production site. Without a doubt, a new day has dawned in Chattanooga, and the vision of a renewed city has blossomed.

CHAPTER ONE

Founders

Chattanooga, it may be said, had two beginnings. The first act belonged to the Cherokee people, who arrived in the 1600s and who, by the time America had become a nation, were accustomed to scattered Europeans living among them. Some, like Daniel Ross, who lived at the base of Lookout Mountain, intermarried with a family of Scottish descent, the McDonalds. In 1816, his son John Ross built a warehouse and trading post on the banks of the Tennessee River, four miles north of his father's farm. It was called Ross's Landing, and it is still known as that today. Billy Long, it is written, managed the site, as part of the Cherokee Nation. That spot was the starting point for the young village. Across the river, a slow stream of farmers set up shop and built farms in US Territory. Some Native Americans, like Dragging Canoe, the rebel Cherokee, fought the encroachment on their native soil. But men like Ross and Indian agent Jonathan Return Meigs worked together as traders; thus, traffic was common between the two peoples.

But in 1838, the world turned upside down for the Cherokee. Pres. Andrew Jackson insisted the Cherokee leave their homeland for the barrens of the west, the Oklahoma Territory. And when they left on the Trail of Tears—some overland to the west, some walking around Moccasin Bend—the second act began. Newcomers from the mountain south like Alan Kennedy and John Long built stores and taverns and had the land surveyed, dividing it into roads with American names from the wilderness like Oak, Cherry, and Walnut Streets. They named the new village Chattanooga, which is a variation on a Cherokee word spelled *Chatanuge* that appeared on an early map and that possibly meant "lookout." By 1850, the glory of the age, the railroad, had reached the town from its beginnings at the Zero Mile Post in the small Georgia town of Atlanta. Robert Craven built a coke furnace on the bluff next to Ross's landing, incorporating a technology few in the South had seen, which created intense heat for iron manufacture. Others like James Whiteside bought real estate and swung deals in that free-for-all manner of frontier capitalism. With the river trade flourishing and families putting down roots, Chattanooga slowly grew into a frontier town of over two thousand during this generation. But the 1860s would change all that, as "war so terrible" bore down on the muddy river town, and a different chapter would be written in the coming days.

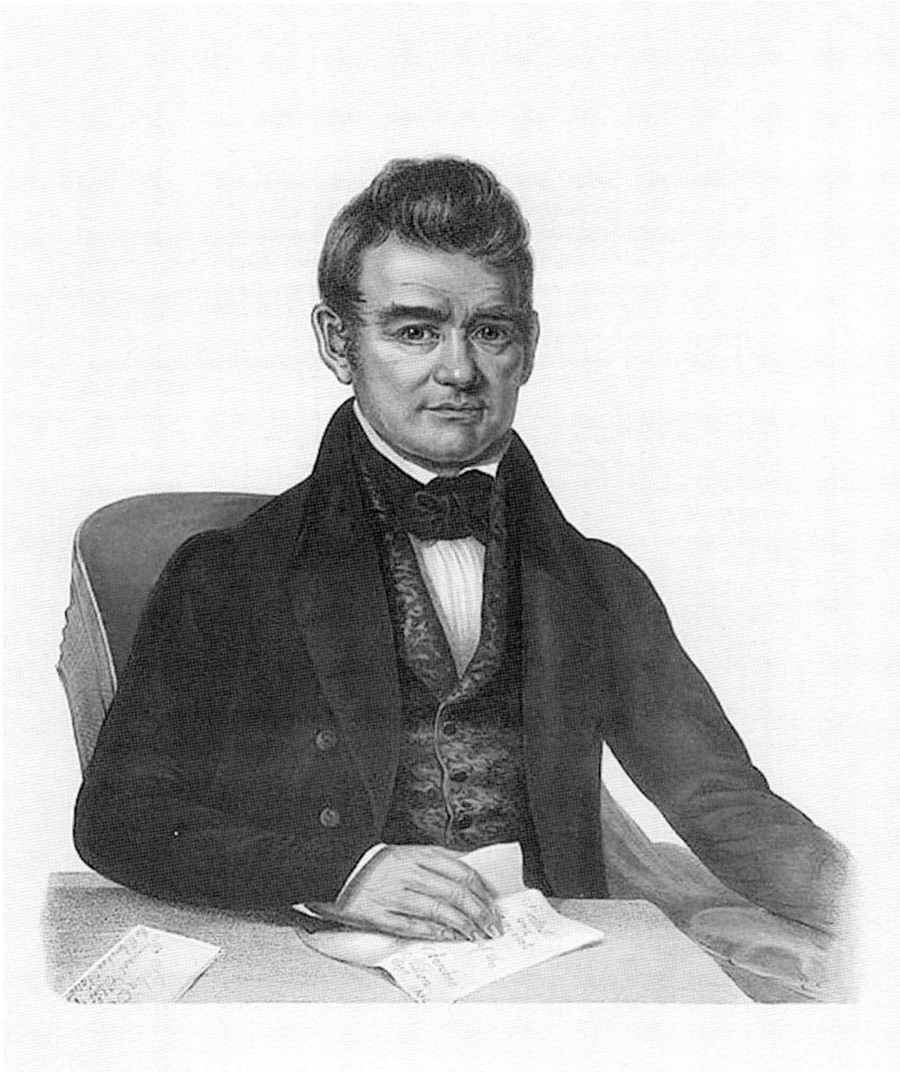

John Ross
Forty years after the United States declared independence, the Cherokee John Ross built a warehouse and landing on the Tennessee River near the present-day Tennessee Aquarium. Called Ross's Landing by travelers and residents alike, it is considered the founding spot, the beginning of Chattanooga. It served as a ferry, a dock for long boats on the river, and a central place for business in this small hamlet in 1816. Ross was the principal chief of the Cherokee Nation and a member of the Bird Clan, and the land where he built belonged to the Cherokee Nation. Across the river, in modern-day North Chattanooga, stood US territory. Ross, a vital figure in 19th-century American history, was born four miles down river in the shadow of Lookout Mountain at the farm of his father, Daniel Ross. A bilingual speaker, who was actually more adept at English than Cherokee, Ross was given a sound education and became the liaison between the American government and his own people as they struggled to hold on to their native lands. His attempts at preserving the Cherokee people against overwhelming difficulty eventually failed, resulting in the removal of the tribes to Oklahoma from Chattanooga on the Trail of Tears. Nevertheless, his tenure as chief from 1828 to 1866 reflects the trust and belief in him by the Cherokee people and their sovereign nation that still survives today. (Courtesy Chattanooga Public Library.)

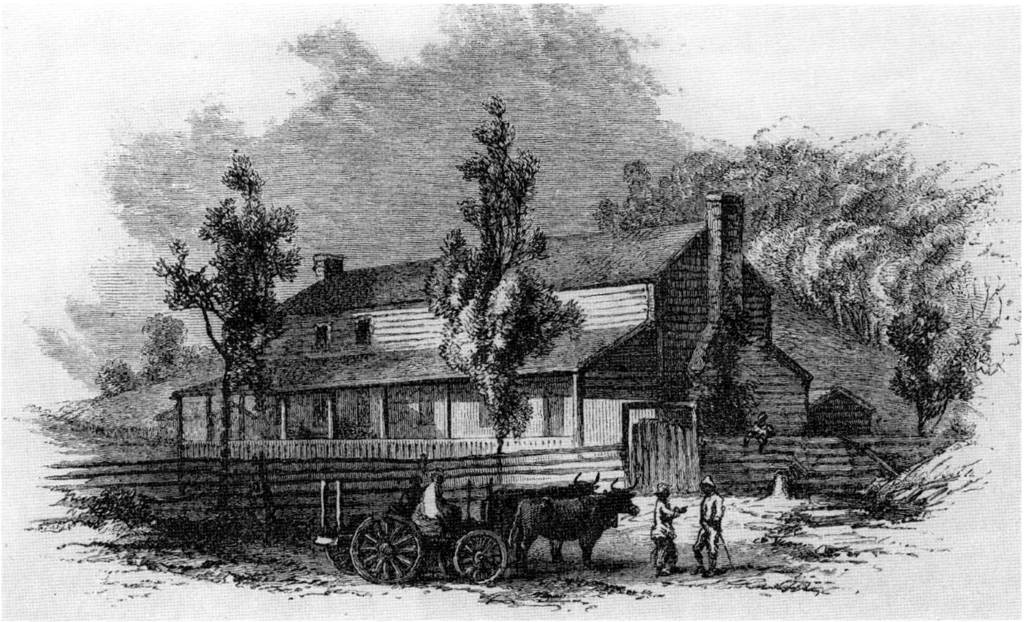

John Ross Home
Built in 1797, the John Ross Home was originally that of his grandfather John McDonald, a Scottish trader who was ubiquitous in the Chattanooga area. Born in Inverness in 1747, McDonald came into the United States through Charleston, South Carolina, and made his way into the Cherokee nation via Fort Loudon, where he made his living as a trader, becoming adept as a negotiator with the English, French, and Native Americans. His only daughter, Molly, married Daniel Ross, also a Scotsman, whom the family saved from hostile Indians; their son John Ross was born in 1790 and lived here after his mother died. Situated on the road from Chattanooga, which goes south to Georgia through the Rossville Gap, the home was built by John McDonald and is a two-story, "plain-style" plantation house, indicative of a family of some wealth. (Courtesy Chattanooga Public Library.)

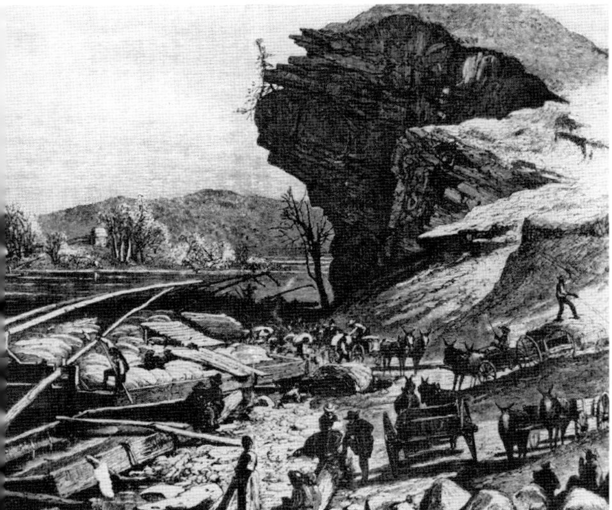

Ross's Landing
Ross's Landing is the founding site of Chattanooga, a usable slope to ground boats traveling on the river. This Harper's engraving depicts the flurry of activity that took place once the site was established. In 1816, Ross built a warehouse and a trading store manned with his brother, Lewis. Ross, a man with many irons in the fire, spent some time here but eventually moved into Georgia and built a plantation. Ironically, it would be in this vicinity where he would spend his final months in Tennessee under guard with his fellow Cherokee before being forcibly deported to the Oklahoma Territory forever. (Courtesy Chattanooga Public Library.)

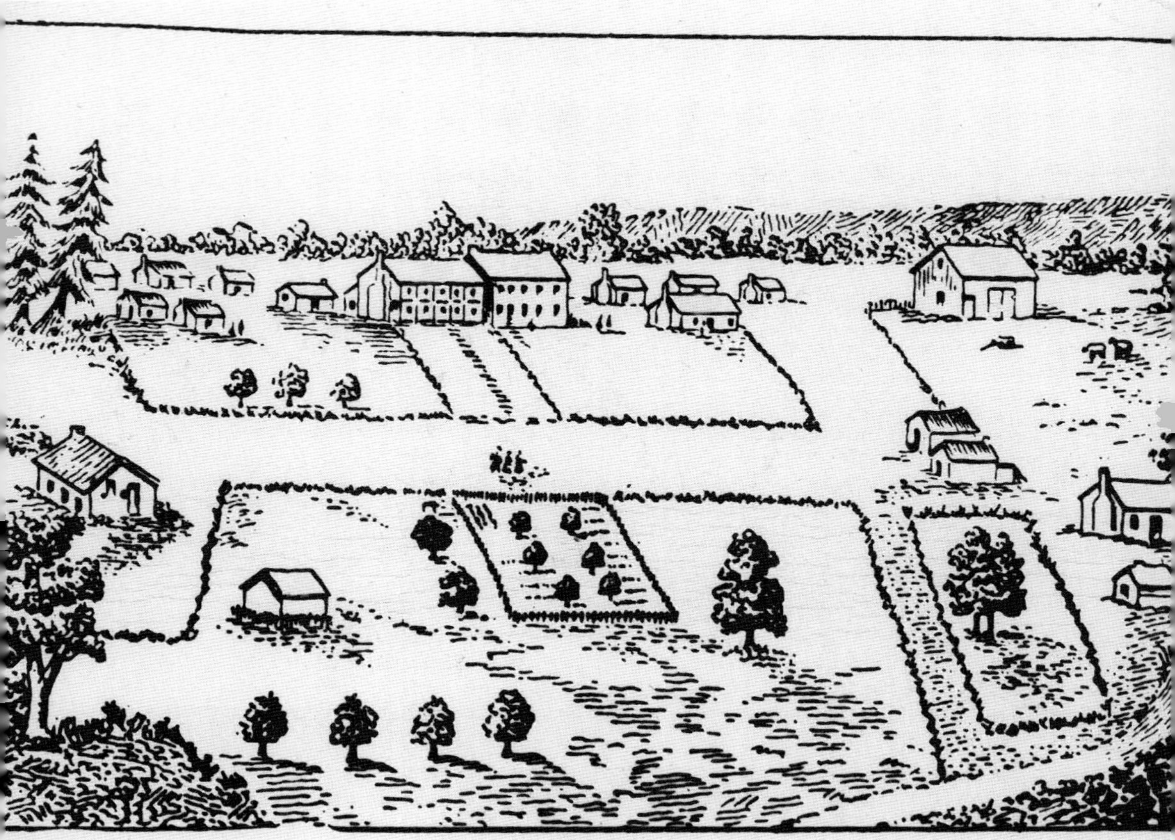

THE STATION AT BRAINERD MISSION
(From a sketch by Thomas E. Paine in 1821)

Brainerd Mission

David Brainerd was a legend in the 1700s for the work he had done bringing the Christian message to Native Americans in New York and New Jersey. Even though he had been expelled from religious studies at Yale University for telling a professor he had "no more grace than a chair," he found supporters for his mission work and overcame physical hardships and major personal trauma such as depression and tuberculosis. The Brainerd Mission established in his name stood nine miles east of Ross's Landing and was a gathering of white clergy, local Cherokee, and some enslaved African Americans. The site was considered important enough that Pres. James Monroe spent the night of May 27, 1819. The mission was closed when the Cherokee left on the Trail of Tears in 1838. (Courtesy Chattanooga Public Library.)

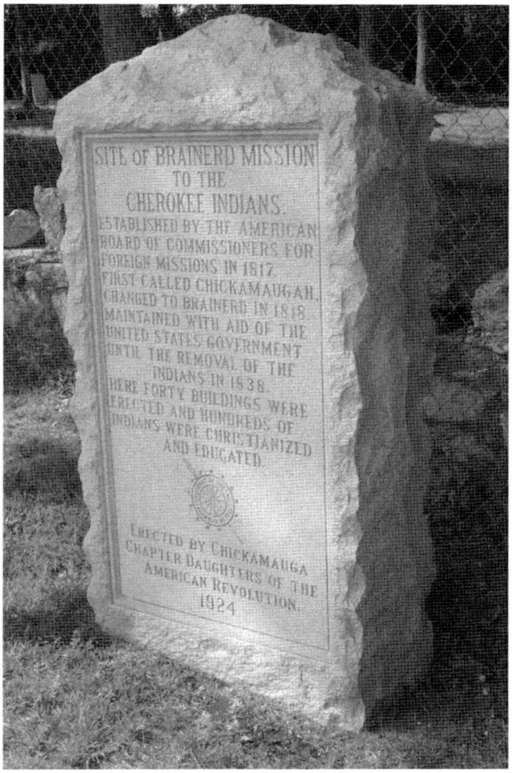

Brainerd Monument
This monument was dedicated by the Chattanooga chapter of the Daughters of the American Revolution (DAR), whose local chapter owns and cares for the land. Though commercial development in the area was not a reality until after World War II, this local history group began taking steps to protect the original site and today, have seen that it is on the Trail of Tears route as designated by the National Park Service. In a classic juxtaposition of history and commerce, the first shopping mall was built next to the site in the 1960s and remains there today. Some large, Southern red oaks thought to date to the 1830s still remain standing. (Author's collection.)

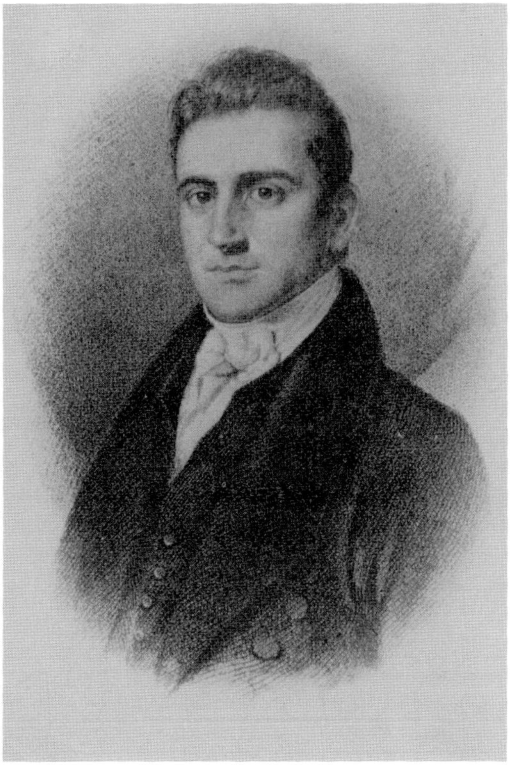

Elias Cornelius
Elias Cornelius was a Yale graduate and a missionary in the Northeast primarily but also traveled in the South. Appointed by the American Board of Commissioners for Foreign Missions, who chartered the Brainerd Mission, his description of Lookout Mountain is one of the earliest written documents by an American in Chattanooga. He ministered to the Cherokee and traveled as far south as Georgia where he encountered and described the Etowah Mounds. (Courtesy Chattanooga History Center.)

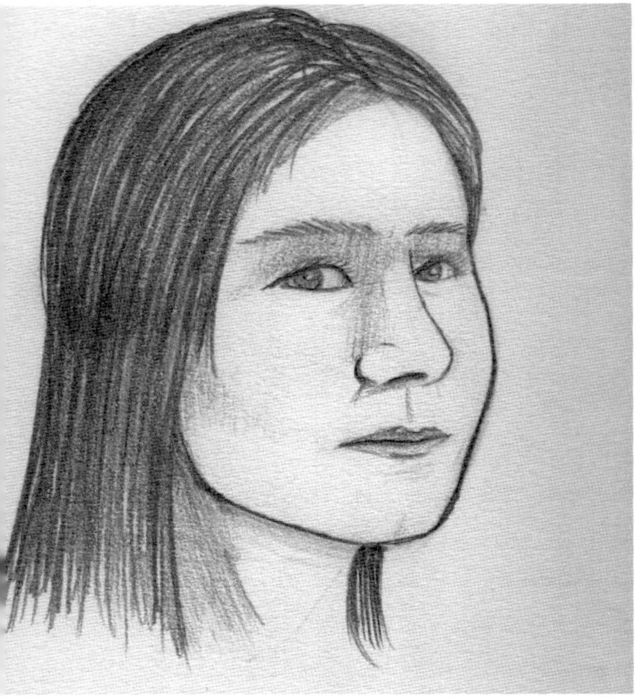

Nancy Ward

Nancy Ward ("Nanyehi" in Cherokee) was a familiar name to Native Americans in the Chattanooga Valley. She was regarded as a "Beloved Woman," one who was respected for her political power. Ward was a skilled negotiator and a believer in peace between the whites and Indians. White farmers were grateful to her for a warning she once provided of an impending attack by Dragging Canoe. On the other hand, Ward was firmly against the repeated sales of Cherokee lands to the settlers. Nevertheless, her efforts to help the Cherokee adapt to the European culture of farming were successful. (Courtesy Andrew B. Hull.)

Dragging Canoe

To modern ears, the name Dragging Canoe may imply someone who is slow or reticent, but to the people of East Tennessee, the name meant independence and ferocity. Tired of seeing vast portions of land disappear in treaties, Dragging Canoe, a warrior, became the iron-willed chief of a rebellious group of Cherokees that became known as the Chickamaugas (or Lower Cherokees). Since he fought on the side of the British, he was shown no mercy by the victorious American colonists when it came time to expand the nation. By the time America became a nation, the Chickamaugas were living around Chickamauga Creek with Dragging Canoe as their chief from 1777 until 1792. "Whole Indian Nations have melted away like snowballs in the sun before the white man's advance" he said in a speech, and the truth of his words was confirmed when in 1782, all their towns were destroyed by US troops. The tribe moved farther down the Tennessee River to new settlements where they continued to battle and confront settlers in the region. Although the Native Americans were no match for the oncoming hordes, he was a fearless spirit to the end when he died in March 1792, apparently of natural causes, during an all night celebration of a new alliance with the Choctaw. (Courtesy Andrew B. Hull.)

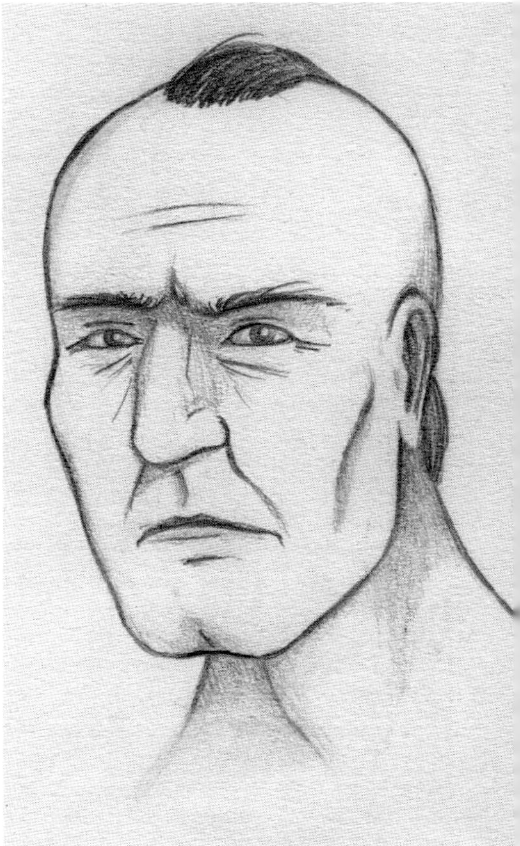

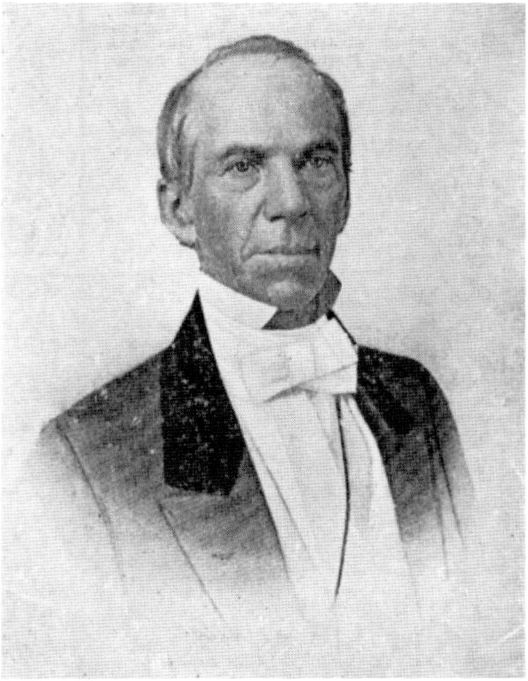

James Whiteside
In small frontier communities, there was often one person who, through wit and work, became a kingpin in his town. In Chattanooga, Col. James Whiteside was without a doubt that person. A member of the state legislature by the age of 24, he brought his family to Ross's Landing as soon as the Cherokee removal was complete and began buying property. He put money into the young railroads that were moving toward town and became president of an iron manufacturing company. For practical purposes, he purchased all of Lookout Mountain in Tennessee and hired crews to cut a road (the Whiteside Turnpike) up its heavily wooded slopes in 1852, only two years after the Western and Atlantic Railroad came to town. With a fine mansion in town, he also constructed a summer home on the mountain and built the Lookout Mountain Hotel. He died at the beginning of the war in 1861. (Courtesy Chattanooga Public Library.)

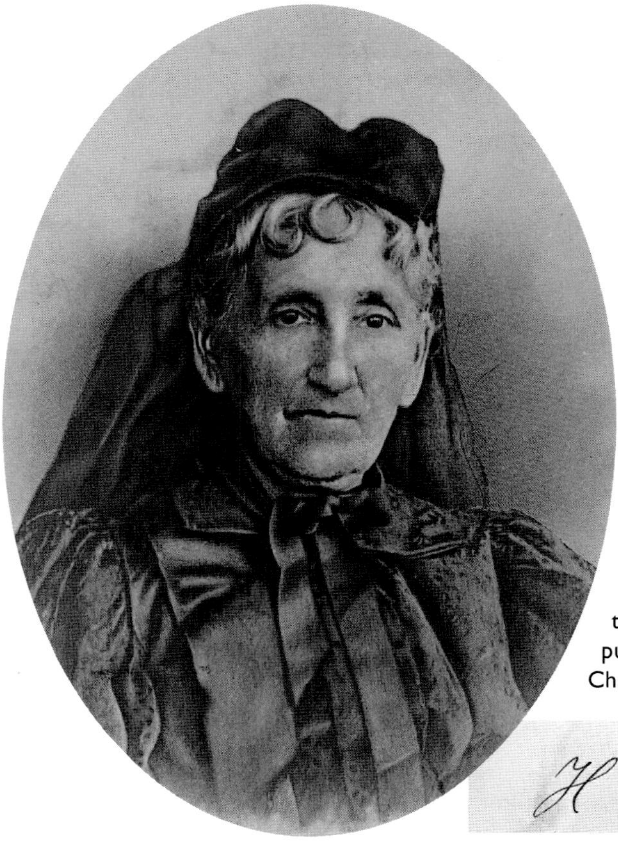

Harriet Whiteside
Harriet Whiteside was no shrinking violet. As the war began in 1861, her husband, James, died. When Chattanooga was captured, she was placed in military detention in Indiana. But she regained her holdings after the war and made anyone who came up Lookout Mountain pay a toll to visit and enjoy the view. Whiteside fought the new rail line up the mountain near her land by successfully backing the construction of another line that put the first out of business. (Courtesy Chattanooga Public Library.)

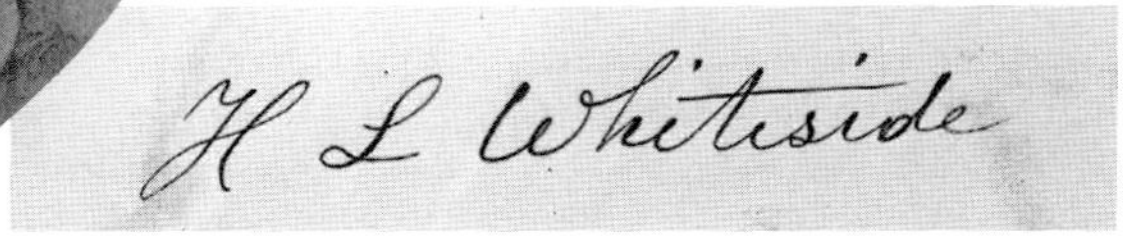

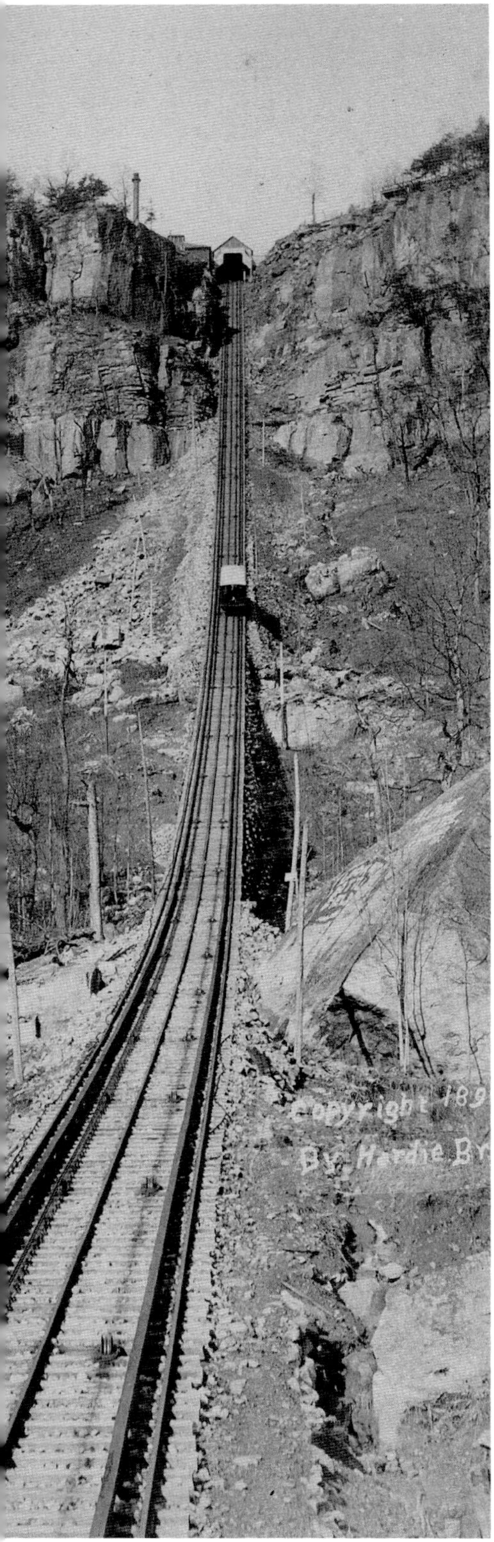

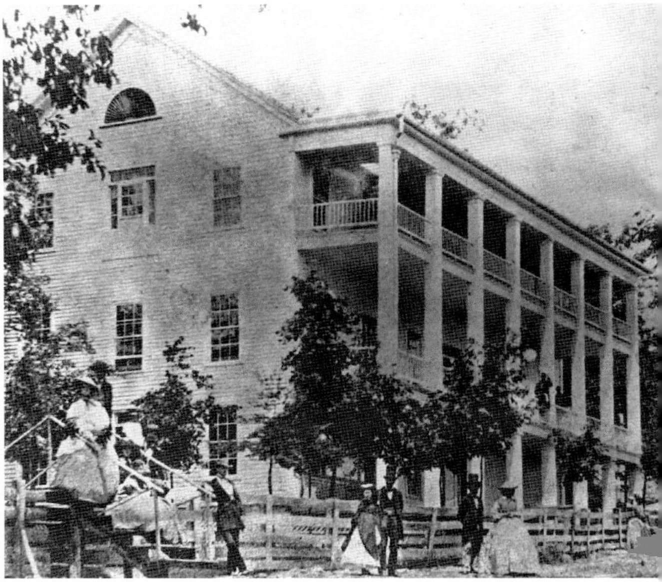

Lookout Mountain Hotel
The Lookout Mountain Hotel was constructed by Colonel Whiteside in 1857 in the community of Summertown. Situated near his turnpike, it featured a spring and some smaller cottages nearby and was a summer retreat for the well-to-do. Both armies used it during the war; it burned to the ground at the end of the conflict. (Courtesy Chattanooga Public Library.)

Lookout Mountain Incline
A true local landmark, the Lookout Mountain Incline is the 100th National Historic Mechanical Engineering Landmark to be so designated, mainly because of the innovative work of Josephus Conn Guild Sr. A graduate of Vanderbilt University, he is still remembered for the Hales Bar Dam that he designed and built on the Tennessee River, one of the first hydroelectrics of its time. Similarly, he also constructed numerous city water and sewer systems in Dixie. Completed in 1895, it has always shuttled tourists and visitors—and a number of residents—up and down the eastern slope. George Duncan, an experienced railroad builder, worked with Guild in the five months it took to construct the line, which reaches a ferociously steep angle of 72.7 degrees at its zenith. (Courtesy Chattanooga Public Library.)

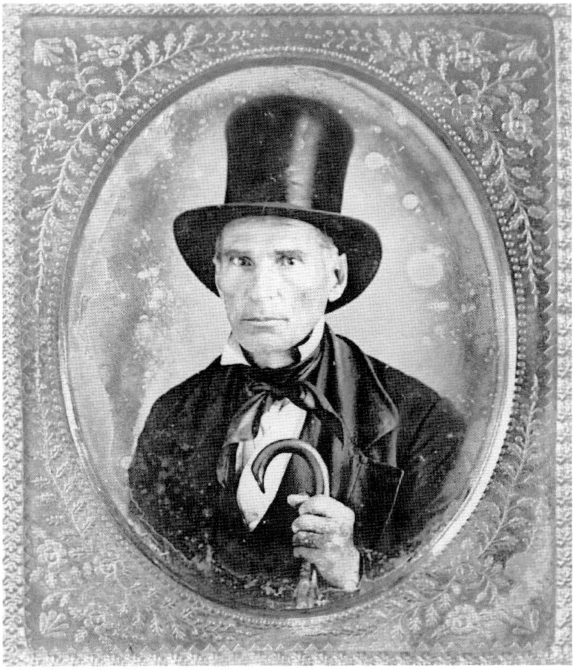

Allen Kennedy
Allen Kennedy was an eager early settler in Chattanooga, coming into the town as soon as it was possible. He built the first tavern, which an English visitor described as "tolerably clean;" later, he built the Kennedy Hotel on Market Street. Before the Cherokee had been removed, he had organized a group to bring the railroad to town. As a commissioner, he was instrumental in making certain that property rights were guaranteed to the new settlers. (Courtesy Chattanooga Public Library.)

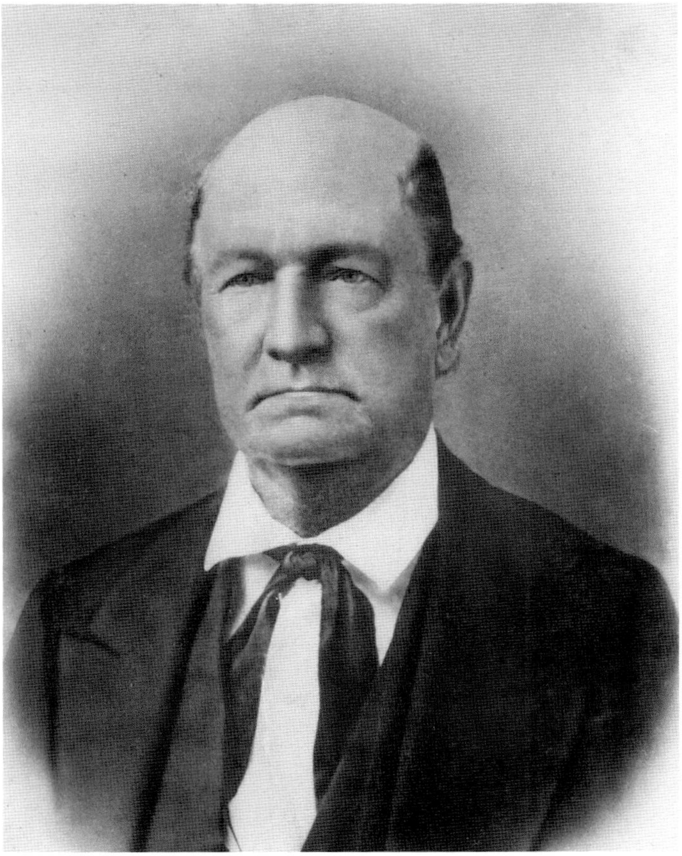

John Long
Once a post office was established in his store, John P. Long became the new town's postmaster. During the early 1800s, a postal carrier riding on a horse from Chattanooga to Washington, DC, had a journey of approximately 10 days. Long is credited as the man who suggested the name of Chattanooga after a spirited debate and gathered much of the early history of the settlement. (Courtesy Chattanooga Public Library.)

Craven's Bluff Furnace

Robert Craven built this 40-foot-high furnace on the banks of the Tennessee River and fueled it with coke—an unusual, forward-looking, and dangerous practice—at a time when charcoal was the standard means to make pig iron. Craven, a practiced ironmaster, had built forges and foundries for 20 years before putting this one in operation in 1856. The first of its kind in the Deep South, Craven's blast furnace set the tone for Chattanooga's long affiliation with heavy industry. With the approach of the enemy, parts of the furnace where sent downstream to Alabama so the Union army could not make use of it. (Courtesy Chattanooga Public Library.)

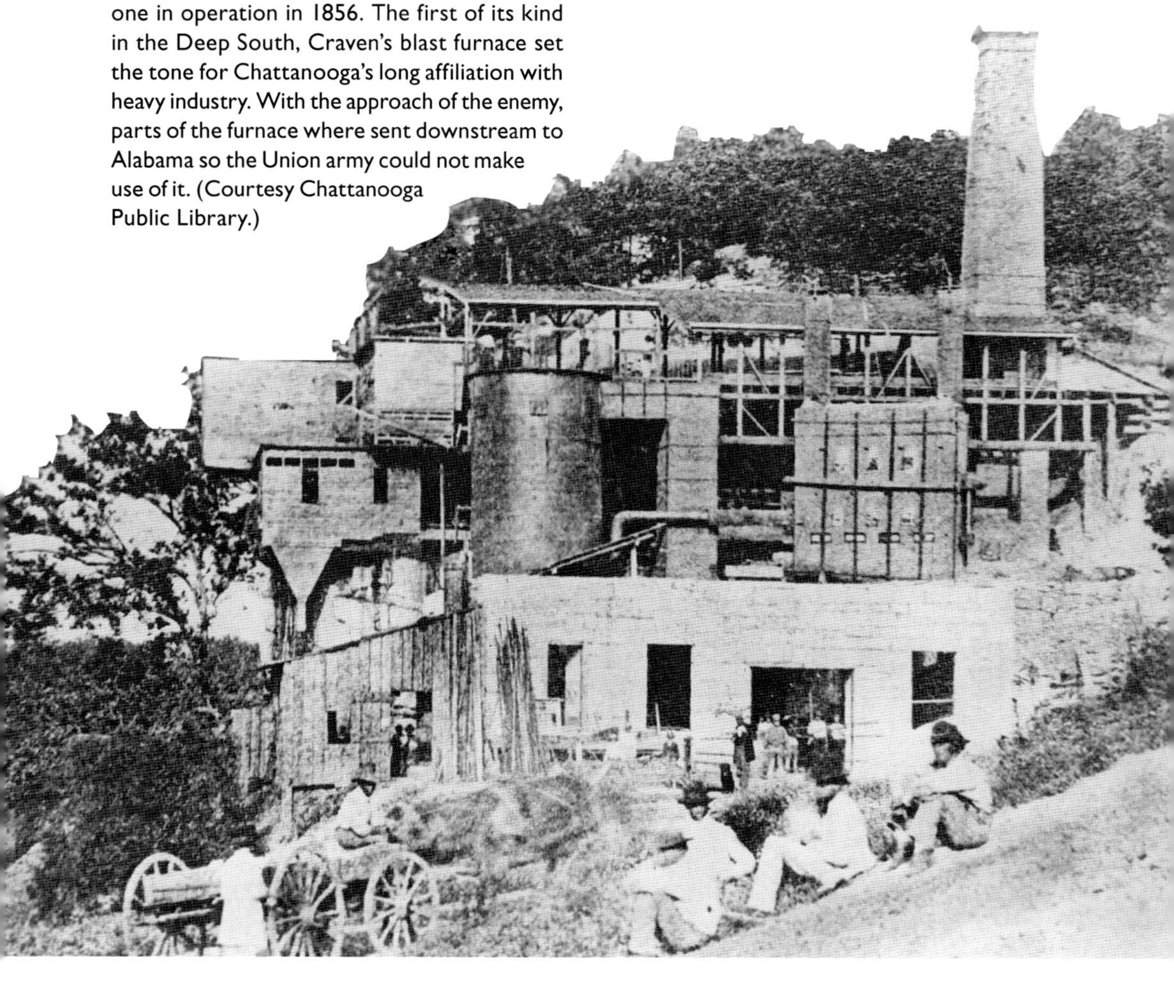

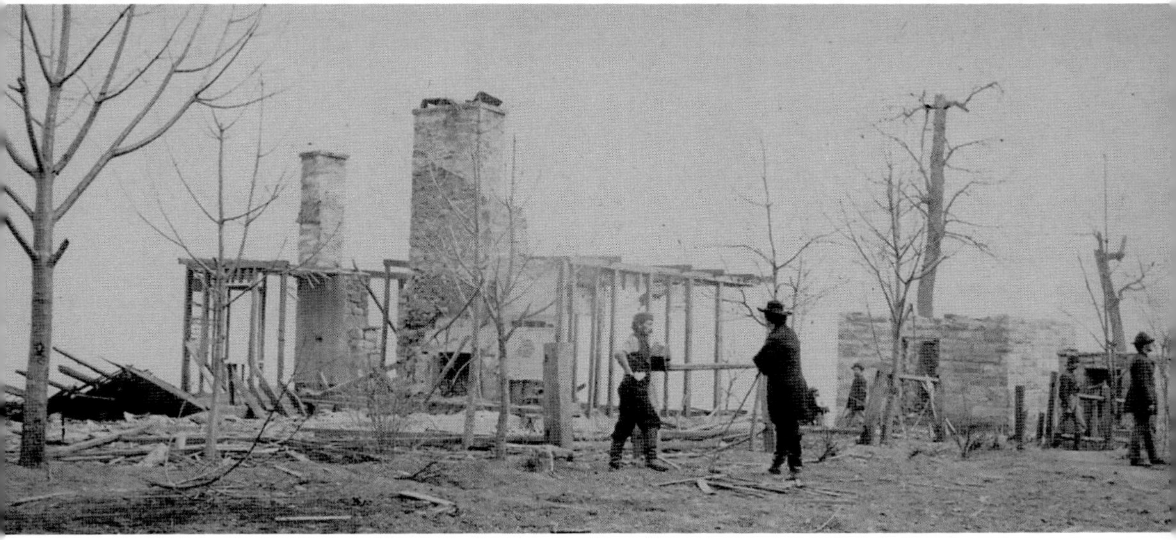

Craven's House
Craven's House was on the side of Lookout Mountain overlooking the city. Built on a terrace of land, it became a battle site as the Federal soldiers advanced toward the top peak. Once this point was secured, the Confederate troops above began to retreat, realizing there was no way to turn back the huge wave of blue coming toward them. This photograph depicts the rebuilding of his house after the war. (Courtesy Chattanooga Public Library.)

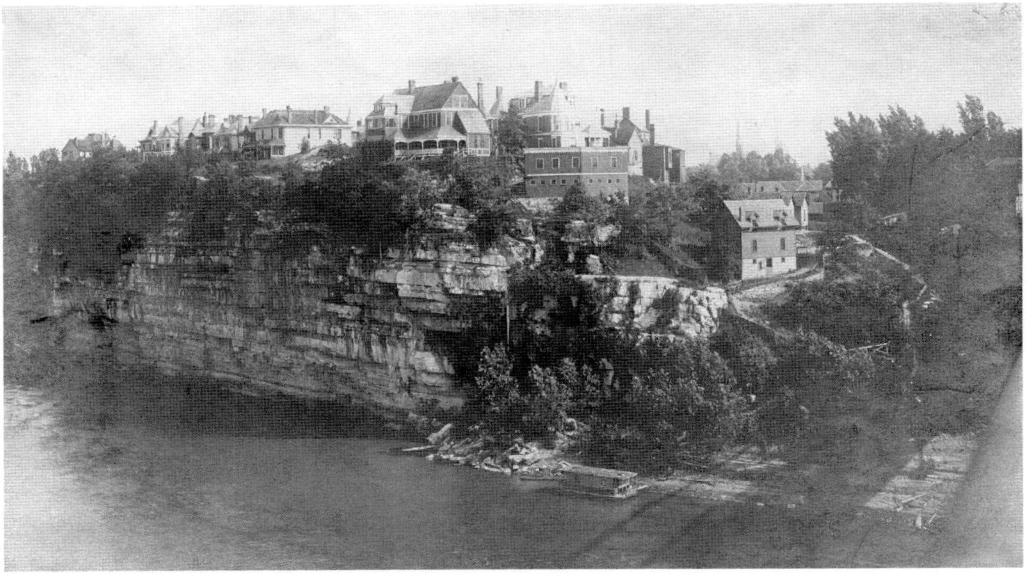

Bluff Houses
Only 40 years after the war ended, the bluff view area had become the most fashionable section of town. Carpetbaggers and others, who had made a fortune in the boom of the 1880s, built fine Victorian homes along the rocky face over the river. Eventually, the Paxton Mansion—known today as the Hunter Museum—would become an even grander replacement for some of these splendid residences. (Courtesy Chattanooga Public Library.)

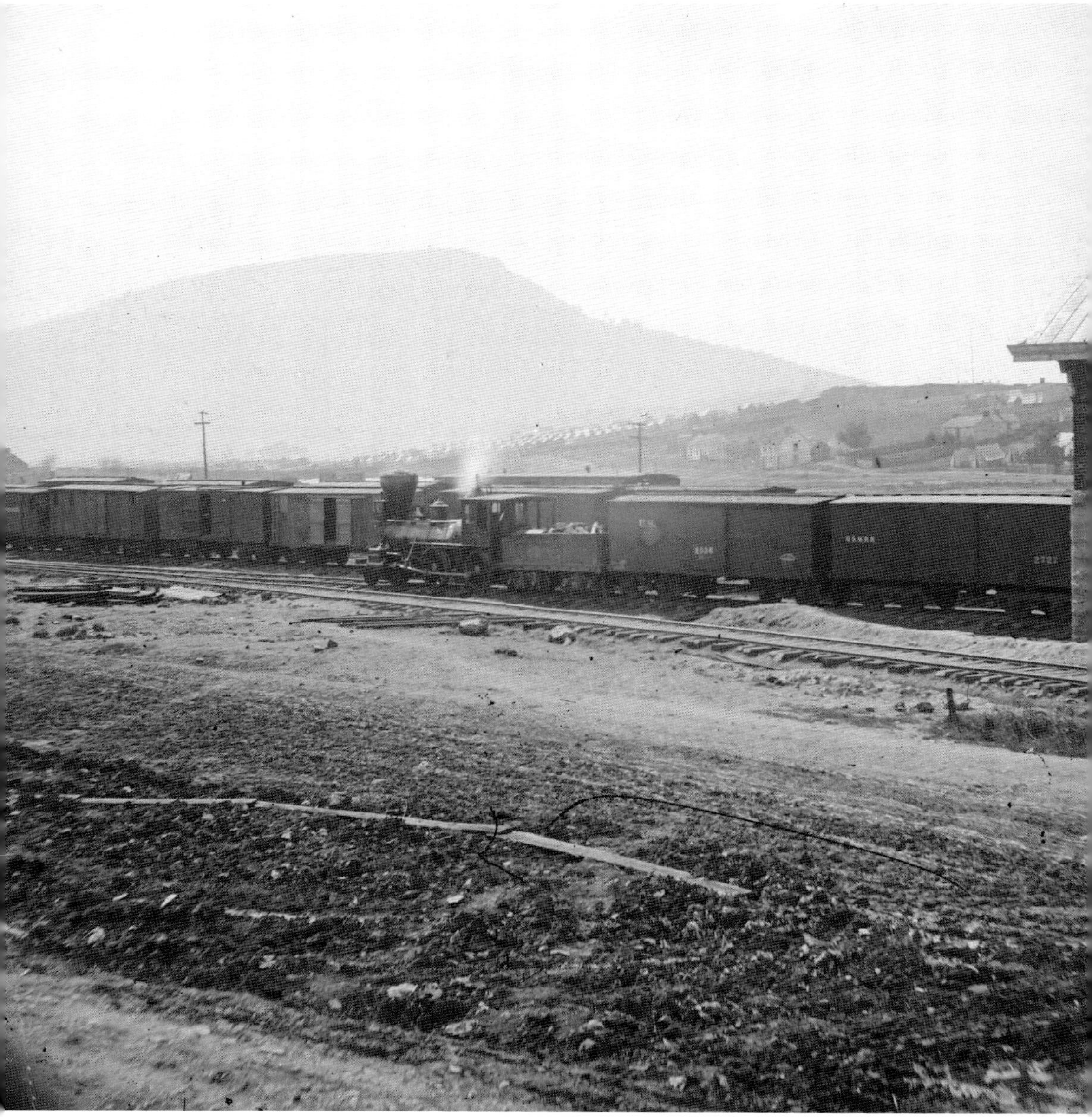

Early Railroad
The railroad was what every 19th-century town sought to bring commerce to their community. The sound of the whistle and smoke of the train was heard in Chattanooga in 1850 when the Western and Atlantic Railroad line reached town from Atlanta. Ending at the depot on Ninth Street (now Martin Luther King Drive), it signaled the beginning of 120 years of Chattanooga as a dominant rail center in the South. The many miles of track ensured that local heavy industry had a gateway to the entire country for its goods and products. (Courtesy Chattanooga Public Library.)

CHAPTER TWO

Entrepreneurs

To use today's parlance, Chattanooga was a "business-friendly" town from the start. Commerce thrived via the river, and cheap land attracted mountain folk from the Carolinas and Virginia to farm and build. But the greatest builder or transformer of the city's infrastructure may have been the Union army of Grant and Sherman. Within only 25 years of the founding of the city, the slate was almost wiped clean by the occupation of the city by Federal forces in 1863. Their large corps of engineers cut down every tree in sight and built a bridge across the river for new supplies. Large frame warehouses on Market and Broad Streets replaced smaller shops. A corral, the quartermaster's supply house, and other units were everywhere. After the war, the US government sold these buildings to entrepreneurs like Gen. John Wilder, who had once lobbed cannon fire into the city and now became an employer and later, a mayor of the city. Men like Z.C. Patten came to town and made patent medicines, a huge business, at the Chattanooga Medicine Co. And Newell Sanders, a native of Indiana, arrived in Chattanooga and built one of the biggest farm implement manufactures in the country at Chattanooga Plow.

Men like Benjamin Franklin Thomas cut a deal with the owner of a refreshing drink named Coca-Cola to bottle his fountain tonic and sell it around the country, spinning off a line of bottling franchises across the United States and making a fortune in the process. Charles James had a big vision for an entire mountain, building a road up wild Signal Mountain and a hotel at the top as well. A man with a mechanical aptitude, Ernest Holmes, designed the first tow truck in the world essentially creating the entire industry of road rescue. Some beloved businesses, like Lovemans Department store or T.H. Payne's office supply and stationery shop, ran for a century and are no more. That ubiquitous snack food, Moon Pie, was born here and still thrives today, as do a number of smaller businesses such as Kelly Cars, Gordon's Cleaners, and Mount Vernon Restaurant, run by families for decades and offering service to generations of citizens.

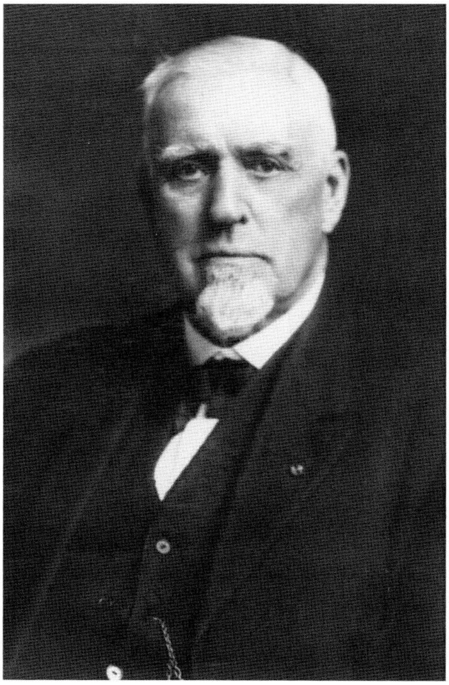

Gen. John Wilder
Gen. John Wilder first encountered Chattanooga as a Union soldier who directed the bombardment of the city from the north side of the river on Stringers Ridge in 1862. Noting the mineral wealth in the mountainous region, he returned to the city after the war and began investing ambitiously in iron manufacturing in the region. He was elected mayor in 1871, with broad support in the postwar town, while expanding his production facilities and promoting a new rail line and then later became the town postmaster. He is buried in the Forest Hills Cemetery in St. Elmo. (Courtesy Chattanooga Public Library.)

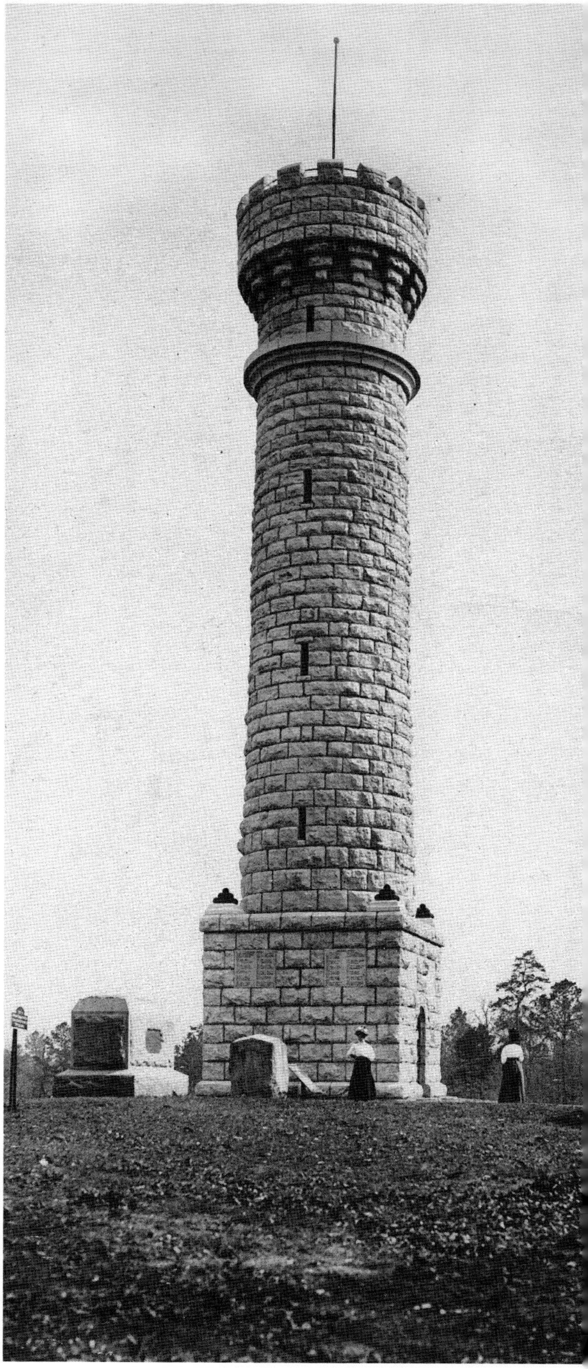

Wilder Tower
One of the outstanding monuments at Chickamauga is the Wilder Brigade Monument, or Wilder Tower, built of hand-hewn stone and still frequented today by visitors who wish to walk to the top for the view. His "Lightning Brigade" was one of the few bright spots for the Union forces during the battle, distinguishing themselves near the Bloody Pond by putting up stiff resistance to the intense Confederate attack that decimated much of the Yankee forces on the second day. (Courtesy Chattanooga Public Library.)

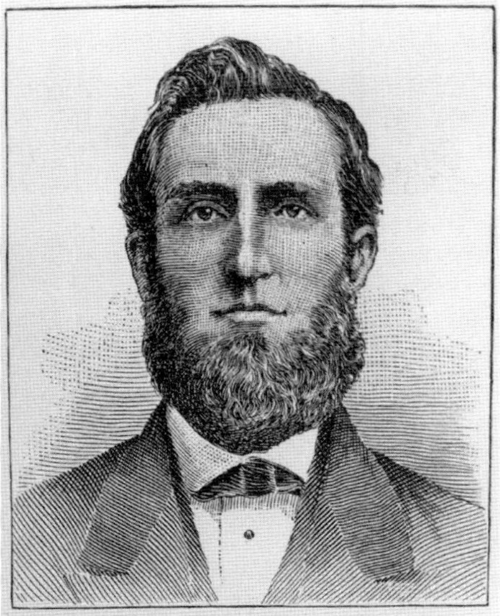

JAMES J. ANDREWS. From a photograph in the possession of Miss Elvira Layton.

James Andrews
James J. Andrews was a spy who worked for the Union army and led a group of men—his "raiders"—from Chattanooga south to Kennesaw, Georgia, close to Atlanta, where he stole a train at breakfast while the engine was waiting for the crew to reboard. They headed north to Chattanooga with the intent of destroying the rail lines and disrupting Confederate supply support. In what was called "The Great Locomotive Chase"—later retold in two motion pictures—he was caught and hung by the Confederate army. His fellow raiders were awarded the first Congressional Medals of Honor. Since Andrew himself was a civilian, he was not eligible to receive the award. He is buried in the national cemetery in Chattanooga. (Courtesy Chattanooga History Center.)

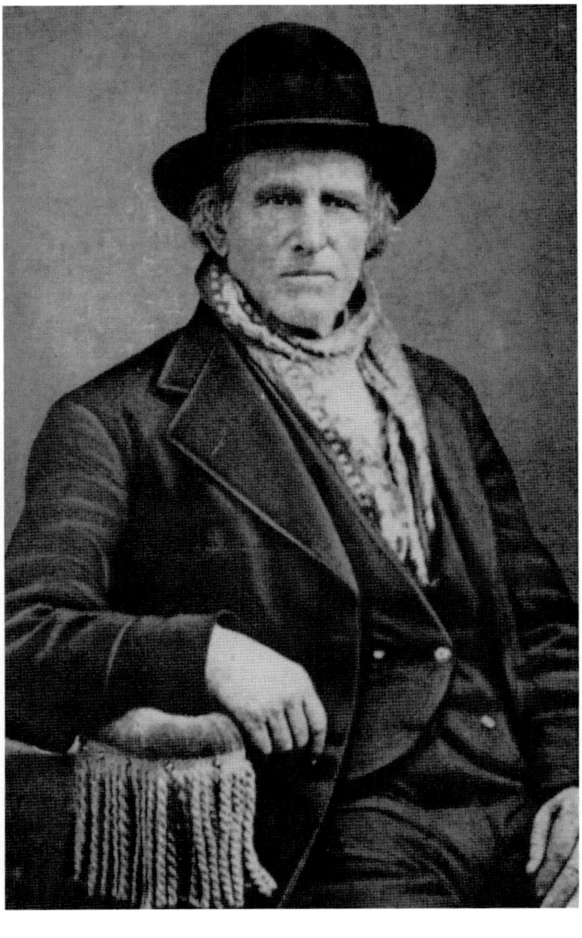

Sam Williams
Often referred to as the "Father of Chattanooga," Williams lived on an island (Williams Island) south of town. Builder of the first plank house in Chattanooga, he captured the escaped James Andrews and returned him to the federal authorities to be jailed. Modern archeology of the island indicates human habitation dating back intermittently 12,000 years. (Courtesy Chattanooga Public Library.)

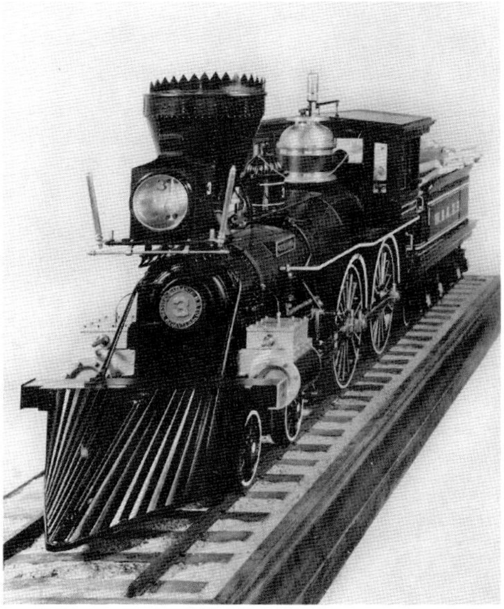

The General

The General was a great point of pride for Chattanooga. The City of Chattanooga kept the General for 100 years in the Union Depot train station facing the Read House, often disputing the State of Georgia for possession of the famous engine. The Civil War locomotive was a must-see for visitors and a landmark for locals. In the 1960s, the legal fight still unresolved, the State of Georgia won a favorable verdict and claimed the train from the City of Chattanooga, much to the chagrin of local citizens, and it was moved to Kennesaw, Georgia. (Courtesy Chattanooga Public Library.)

The General Replica

Visitors interested in the Civil War often spend time in Chattanooga's beautiful national cemetery. One of the striking sites is the stone monument dedicated to Andrew's Raiders with the replica of the General on top. Here, a group of veterans, including Medal of Honor winner Charles Coolidge (top row, second from right), stand in front of it as they prepare to tour the country with a replica of the famous engine. (Courtesy Chattanooga Public Library.)

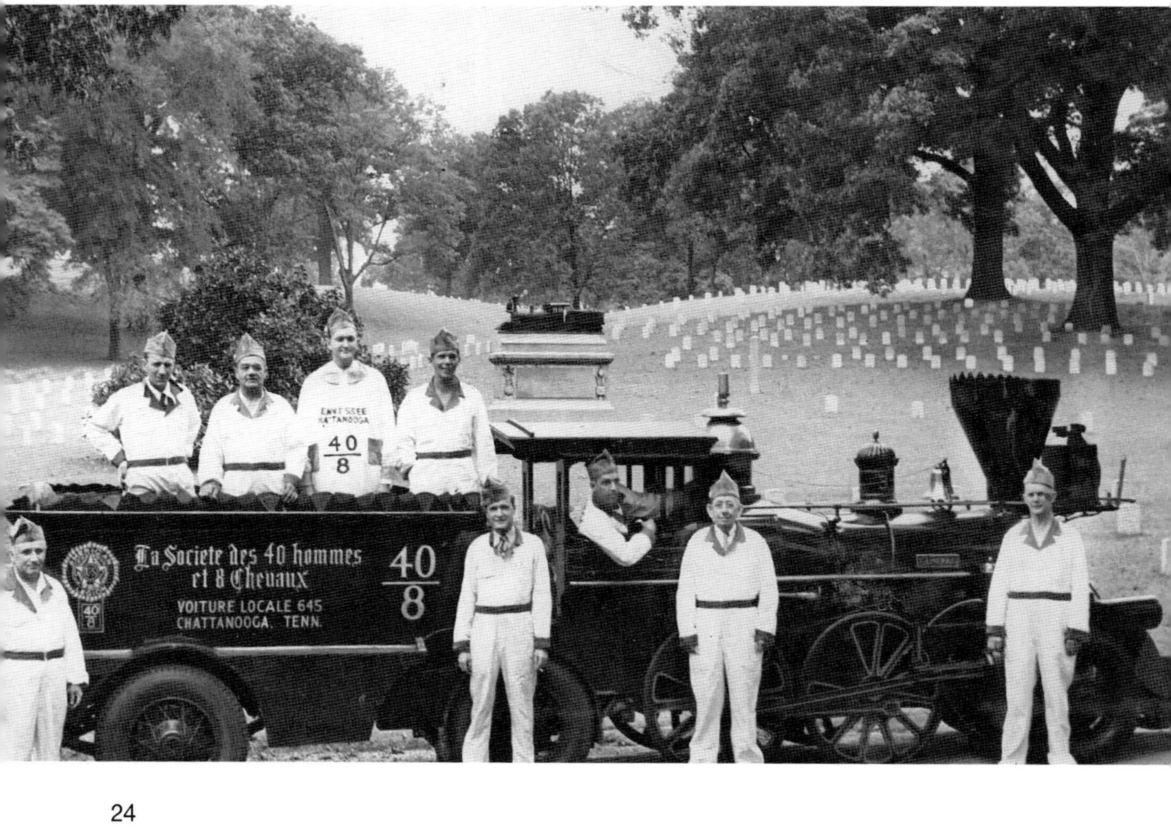

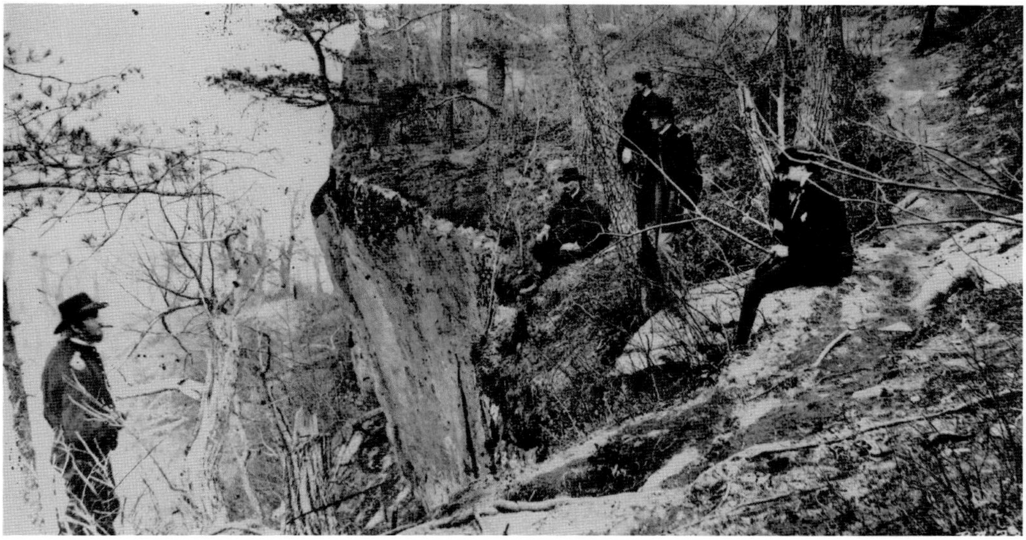

General Grant

Although his stay here was short, it had, to quote a current phrase, "maximum impact." Gen. Ulysses S. Grant arrived in Chattanooga on October 23, 1863, on horseback from northern Alabama. He found a huge Union army surrounded by Bragg's Confederate soldiers who had beaten them badly at Chickamauga. Within 33 days, he punctured the rebel line and brought in supplies; drove the Southern troops off of Lookout Mountain; and then faced his enemy and assaulted Missionary Ridge, pushing the rebels back into Georgia. But his permanent imprint came from the fact that he built relentlessly throughout the city. His engineers measured, cut, and built warehouses and service buildings everywhere. And they were all built at the federal government's expense. And so, they would remain after the final shot had been fired and would lay the urban foundation for the next generation of leaders (carpetbaggers) that would arise to renew the city. (Courtesy Chattanooga Public Library.)

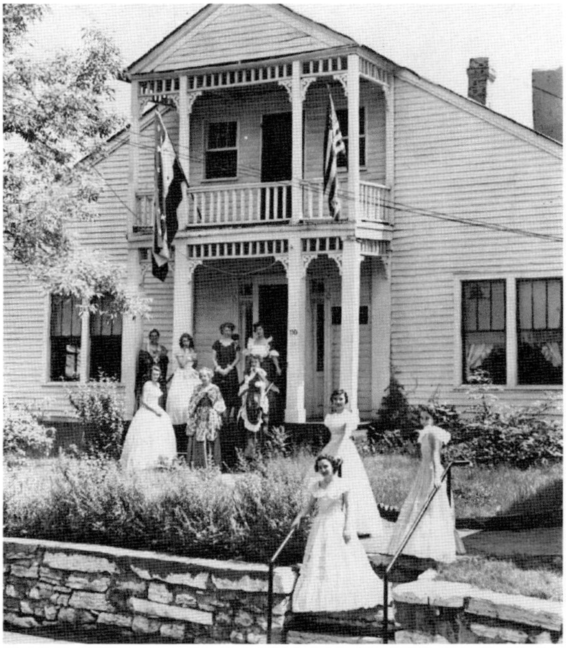

Belles at Grant House

Grant's headquarters stood on First Street by the river for years. A private residence, it finally gave way to the proverbial highway that urban developers ran through downtowns in 1950s and 1960s. Somewhat shabby by the time this photograph was made, the house still had the mystique to serve as a backdrop for southern belles posing for the camera. (Courtesy Chattanooga Public Library.)

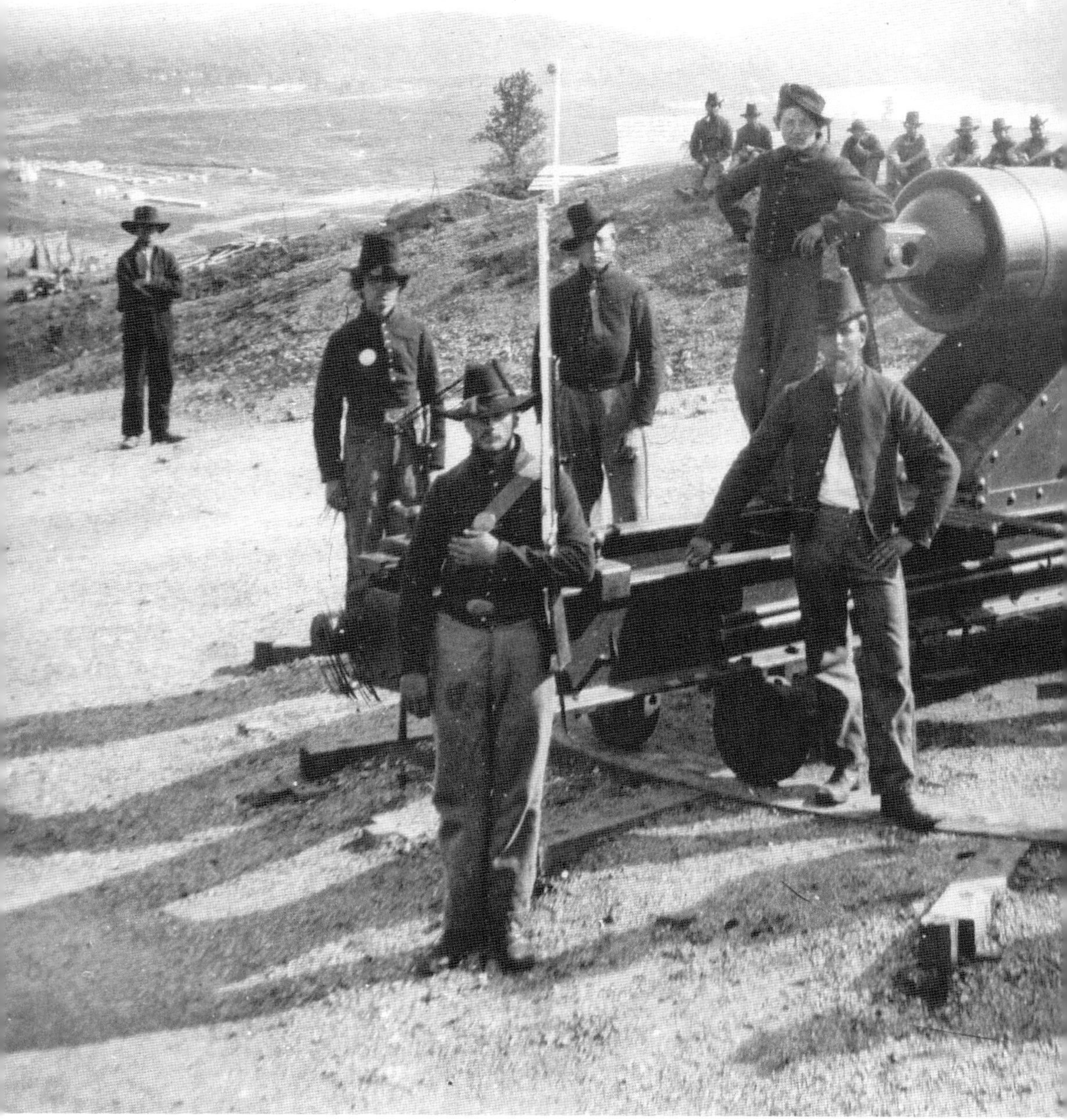

Soldiers on Cameron Hill

Cameron Hill towered over the young city and made a perfect place for a cannon emplacement. With Lookout Mountain in the background and the Tennessee River below, this high ground was ideal for

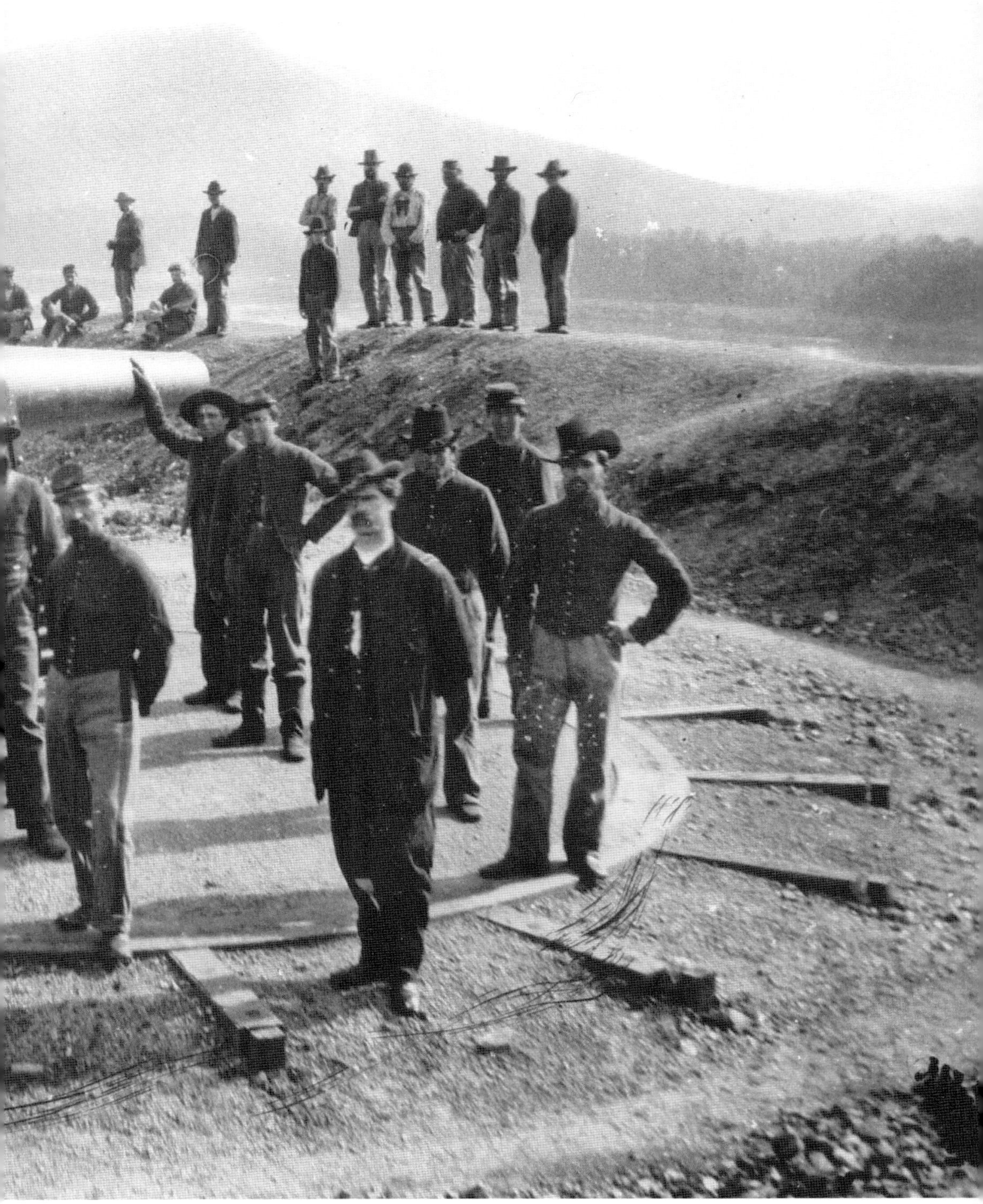

shelling any intruders. The attitude of the Union soldiers indicates they meant business. (Courtesy Chattanooga Public Library.)

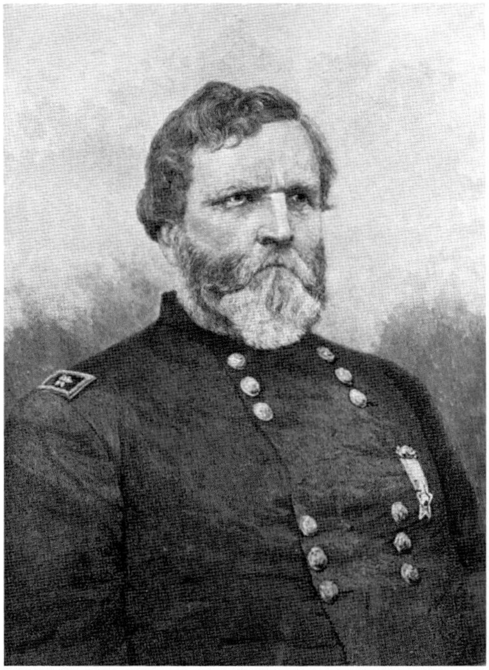

General Thomas

General Thomas was known as the Rock of Chickamauga for his defiance of the onslaught of Confederate troops that mauled the Union troops on September 19, 1863. With troops on the right flank in retreat, Thomas quickly rallied his troops of the XIV Corps to face Longstreet's charge through the line. During the battle, future president James Garfield saw Thomas "standing like a rock" in spite of the desperate situation. Thomas then replaced Rosecrans as commander of the Army of the Cumberland. The sight of Thomas on his famous bay horse, "Billy"—named for Gen. William Sherman—became a rallying point for his troops. (Courtesy Chattanooga Public Library.)

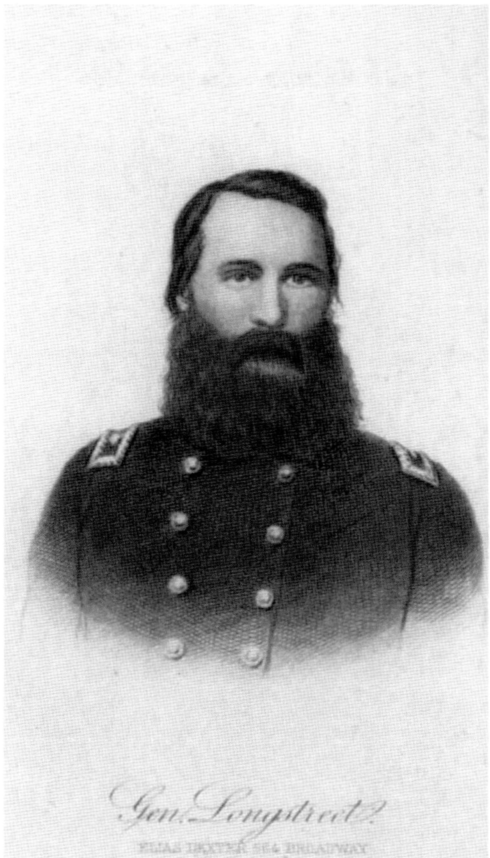

General Longstreet

General Longstreet was an experienced veteran of the war by the time he arrived at Chickamauga. Lining up troops for what would become his famous charge, he realized an incorrect command had left a gap in the Union line, and he took advantage of it. His charge was overwhelming, and Federal troops scattered in disarray and disbelief. The triumph would have been complete except that he was contained by George Thomas's defense, and at nightfall, the Union troops were able to retreat. Nonetheless, the lion's share of praise belonged to him for the victory. (Courtesy Chattanooga Public Library.)

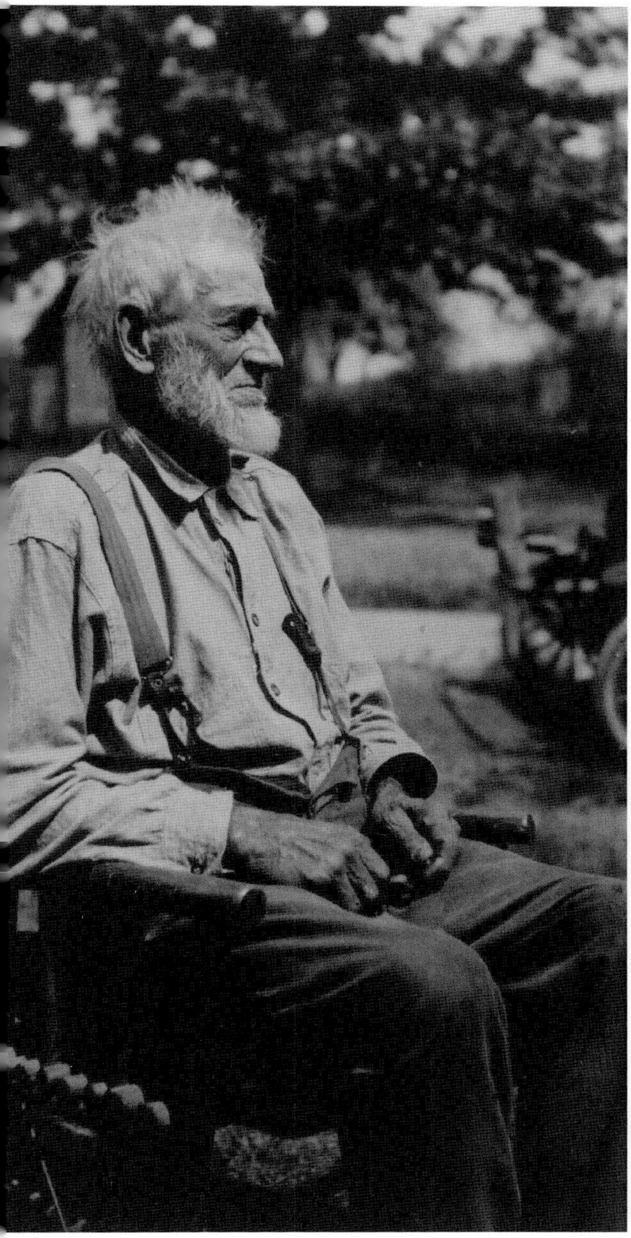

Larkin Poe

Larkin Poe was a lad when the armies massed at Chickamauga. The first Union soldiers he encountered were foraging for food, and as it became clearer that fighting was imminent, he and his family went to the woods to hide. Living for days on almost nothing, they returned to their home to find it burned. He was one of the last civilian survivors of the days of September 1863. (Courtesy Tennessee State Library and Archives.)

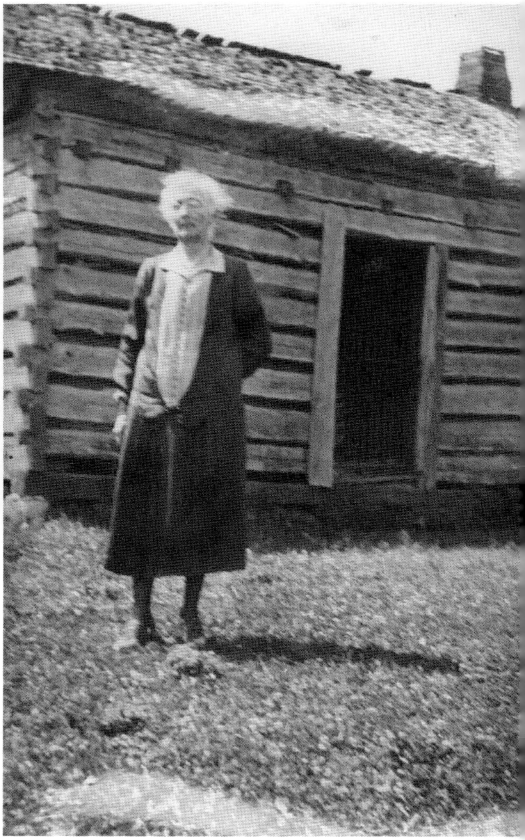

Julia Snodgrass

Julia Snodgrass is standing at the battlefield in her later years. Her family lived in this log home, the Brotherton House, when the fighting began, caught by surprise like the other families. The home where General Thomas made his stand is a frequently visited site at Chickamauga. (Courtesy Tennessee State Library and Archives.)

Mark Thrash

Mark Thrash did not live an ordinary life. Born in Richmond, Virginia, in 1820, his owner, Doctor Thrash, sent him to Georgia to clear new property he had acquired when he was 20. During the Civil War, he was sent to Chickamauga to search for his own son and his master's son, where he witnessed the thousands of dead soldiers and decaying horses that were on the battlefield. The horrific site was "full of obnoxious odors" that he described later. He was part of the crew ordered to bury them and claimed he talked to future president Garfield in the 15 days it took to dispose of the bodies. Now a free man, he decided to settle down at Chickamauga and worked there until the astounding age of 108 when he was asked to retire. Federal officials were shocked by his age and gladly gave him his pension. Gradually, he became a local celebrity, and tourists such as this Georgia camera club traveled miles to see him. At the age of 117, he was reunited with his twin brother and became the oldest living twin as well as the country's oldest-living citizen. When he died in 1943, he was eight days shy of his 123rd birthday. Married five times and the father of 29 children, he is buried in his trademark white apron in the old Haselrig Cemetery at the park where an engraved headstone was placed in 1982. (Courtesy Chattanooga History Center.)

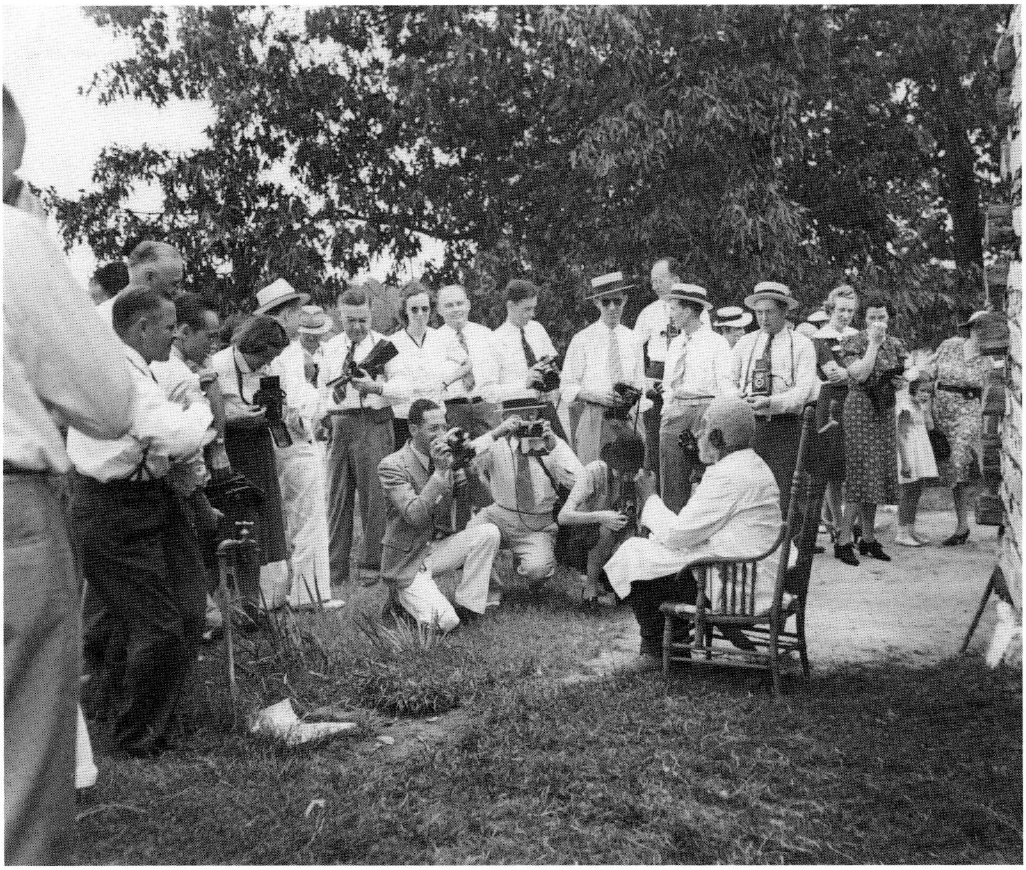

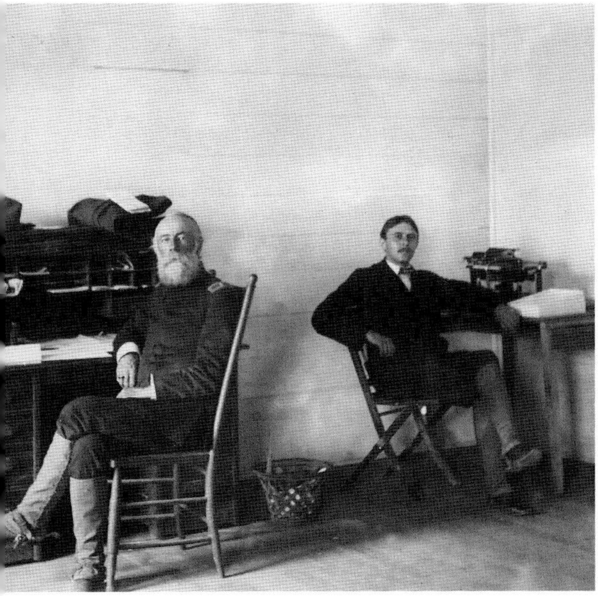

Henry Boynton

As the years passed after the war, a movement of reconciliation swept through the remaining veterans on both sides. By the early 1890s, the decision to create a park to commemorate the battle at Chickamauga was made. Henry Boynton was a Union officer who won the Medal of Honor at Missionary Ridge and a prime mover in the creation of the Chickamauga and Chattanooga National Military Park. The park was the first battlefield in the nation to be established by the federal government. When the park was dedicated in 1895, Boynton became the park historian and commissioner and wrote the first detailed tour guides for visitors. Following his time at the park, he served as commander of nearby Camp Thomas during the Spanish-American War. (Courtesy Chattanooga Public Library.)

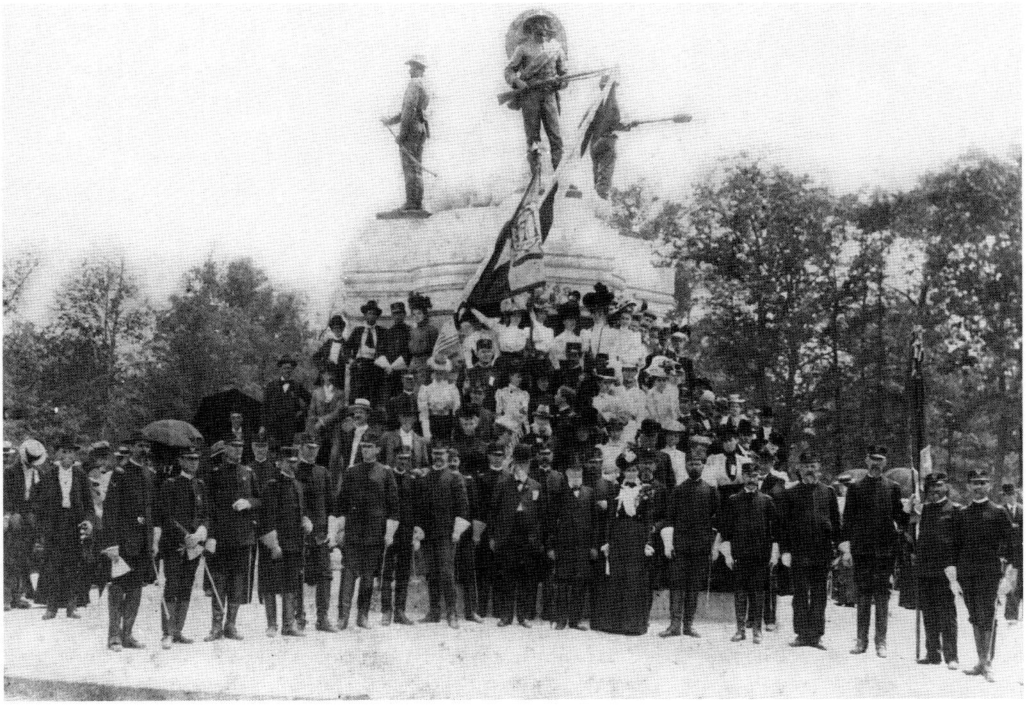

Georgia Monument

In May 1897, two years after the park opened, the Georgia Monument was completed and dedicated. Governor Candler made a speech and tendered the blue granite memorial to the federal government. The tall, vertical monument stands near the center of the park, close to where Georgia troops made their charge. The color bearer on top points toward Chattanooga with his right hand while the base of the monument is appointed with three bronze figures designating the three branches of the Army: infantry, artillery, and cavalry. (Courtesy Chattanooga Public Library.)

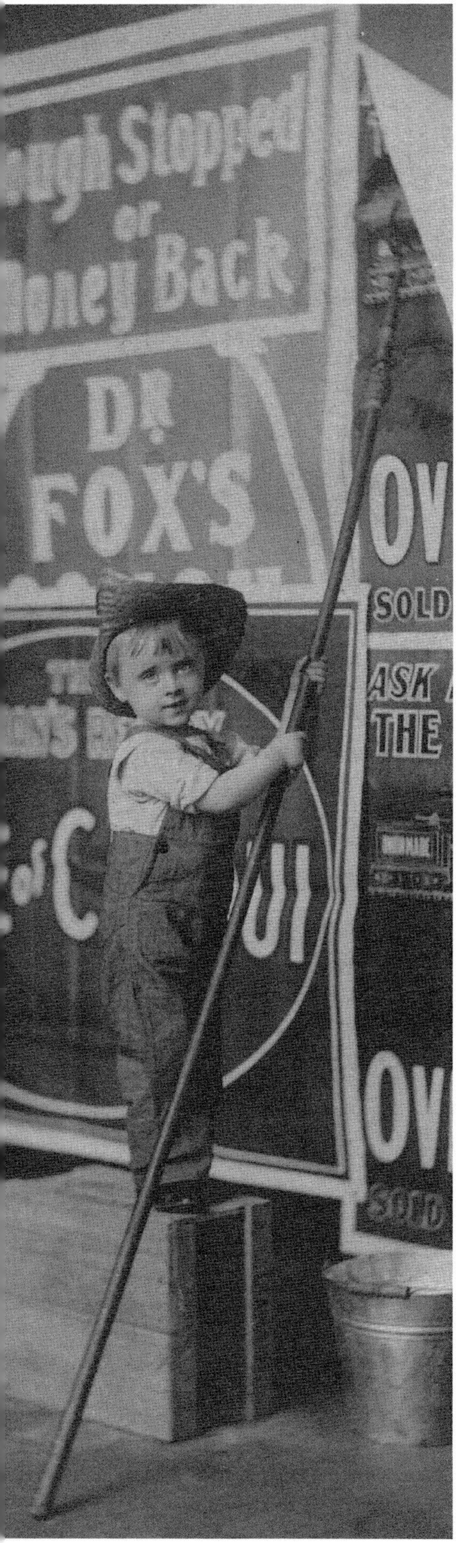

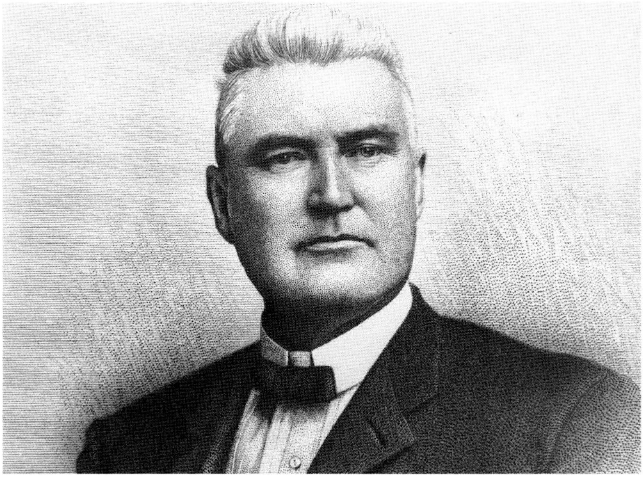

Z.C. Patten

Zeboim Cartter Patten was one of several Yankee soldiers who fought in Chattanooga during the Civil War and then returned to make a career here. Originally, he opened a bookstore with his friend T.H. Payne. But his claim to fame and his own fortune was the Chattanooga Medicine Company, manufacturer and promoter of a number of patent medicines that began in 1879. A man with a keen sense of salesmanship, he created two wildly successful tonics, Black-Draught and Wine of Cardui. Wine of Cardui was "a vegetable bitter tonic and stomachic with antispasmodic properties" for the relief of menstrual cramps. Among its several ingredients was a hefty 38-proof dose of alcohol which no doubt increased its appeal. Black Draught was a laxative made of senna and magnesium. As a youngster, Dolly Parton made a singing commercial promoting the medicine that "makes you smile from the inside out." The company became so successful, it was given its own government-paid post office on the premises and used that facility to distribute a calendar with company images of Cardui emblazoned in bold type. Patten would become director of the chamber of commerce and was instrumental in the last great Civil War veterans' reunion in 1913. His involvement in real estate resulted in the building the town's first high rise, the Patten Hotel, and with his son-in-law, John T. Lupton, he built Volunteer State Life Insurance. He was a founder of American Trust and Banking Company. His beautiful estate, Ashland Farms, still stands today in Flintstone, Georgia, in the shadow of Lookout Mountain. (Courtesy Chattanooga Public Library.)

Stoops Boy

Little Frank Stoops reaches as high as he can with his brush to smooth out the paste under the posted signs. A close look to the left reveals the poster for Wine of Cardui, the Chattanooga Medicine Company concoction, as it competes for space with other printed posters. The Stoops were well known for their clever advertisements, as was Chattanooga Medicine. (Courtesy Chattanooga Public Library.)

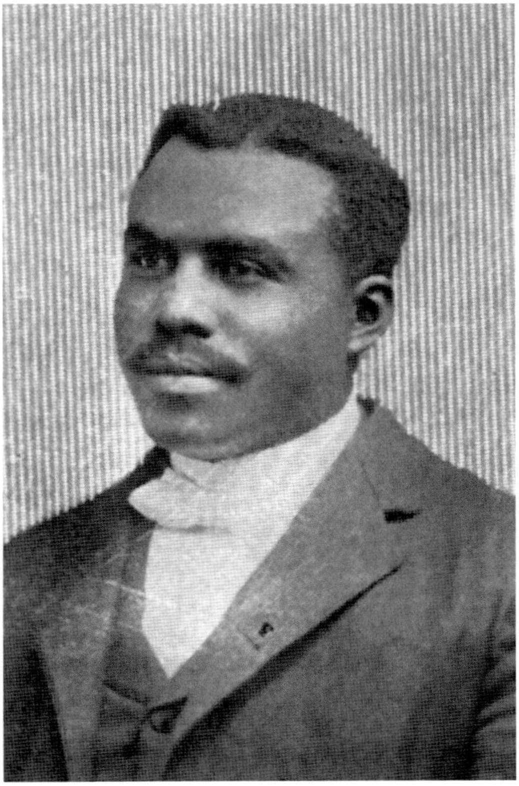

G.W. Franklin
G.W. Franklin was born in South Georgia in 1865, grew up in Rome, Georgia (70 miles south of Chattanooga), and was engaged in four businesses at a young age. He ran a coal yard, drove a hack (a taxi), practiced blacksmithing that he learned from his father, and worked as an undertaker. Focused and a tireless worker, he moved to Chattanooga to become an undertaker full-time in 1894 and became quite successful. His descendants still live in Chattanooga and carry on that business today. Franklin then expanded his business by purchasing two cemeteries, East View and Pleasant Garden, and maintained a sizable farm of 111 acres for his family as well. He was a prime example of black entrepreneurship and claimed Booker T. Washington, a promoter of the gospel of self-improvement, as a friend. (Courtesy Chattanooga Public Library.)

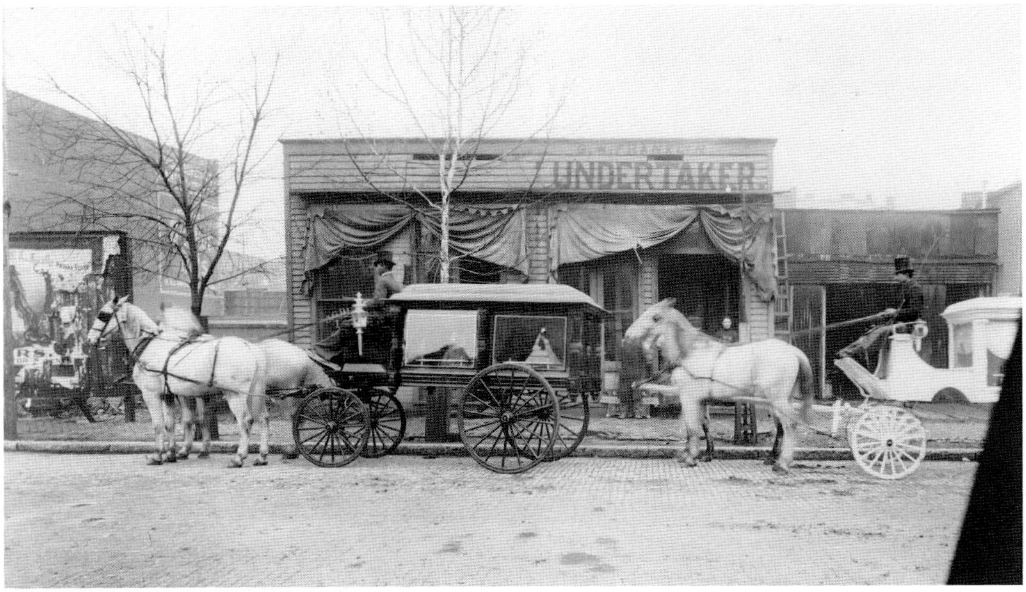

Funeral Home
A horse-and-buggy hearse stands outside the G.W. Franklin Funeral Home apparently ready to go to the cemetery. One of the oldest running funeral homes in the state, the family-owned business still stands today, a testament to the quality of service that the Franklin family offers to the local community. (Courtesy Library of Congress.)

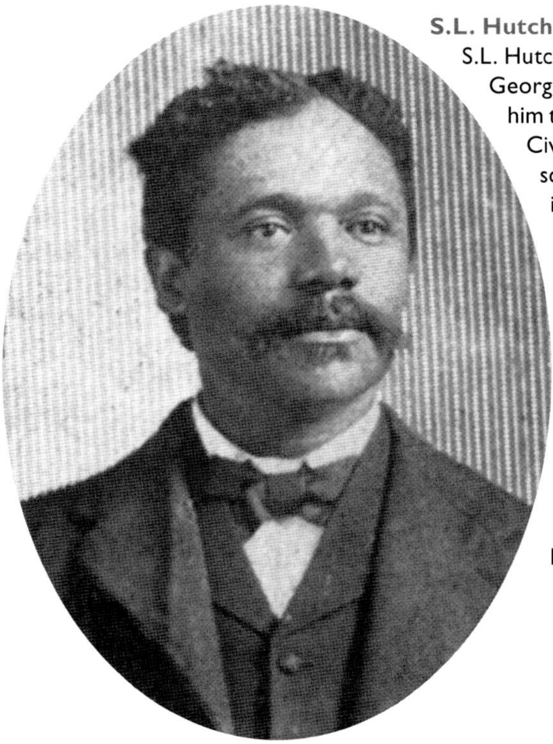

S.L. Hutchins

S.L. Hutchins was a determined man from Lawrenceville, Georgia. Unusually, his parents had the means to send him to the newly minted Atlanta University after the Civil War, and following his graduation, he taught school, becoming the principal of Knox Institute in Athens, Georgia. Furthering his education, he graduated law school and against overt resistance from authorities, he became the first black man admitted to the Georgia Bar, which was no small feat. He moved to Chattanooga as blacks gained more power and was highly successful. He ran for office in 1882 against local Democrats that tried to have him unseated even after he won the election. His defense of lynching victim Ed Johnson brought him intense criticism from the white community. He finished his career as a US revenue gauger. (Courtesy Chattanooga Public Library.)

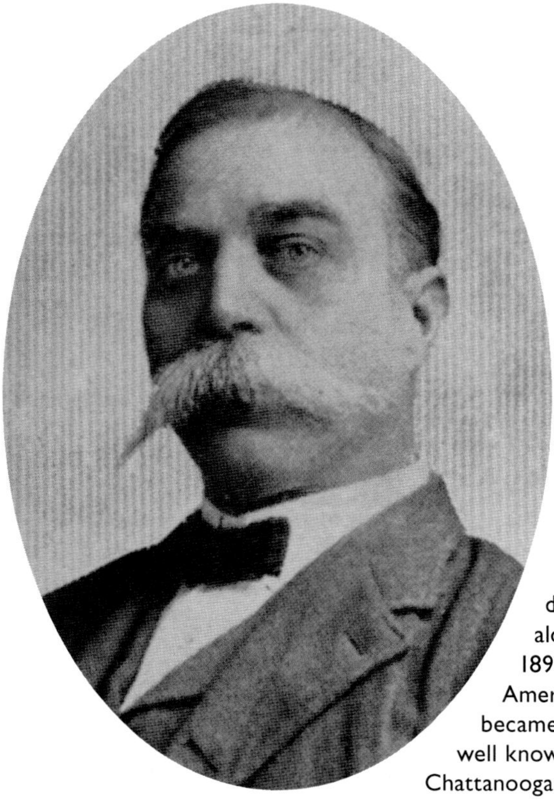

Hyram Tyree

Hyram Tyree is an example of a man who overcame real adversity. Born a slave in Virginia, he was 19 years old when the war ended. Before that time, he had learned the craft of shoemaking, but when he came to Chattanooga in 1867, railroad work was what he could find. Eventually he became a foreman, constructing the Wills Valley Railroad and working his way up to general yardmaster. But in September 1881, he lost his right leg and had to return to making shoes for a living. Undeterred, he decided to run for office in town and became an alderman in the old fourth ward as a Republican in 1899. It was a period of political power for African Americans in Chattanooga before the Jim Crow laws became widespread. Known as a "race man," he was well known and respected in his community. (Courtesy Chattanooga Public Library.)

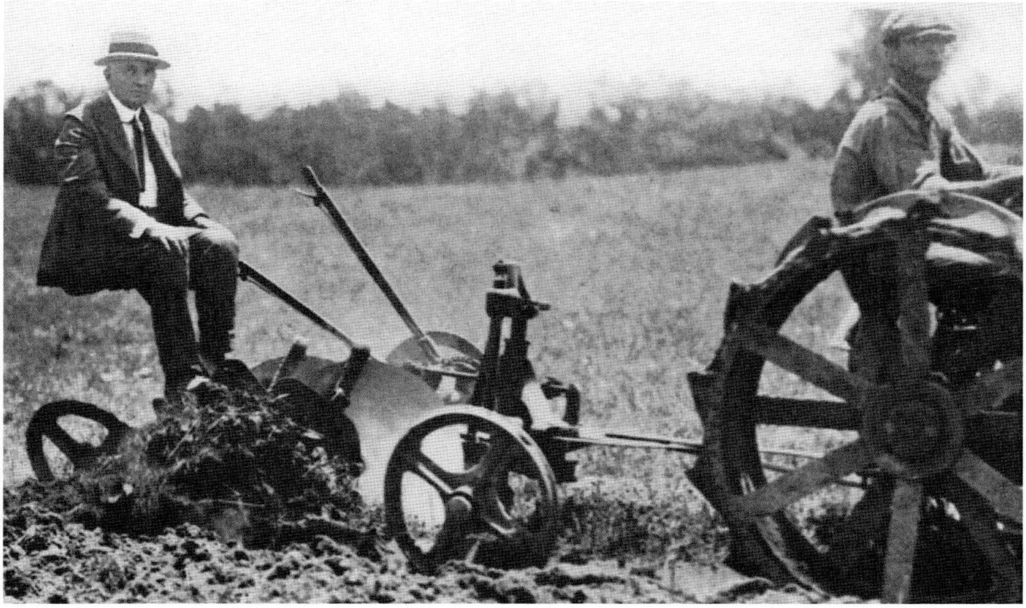

Newell Sanders
Newell Sanders came to Chattanooga about 10 years after the Civil War when the city was beginning to recover. Encouraged by fellow Indiana native John Wilder to come south, he borrowed $3,000 and started the first plow factory in the South, Chattanooga Plow, a business that became one of the leading producers in Chattanooga's large industrial base. Its products, such as cane mills and evaporators, served the agrarian southland for decades, and the manufacturing site at one time covered six acres with 250 employees—the biggest factory in town. But soon he expanded into the Western states with some forays into international markets like Jamaica and South America. Eventually, Sanders introduced the disc plow, an implement especially useful in rocky soil that could be rigged to the then-new farm vehicle known as the tractor. So successful was his brand that the International Harvester Company purchased it for $1 million in 1919—an enormous sum for its day. He was appointed to the US senate for almost a year in 1912 and was a staunch proponent of equal suffrage for women as well as a supporter of the national amendment that became law when Tennessee passed it. His wife, Corinne Sanders, then became the first woman in the state to cast a vote. He died in 1938 in his home on Lookout Mountain, which stood next to the Lookout Mountain Incline Railway. (Courtesy Chattanooga Public Library.)

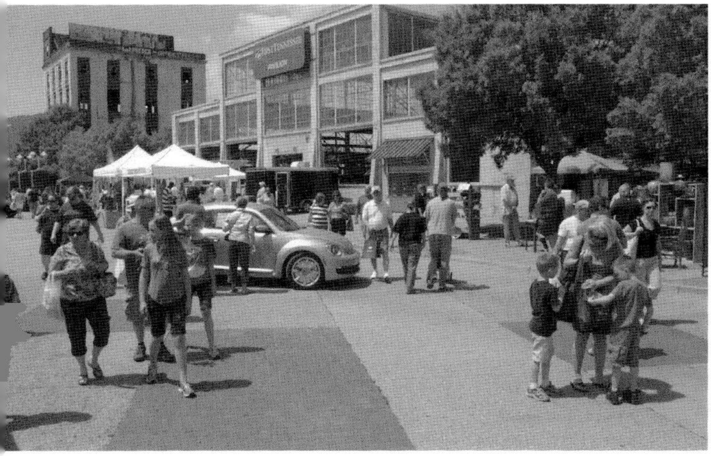

Sunday Market
In an odd twist in time, the enormous site that Chattanooga Plow once owned now hosts a popular Sunday market. Considering that the implements of agriculture that poured from the noisy factory for many years went to farmers to till the soil, there is something continuous about having a place for small farmers to sell their fresh vegetables directly to the public. (Author's collection.)

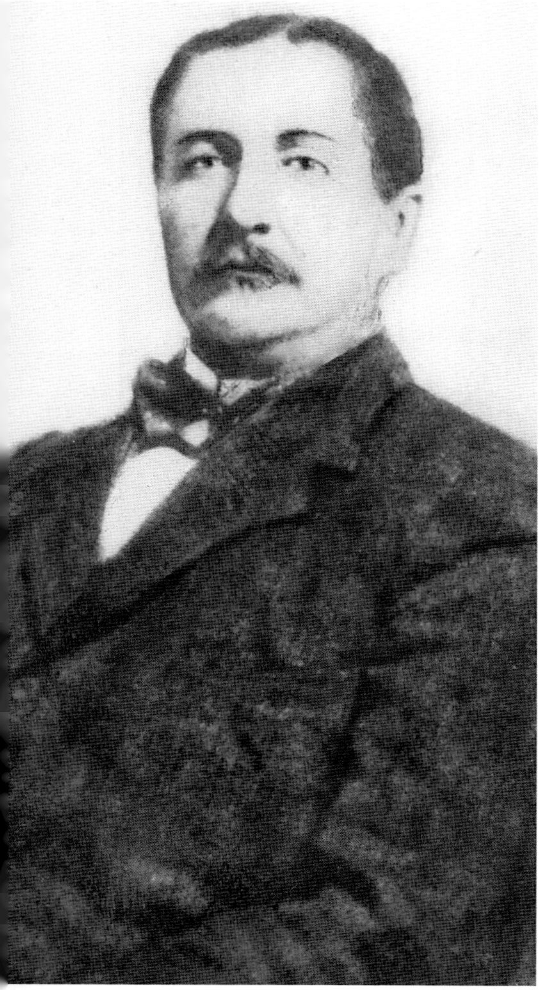

B.F. Thomas
Like many entrepreneurs, Benjamin Franklin Thomas tried his hand at many things. But his talent was best served with a law degree, which he obtained from the University of Cincinnati in 1887 before he settled in Chattanooga. Anecdotes reveal a man with ambition, energy, and curiosity. While serving in Cuba during the Spanish-American War, he tasted some fruit drinks in bottles and wondered how he could do that back home in Chattanooga. With the support of his wife, Ann Taylor Thomas, he and a friend, Joseph Whitehead, took the train to Atlanta in the spring of 1899 to call upon Asa Candler, the owner of a local drink called Coca-Cola, hoping to convince him to let them bottle his carbonated drink and sell it outside of Georgia. Candler reportedly was dubious that people would buy his soft drink in a bottle. According to family legend, the deal was made on a handshake and the exchange of a single dollar. Thomas wasted no time in setting up a small bottling plant off Georgia Avenue and the Patten Parkway in late 1899, and the explosion of the world's most famous soft drink was underway. The two men added a third partner, John T. Lupton, dividing the country operations into territories where they could franchise their operations. The resulting fortune for the principals was the stuff of dreams. Thomas chose the Eastern United States and the three Western coastal states, including California. As the popularity of the drink grew, he had little trouble in finding men who wanted to start a bottling operation in their town, and Thomas's business grew exponentially. A wealthy man, Thomas became a generous giver to social and civic causes in Chattanooga, not to mention a major creator of jobs in his hometown. (Courtesy Chattanooga Public Library.)

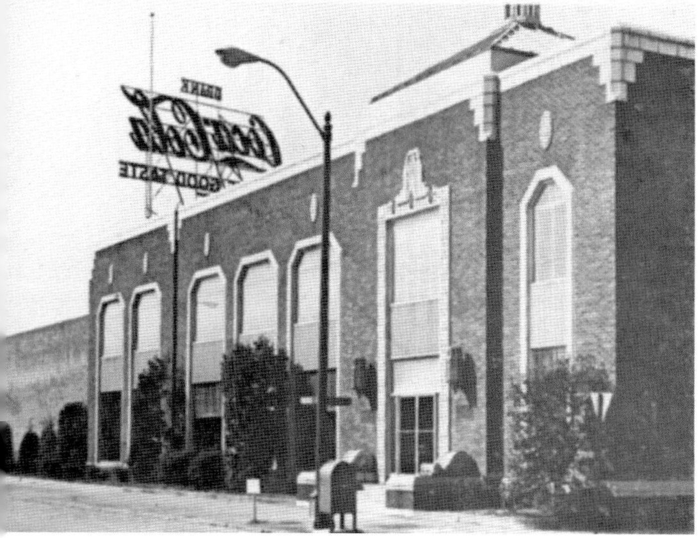

Coca-Cola Building
The Chattanooga Coca-Cola Bottling building was a landmark in downtown for years. With its large glass windows, the operation inside was visible for many to see, and the assembly line was part of many elementary school trips. When the modern plant moved to Amnicola Highway, the Broad Street building changed hands and currently houses an ice-cream and pizza business, selling foods that go better with Coke. (Courtesy Chattanooga Public Library.)

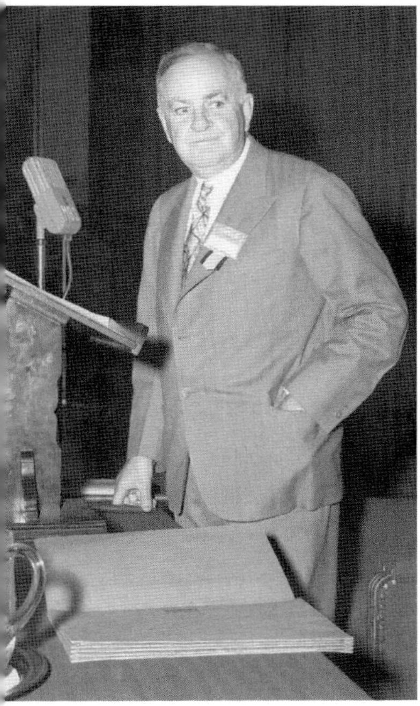

G.T. Hunter

In 1904, George Thomas Hunter came to live with his uncle Benjamin F. Thomas and his wife. He attended Baylor School to round out his education and while in school, began learning the bottling business. Working as a clerk, he eventually rose to secretary of the company, and when his uncle died in 1914, Hunter, the heir apparent, became president. He renamed the company the Coca-Cola Bottling Company in honor of his uncle Thomas and expanded his bottling business significantly as Coca-Cola essentially became the national soft drink. Like his uncle, philanthropy was an important part of his life, and in 1944, he created the Benwood Foundation, which also was named for his uncle Thomas. An activist in the life of the city, the foundation's name reflects his positivism in the respelling of the phrase, "Ben would." Fully funded at his death in 1950, the foundation has been one of the standard bearers of philanthropy in Chattanooga for decades and a linchpin for civic causes. His most notable legacy is the Hunter Museum of American Art, which came to life in 1952 at his former residence, the Faxon-Hunter mansion on the bluff above the Tennessee River. Today, the columned, brick building is home to the museum's 19th-century collection and offers visitors a unique, hushed ambiance to view the fine portraits and landscapes that grace its walls. (Courtesy Chattanooga Public Library.)

Hunter Mansion

Today, the Hunter mansion looks over a renewed townscape. Gone is the neighborhood that surrounded it, and now, a plaza dotted with a variety of American sculpture stands before it. Adjoining its right flank is a 21st-century, swooping-roofed addition with an aluminum facade that makes quite a contrast to the proper classical proportions embodied in its architecture. (Author's collection.)

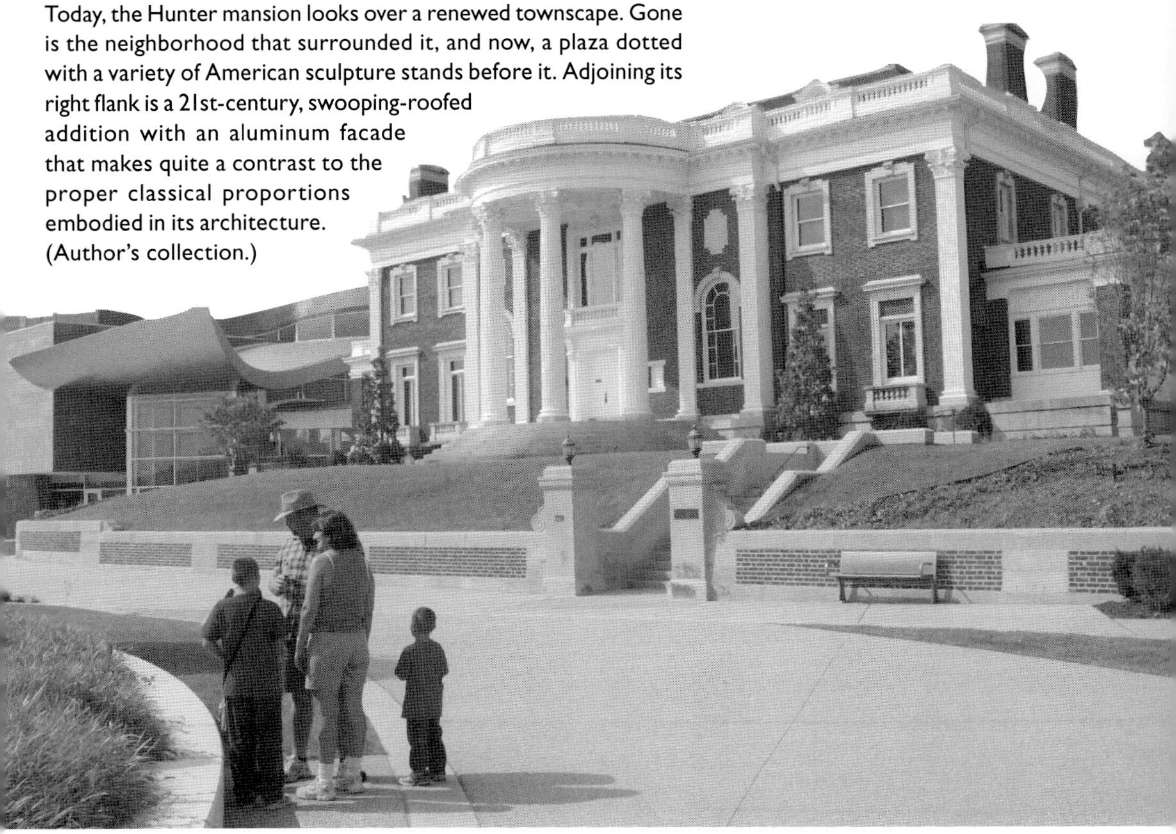

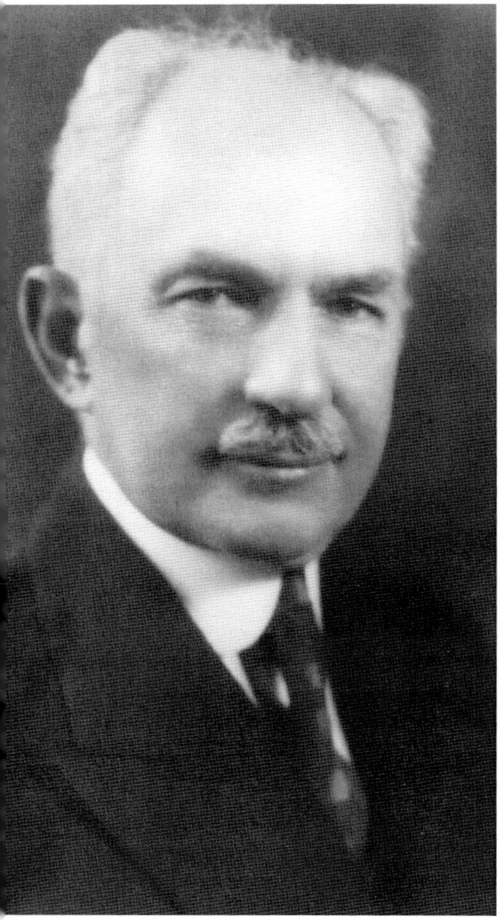

John T. Lupton

John Thomas Lupton made the most of an opportunity. Hailing from the town of Winchester, Virginia, in the northern Shenandoah Valley, he moved to Chattanooga at the height of the economic boom that followed from the Civil War. A graduate of the University of Virginia law school, he became a law partner of William Gibbs McAdoo, who later became Woodrow Wilson's secretary of the treasury. Two years after his arrival, he met and married Elizabeth Oliver Patten, daughter of Zeboim Cartter Patten, the founder of the Chattanooga Medicine Company, for whom he became legal counsel. Life was good, but the best was yet to come. In 1899, Benjamin Franklin Thomas and Joseph Brown Whitehead asked him to join them in their new venture to bottle a new drink in the South called Coca-Cola. Lupton offered them the financial support they needed and was given exclusive rights to license bottlers of the drink in the South and most of the West. When Whitehead died in 1906, Lupton actively expanded his role in growing the bottling business, which was taking off. The same year, he and his father-in-law organized the Volunteer State Life Insurance Company. By 1923, his textile mill, Dixie Mercerizing Company, was in production with 12,000 spindles. The site contained a mill village known as Lupton City, adjacent to the plant with homes for the workers featuring modern conveniences like indoor plumbing and electricity. In later life, philanthropy became important to him. Lipton supported a number of schools such as the Baylor School, the University of Chattanooga, and Oglethorpe University in Georgia, all of which have buildings named for him. (Courtesy Chattanooga Public Library.)

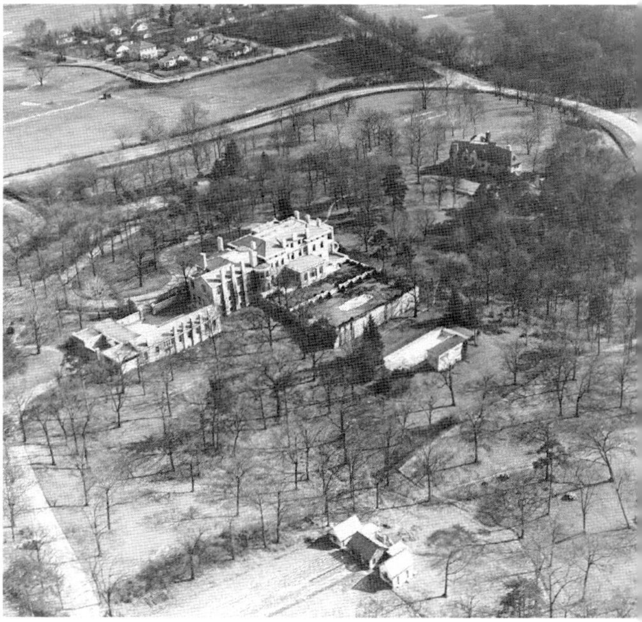

Lupton Mansion

John Lupton did things in a large way. His home, Lyndhurst, built in 1909, was no exception, a monument to his ascendancy in financial circles. It was an enormous, 34,000-square-foot Georgian style mansion with walls 18 inches thick. Built in Riverview by famed Atlanta architect, W.T. Downing, near the Riverview Golf and Country Club, the handsome dwelling was comparable in its size and scope to the Cheek House in Nashville or the Swan House in Atlanta. Unfortunately, when his wife, Elizabeth, died there was no one with the means or desire to keep it up and it had to be taken down in 1960, and the land divided into smaller lots. (Courtesy Chattanooga Public Library.)

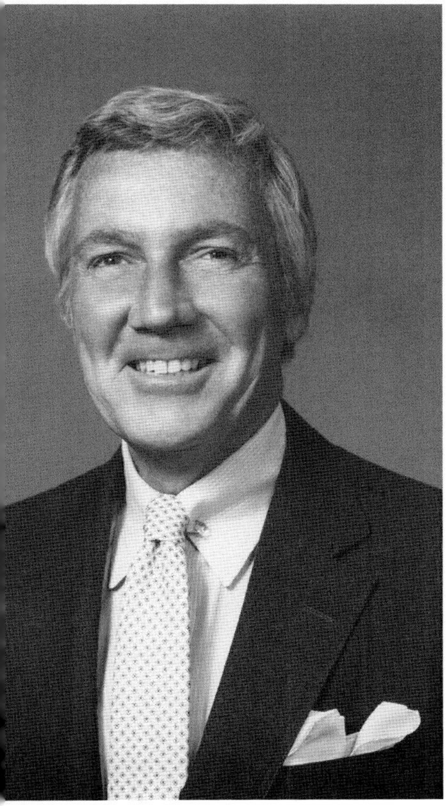

Jack Lupton

At the heart of philanthropy is devotion and Jack Lupton's love of his hometown was remarkable. The grandson of John Thomas Lupton, the Coca-Cola Bottling magnate, Lupton attended Baylor School where he excelled and graduated going straight into the Army in 1944 and serving on a PT boat in the South Pacific. In the style of the day, he entered his father's business at Coca-Cola by becoming a bottle washer in Macon, Georgia, and learning the business from the ground up. In time, he became head of the Chattanooga bottling enterprise, expanding the family empire until what was then known as the "JTL Bottling Empire" was sold to the Coca-Cola Company for a staggering $1.2 billion in 1986. But in many ways, his work was just beginning. He began to steer his family charity, the Lyndhurst Foundation, towards funding local education, promoting the arts, and sustaining the environment. Cognizant of the severe economic woes of the city and its questionable future at the time, he pledged a hefty $20 million in 1985 toward the development of a desolate riverfront, more particularly, the building of the proposed Tennessee Aquarium. This one bold act was a critical ingredient in what is now widely recognized as a major urban renaissance in the United States. In 2001, he donated $25 million to the University of Tennessee at Chattanooga, an example of the attitude of excellence that permeated his many beneficent activities. (Courtesy Chattanooga Public Library.)

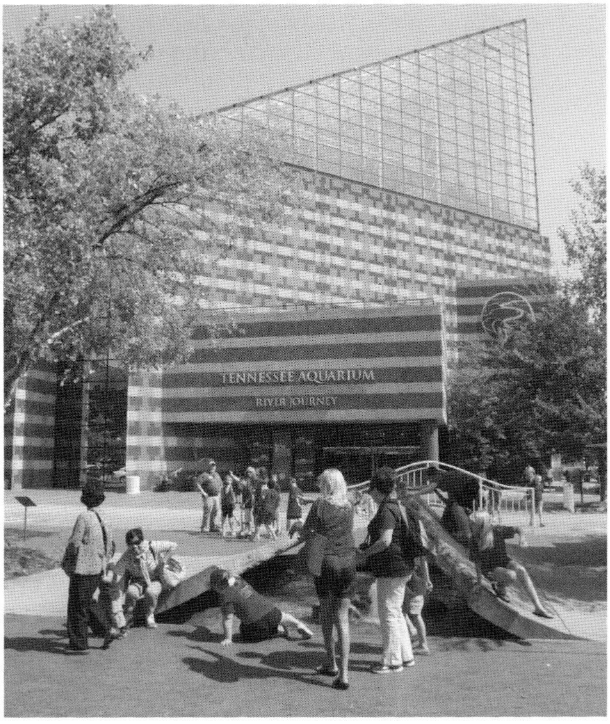

Lupton Legacy

It is difficult to cite only one instance of Jack Lupton's legacy, but the Tennessee Aquarium on the banks of the Tennessee River is hard to ignore. Many people played a role in its realization, but Lupton gave the idea the big kick it needed. For citizens at that time who had a long memory in Chattanooga, the aquarium was either going to be a grand boondoggle or a showstopper. For a city financially on its back in the 1980s, it turned out to be the latter when it opened in 1992. (Author's collection.)

Chattanooga Glass

The Chattanooga Glass Company came into being in 1901, shortly after the Coca-Cola Bottling Company got its start. Originally, a bottler of beer, the company, founded by Charles Rief, soon became a steady producer of Coca-Cola bottles for the booming soft drink maker. Prohibition forced Chattanooga Glass to discontinue alcohol-related bottles and focus on carbonated beverages. The first stoppers for these bottles were made of rubber and when opened and made a popping sound, creating the term "pop," or "soda pop," for drinks like Coke. In 1925, J. Frank Harrison purchased the company and ramped up production considerably, making the company a vital part of Chattanooga's thriving industrial economy and an employer to many. (Courtesy Tennessee State Library and Archives.)

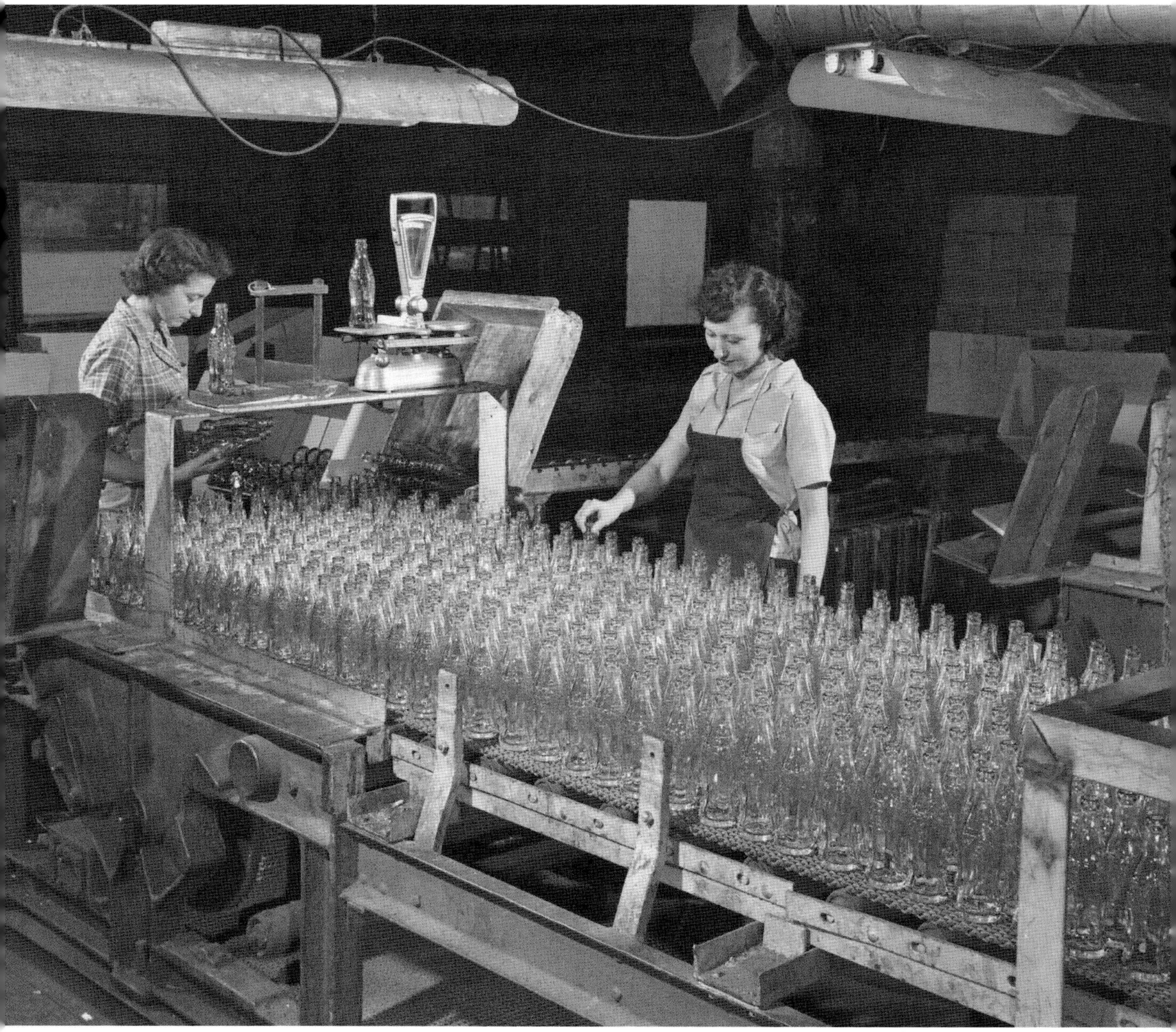

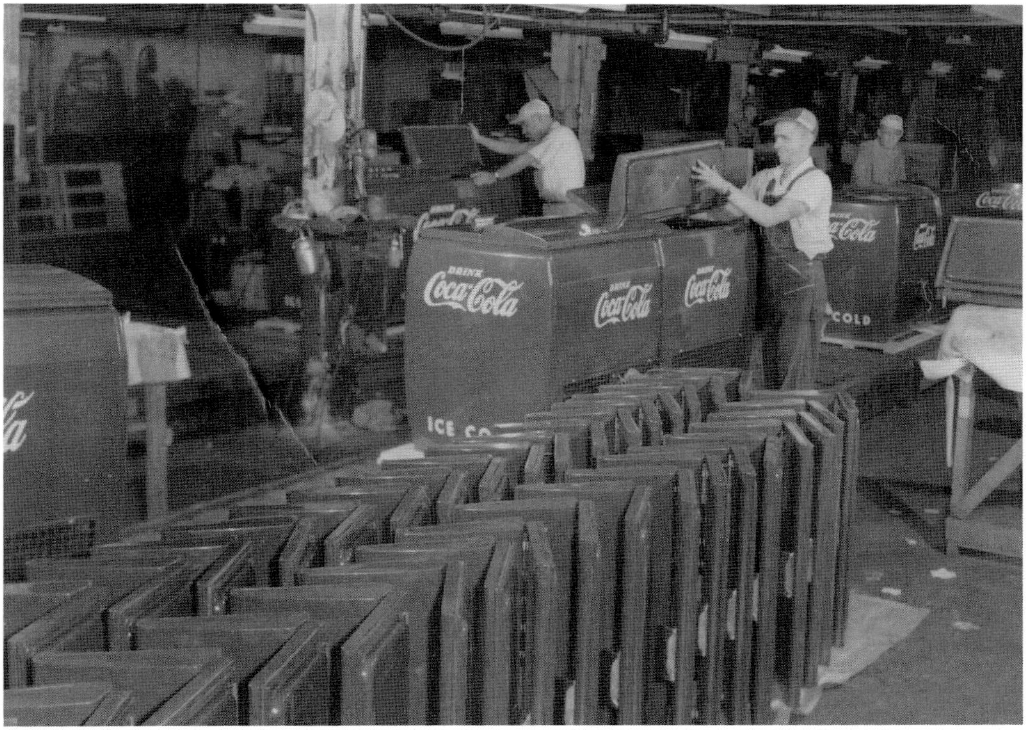

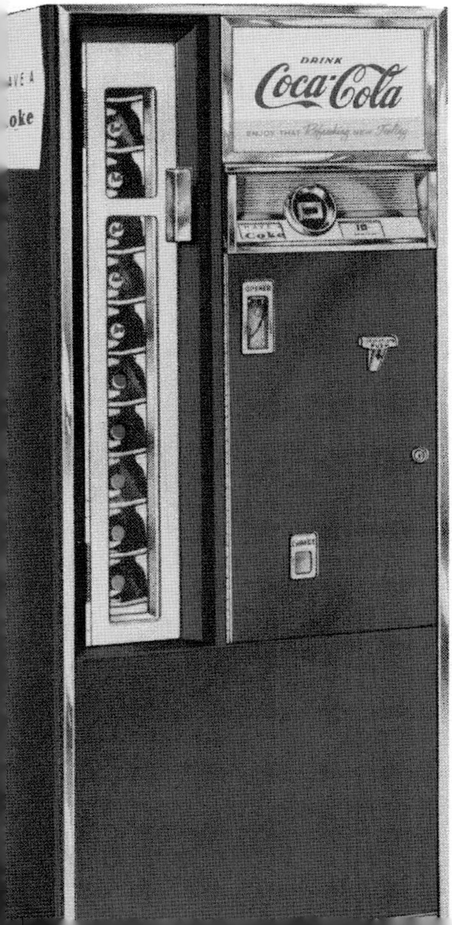

Cavalier Corp.

Another company that benefited from an association with Coca-Cola Bottling was the Cavalier Corporation. A division of the Tennessee Furniture Company of Chattanooga dating back to 1865, Cavalier began making cedar hope chests and then coolers for ice under the direction of Gaston C. Raoul. In 1935, Cavalier they began making cold drink coolers and upright vending machines specifically for the Coca-Cola Company. The introduction of the iconic Coca-Cola vending machine around the country became an enormously successful venture. Soon, the company introduced the first standing machine—the collectible CS-72 with its "Have a Coke" button that lights up—with an internal shelf storage system that enabled it to hold nine different kinds of drinks. Cavalier also created a machine that could dispense bottles or cans. Profitable for years, the company fell on hard times, declared bankruptcy in 1987, and closed for good in 2000. (Courtesy Tennessee State Library and Archives.)

Cavalier Product (Soft Drink Machine)

Cavalier was an early developer of the soft drink machines that seemed to be everywhere by the 1960s. They constantly adapted the machines to deliver more products and look more appealing. Like jukeboxes or pinball machines, these machines have a nostalgic appeal and are coveted by collectors. (Courtesy Chattanooga Public Library.)

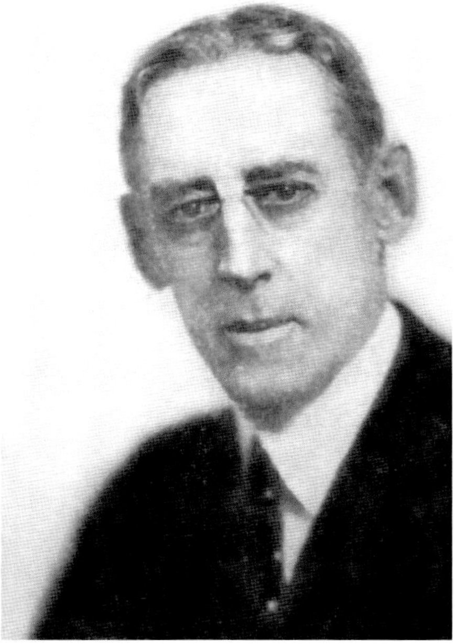

William Emerson Brock, Sr.
William Emerson Brock was an entrepreneur who moved to Chattanooga in 1906 from North Carolina, where he had been one of the first salesmen with R.J. Reynolds Tobacco. With the dream of manufacturing candy on a large scale, he began working with the Trigg Candy Company and then founded his own business. By the 1930s, his chocolate-covered cherries were widely popular in the South. Jellied candies became a specialty of Brock. He also was a leader in introducing cellophane packages made by the DuPont Company as a way to keep candy fresh. Appointed as a US senator for a short term, his candy company was the largest in the South when he died in 1950. (Courtesy Chattanooga Public Library.)

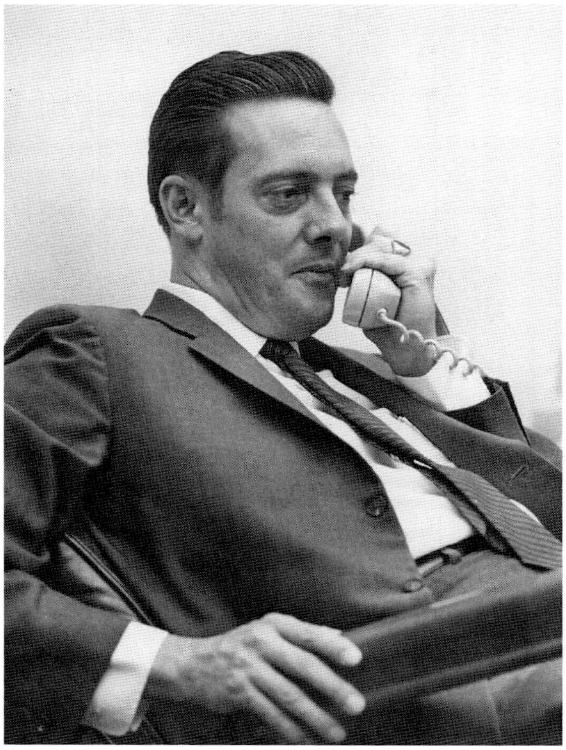

Bill Brock III
Bill Brock III, a McCallie School graduate, became Chattanooga's congressman in 1962 in a significant election. Part of the new wave of Republicans in the South, Brock broke a 40-year-old lock that the old New Deal Democrats had on the district when he was voted in. He held the seat until becoming a US senator in 1971 for one term. Brock later headed the Republican National Committee and was US secretary of labor for Ronald Reagan. (Courtesy Chattanooga Public Library.)

Brock Jellies (OPPOSITE PAGE)
Brock Jellies were a popular candy for thousands of sweets-lovers, particularly folks in small towns where the Brock Candy Company concentrated its sales efforts. In the early days of the company, fudge was a constant seller, and at one point, its nickel peanut stick was a delight to the business's bottom line. But eventually, William Brock found that marshmallow and jelly snacks were the favorite treat that many customers craved and emphasizing them sent sales steadily up. (Courtesy Tennessee State Library and Archives.)

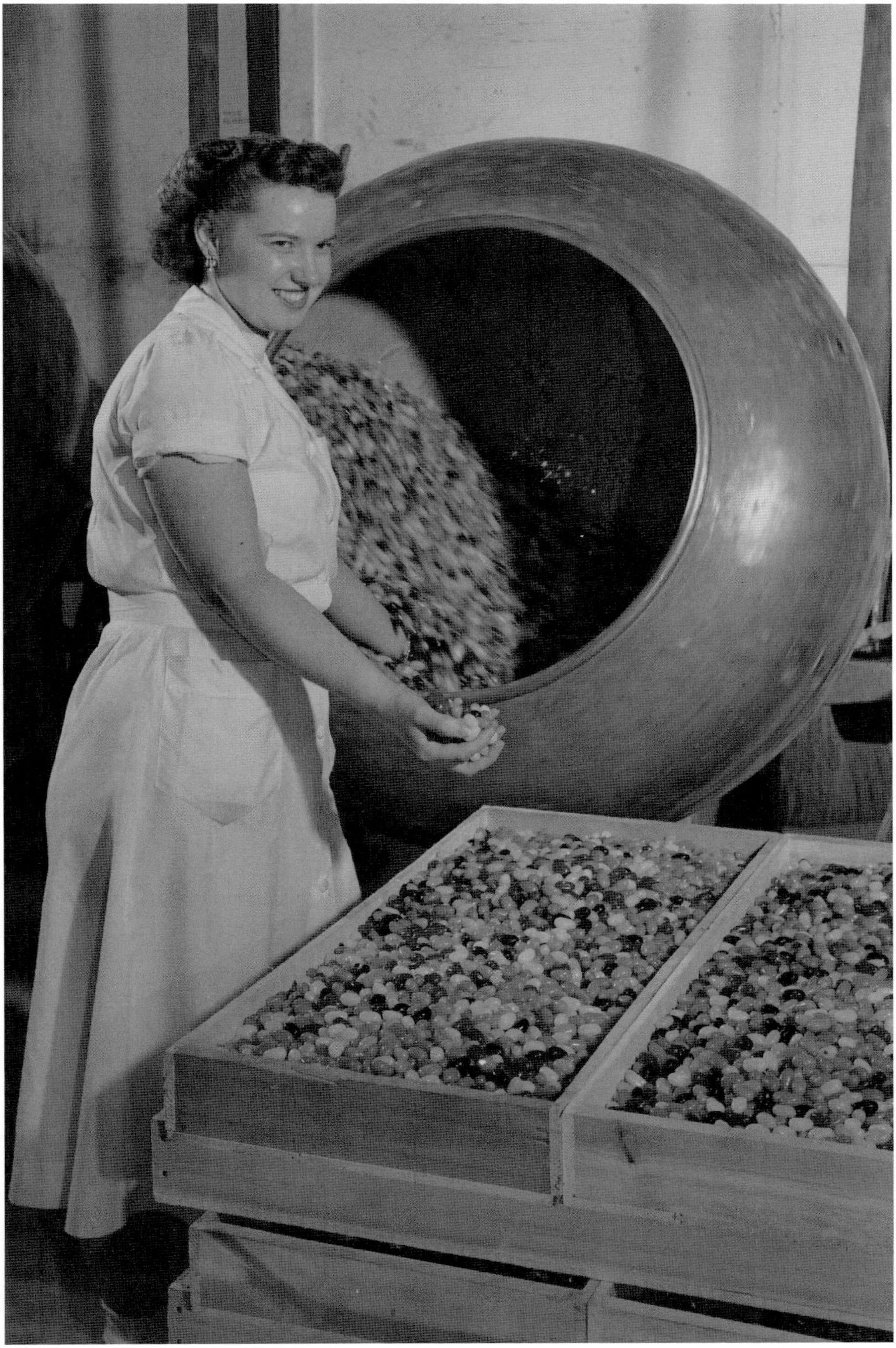

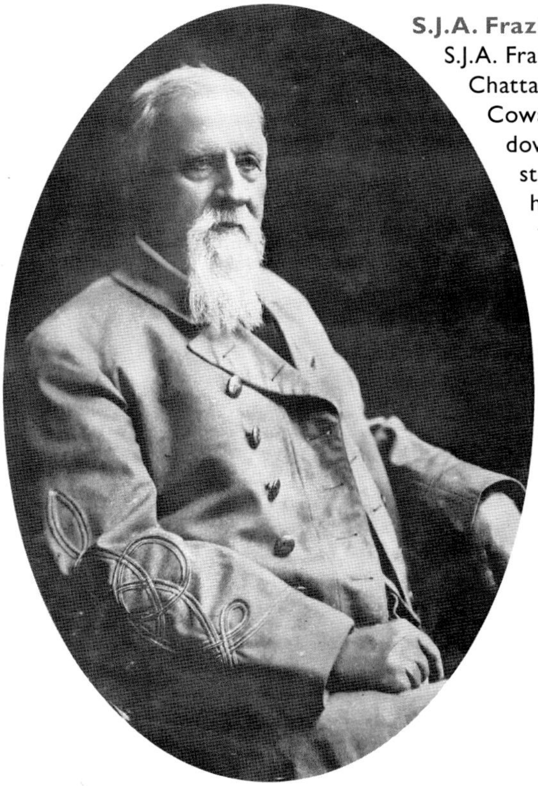

S.J.A. Frazier

S.J.A. Frazier could rightly be called the planner of North Chattanooga. A Civil War veteran, he purchased the Cowart property in the area across the river from downtown and began laying out tracts of land and streets as he planned the new "suburb" in 1882. He helped start a regular ferry across the river and was a major backer of the Walnut Street Bridge that spanned the river 10 years later. During a time of prosperity for Chattanooga, the new neighborhood grew steadily and by the early 1900s, was in need of its own post office. Frazier and his family happily saw all this happen from his home, The Cedars, on Frazier Avenue. (Courtesy Chattanooga Public Library.)

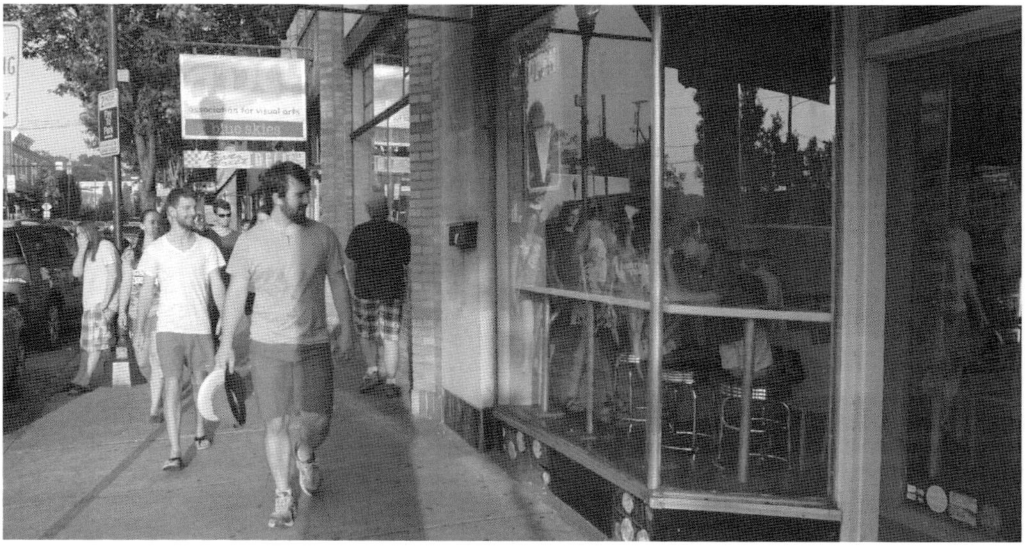

Frazier Today

Frazier Avenue on a typical weekend is home to a variety of people—tourists, teenagers, families, artists, and urban trekkers. The street is still lined with many of the buildings from the early 1900s that house restaurants, beauty salons, antique stores, bicycle shops, and a potpourri of other offerings. Situated next to the Walnut Street Bridge, a pedestrian thoroughfare, the area is just a mile walk from downtown Chattanooga across the river and an easy area to navigate and enjoy. (Author's collection.)

Walnut Street Bridge

The Walnut Street Bridge was the first permanent span to connect Chattanooga south of the river to the wooded north side in 1891. The beautifully massive, stacked stone piers that support the Walnut Street Bridge were laid by stone contractor William Andrew Slayton and his crew. Slayton actually lived on the north side of the river at the end of the bridge on Frazier Avenue at the location of the "Little Art Shop." There, he could constantly monitor and inspect the progress of the construction. Many people believe that the numerous, residential walls around old North Chattanooga were formed from small rocks that were discarded in the building process. Oddly enough, at his burial site, the mason has no stone to mark his grave. (Courtesy Chattanooga Public Library.)

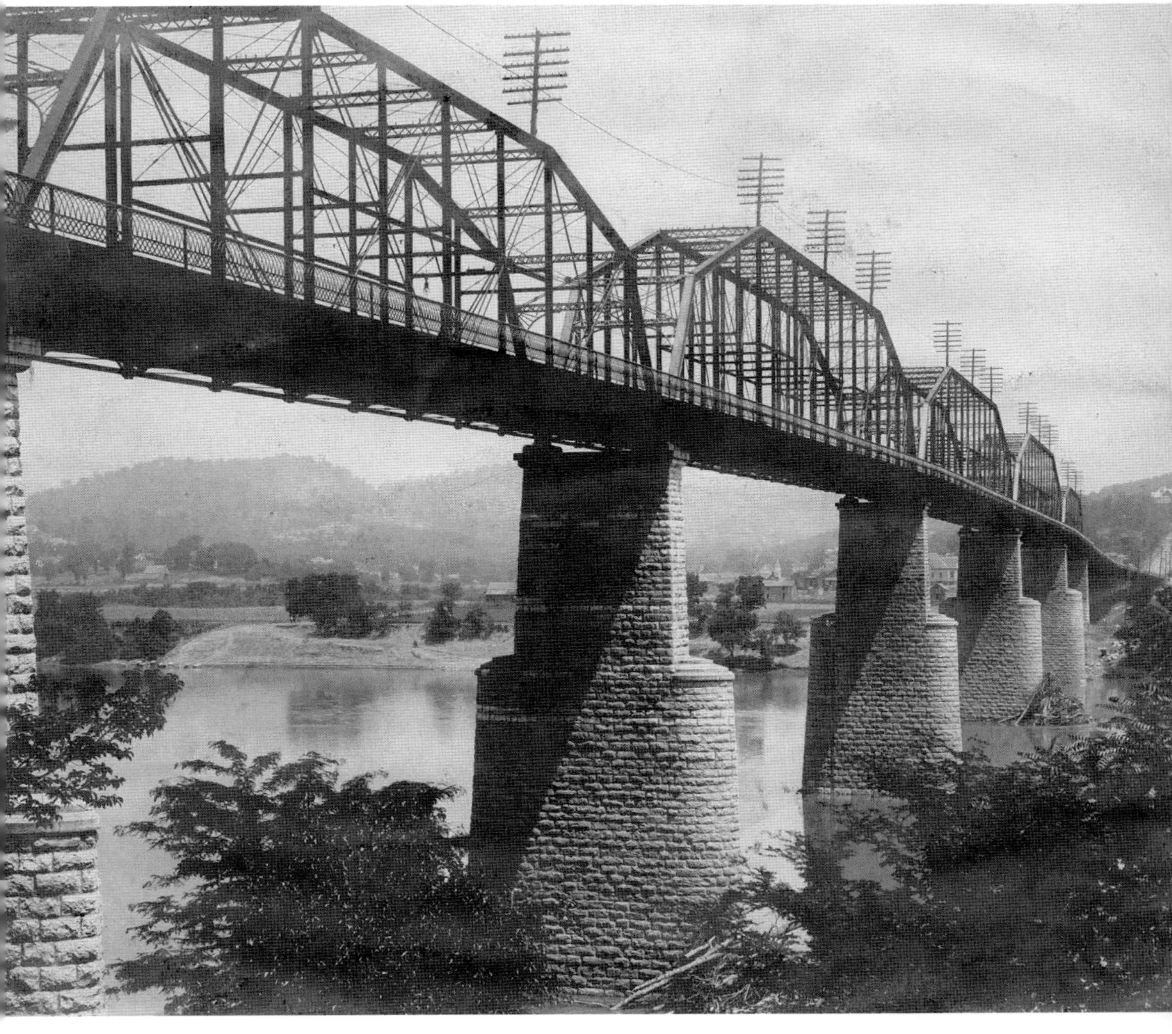

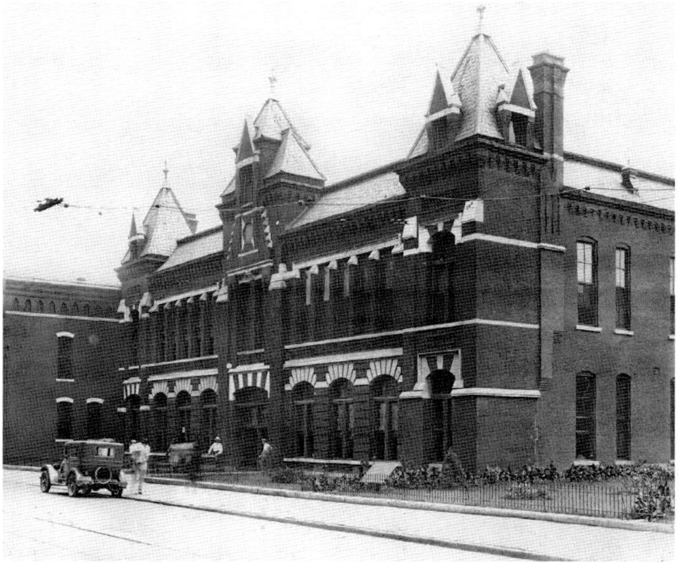

Railroad
The Union Depot was completed in 1881 when the waiting rooms and offices were added to the old depot to handle the traffic at the popular departure point. Called "Union" because it served several different rails, the depot faced the Read House on Martin Luther King Boulevard (formerly Ninth Street). With an interesting facade of variegated brick and pointed towers, it faced a sad fate when the last passenger train left on May 1, 1971; it was razed in 1973. (Courtesy Chattanooga Public Library.)

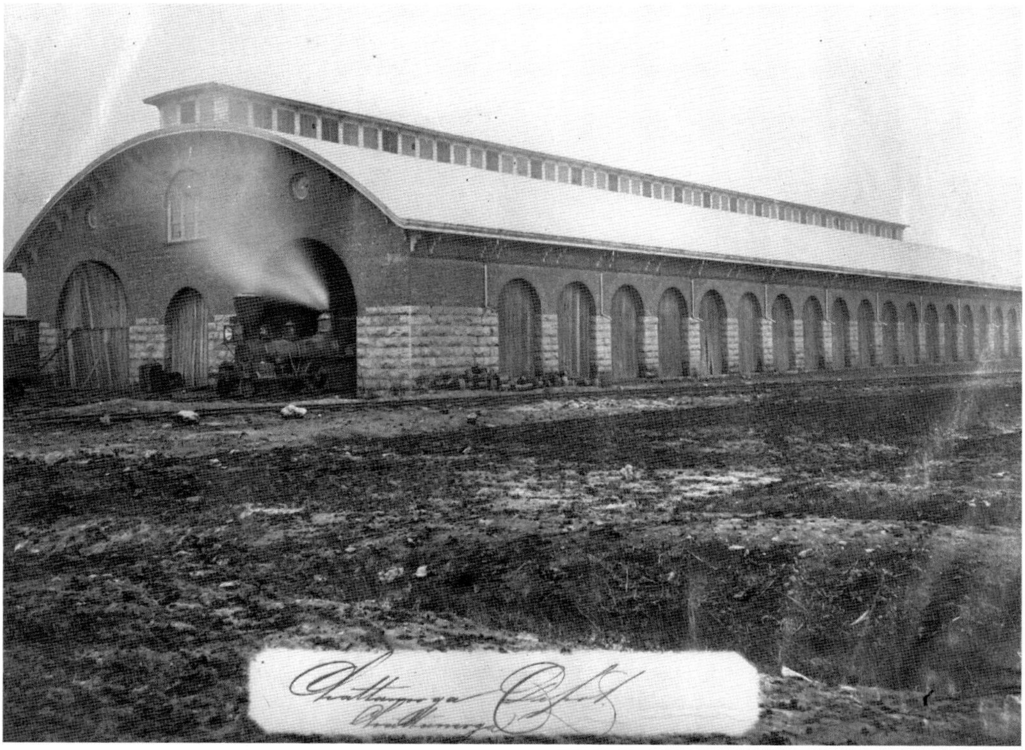

Railroad Shed
This long railroad shed was originally where everyone caught the train in 1858. The huge archway of stone was over 300 feet long and was the center of town in a manner of speaking. It sat near modern-day Tenth and Broad Streets, and when the Confederates retreated from Middle Tennessee, it served as a hospital. Later, after Chickamauga, the wounded and bloodied Federal troops crawled back to Chattanooga to use it as a sanctuary as well. (Courtesy Chattanooga Public Library.)

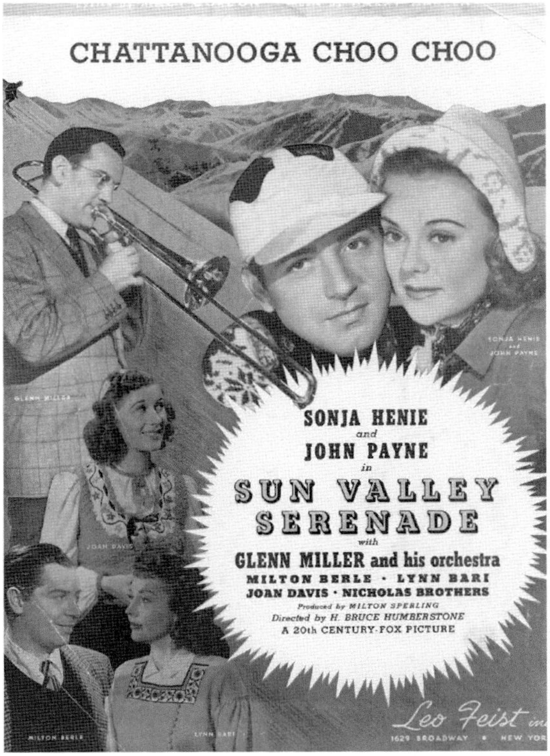

"Chattanooga Choo Choo," Glen Miller
Ask someone from around the country what goes with the word, "Chattanooga," and you are bound to hear the phrase "Chattanooga Choo Choo," something that is remarkable considering it is the title of a song that was written 70 years ago. With its catchy rhythm, punchy horns, and syncopated syllables, the tune made famous the local locomotive that plowed up and down the railroads of the east coast. Or did it? The fact is that the steam-blowing train only exists on record and the airwaves of oldies-playing radio stations. The song was written and made popular by Glenn Miller during his great reign of popularity in the Big Band era and takes credit for being the first million-selling record in American history. Artists as diverse as Carmen Miranda, Cab Calloway, and Hank Snow have recorded versions of the tune. Local entrepreneurs have always looked for a way to capitalize on the song, and since 1973, the Terminal Station on Market Street has claimed the title. (Courtesy Chattanooga History Center.)

Chattanooga Choo-Choo, Station
The Terminal Station on Market Street stands on the site of the former Stanton House. Opened in 1909, the station is a Beaux Arts–style building with an 82-foot dome in the lobby. A property of the Southern Railway, it saw the last passenger train depart in 1970 and its fortunes with it. Reopened several years later, the Chattanooga Choo-Choo serves as a hotel, featuring period train cars that are available as rooms if one prefers the experience of a night on a stationery sleeper car. (Courtesy Chattanooga Public Library.)

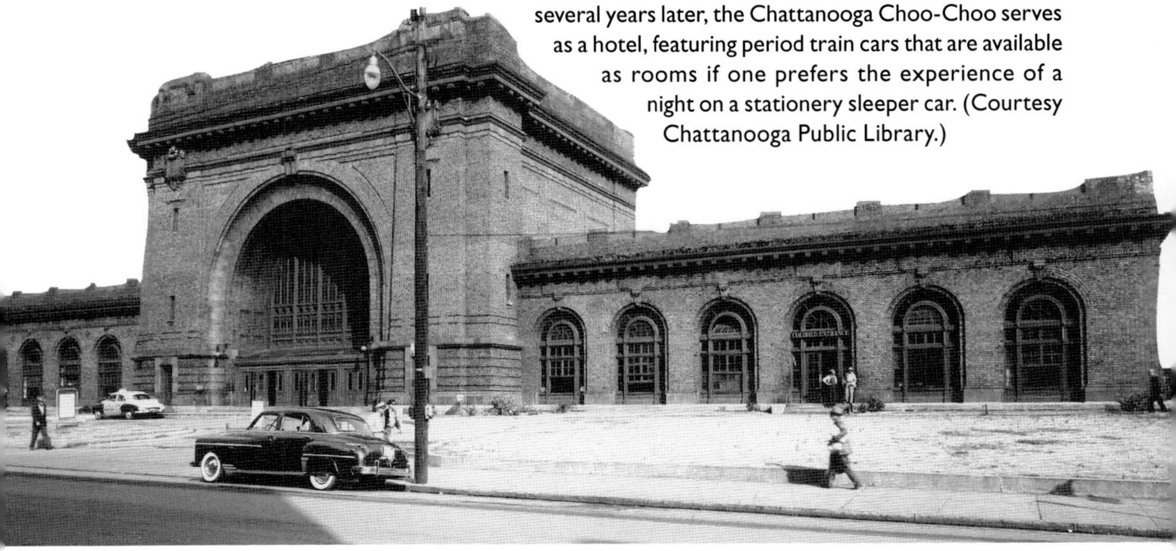

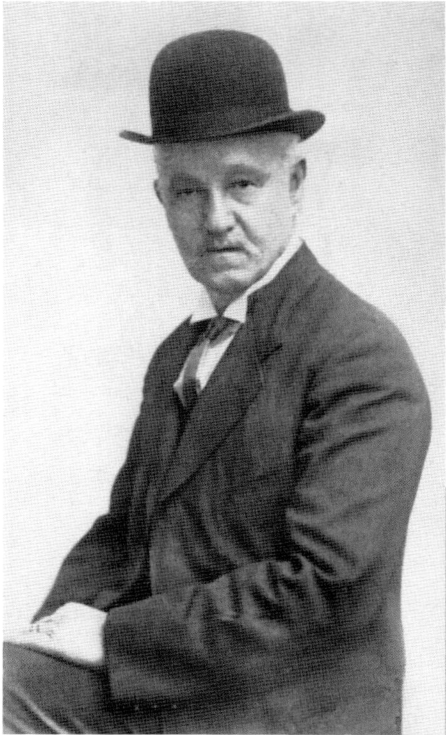

Charles James

Charles James was a man on a mission to build and earn, and his portrait shows it. He decided to open up what was a backwoods mountain and make it a resort and residential area. To that point, he built a road up Signal Mountain and then an inn. He was a backer of the power dam at Hales Bar, the first on the river, and as a symbol of his prowess, he constructed Chattanooga's first skyscraper, the James Building on Broad Street. Often referred to as the "Jay Gould of the South," James was the town's first millionaire. When he died in 1925 from congestion, he was buried in historic Forest Hills Cemetery with his solid gravestone facing towards Signal Mountain. (Courtesy Chattanooga Public Library.)

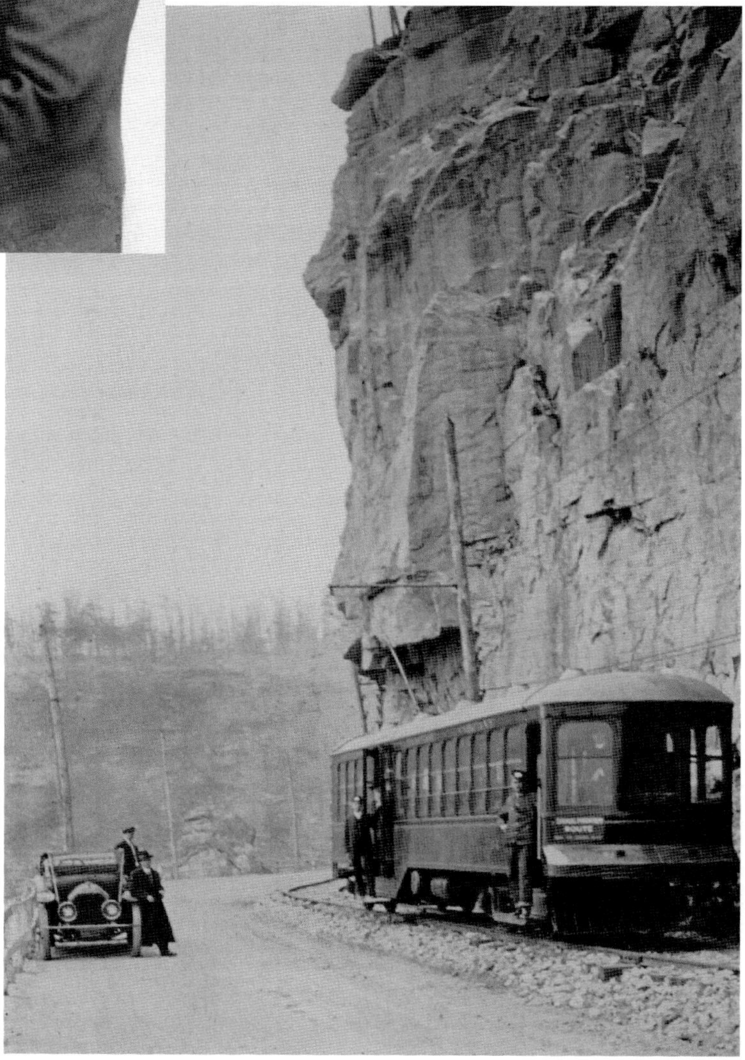

Road Up Signal Mountain

The palisades up Signal Mountain are steep and cutting a road up the mountain was no easy task, plus in 1913, it seemed miles from nowhere. But a trolley made it less difficult, and a beautiful inn in a neighborhood, now called Old Town, made it more tempting. (Courtesy Chattanooga Public Library.)

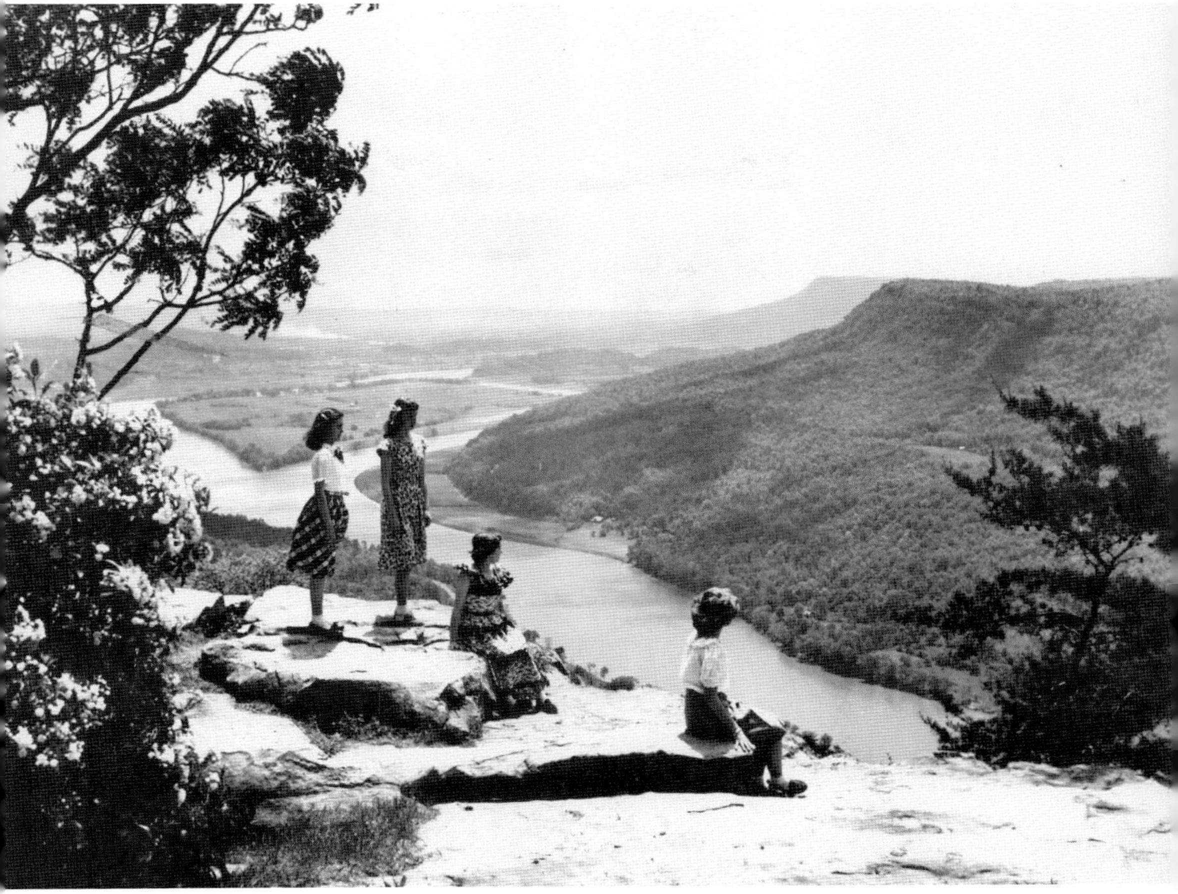

Signal Mountain Vista

Signal Mountain was an important first stop for the Union army coming into the valley. From Brady Point, where these children stand, the view of the river and Lookout Mountain in the distance is unparalleled, and troops used it to signal across the distance to soldiers below. The point is a park today and the starting point for trails into the Tennessee River Gorge. (Courtesy Chattanooga Public Library.)

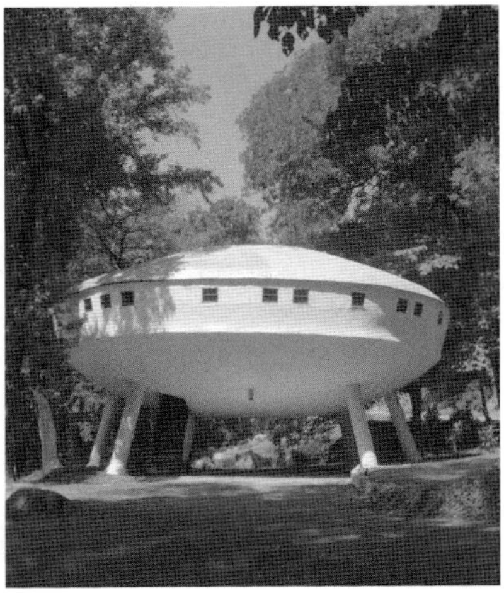

Flying Saucer House

Curtis W. King was fascinated with space travel as were many Americans in the 1960s. King, along with his two sons, decided to build one on the side of Signal Mountain in 1972, joking it could be "a bachelor pad for my son." Supported by sturdy concrete pillars that contain the plumbing and electrical workings, the house has a drop-down ladder with 13 steps that curious earthlings may use to enter the house where they immediately encounter a bar with 13 mysterious mirrors and 13 light fixtures. More steps up a spiral staircase reveal the living quarters with endlessly rounded walls and a creative use of "mood lighting." King thought this house might be a prototype for future dwellings, but the expense of this circular domicile convinced him to settle for just this one spaceship. (Author's collection.)

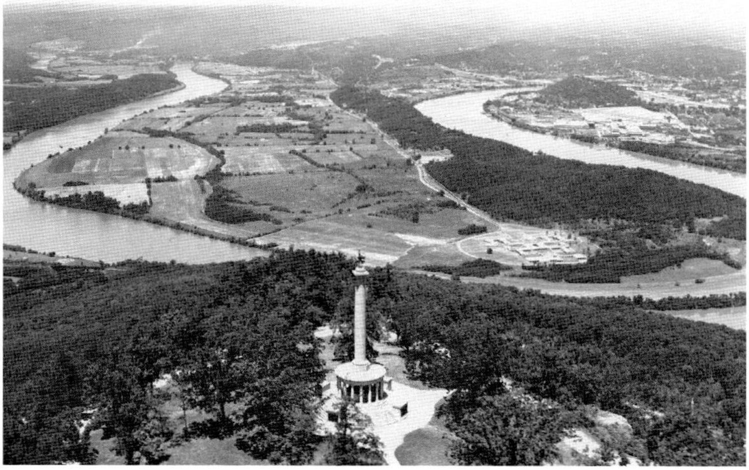

Lookout Mountain Vista
This sweeping panorama of the Chattanooga Valley is one reason people have sought out the peak of Lookout Mountain. Below, Moccasin Bend appears in the distinct shape of a foot, the location of centuries-old traces of human communities that have lived off its rich soil and fished its waters. This new century has seen the national park system make a substantial portion of this land public property to be protected in perpetuity. (Courtesy Chattanooga Public Library.)

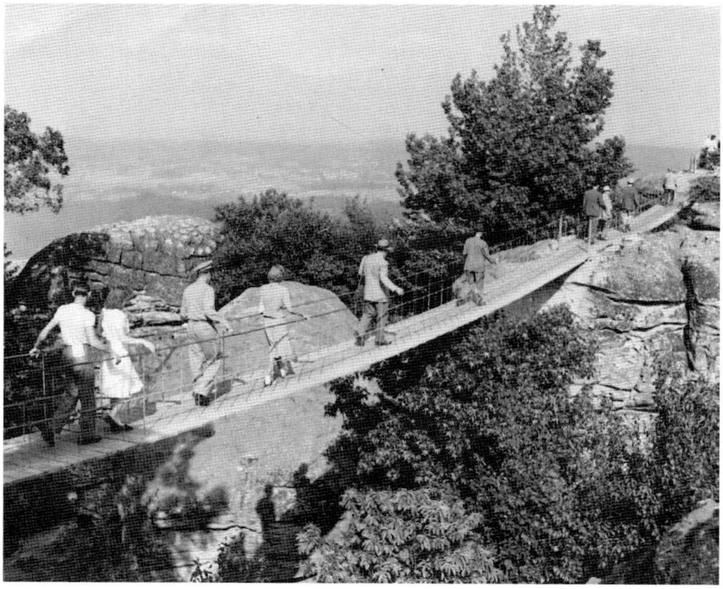

Lookout Mountain Rope Bridge
There is no bridge like a rope bridge, and this one still makes a lot of people nervous. Though it is completely safe, the feeling of walking on it with a group of strangers is a bit unnerving. Interestingly enough, ropes courses are currently popular on the mountain as a way to have fun while paying to feel some real unsteadiness. (Courtesy Chattanooga Public Library.)

Lovers Leap
A view from Lovers Leap shows the eastern valley below stretching back into Georgia. Huge boulders protruding from the palisades of the mountain offer dynamic viewing and great climbing opportunities for today's outdoor adventurer. The soft rock atop many of the mountains in the southern Appalachians tends to erode over time, giving way to a sheer wall of rock near the top, which is framed by hardwood forests above and gently swooping woods below. (Courtesy Chattanooga Public Library.)

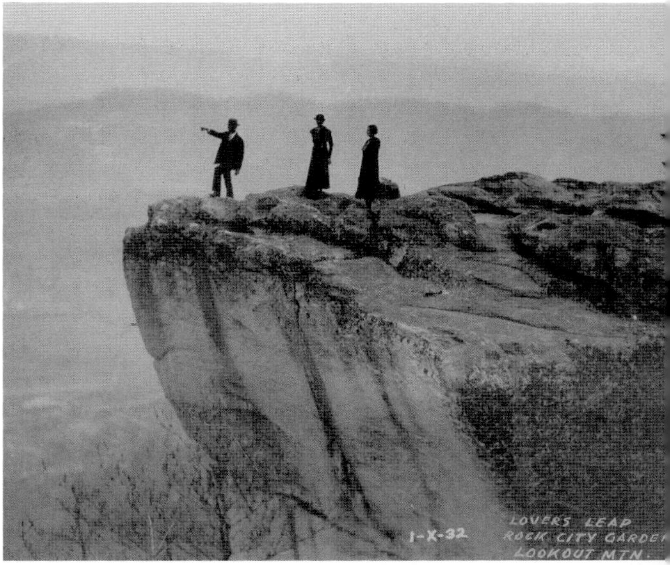

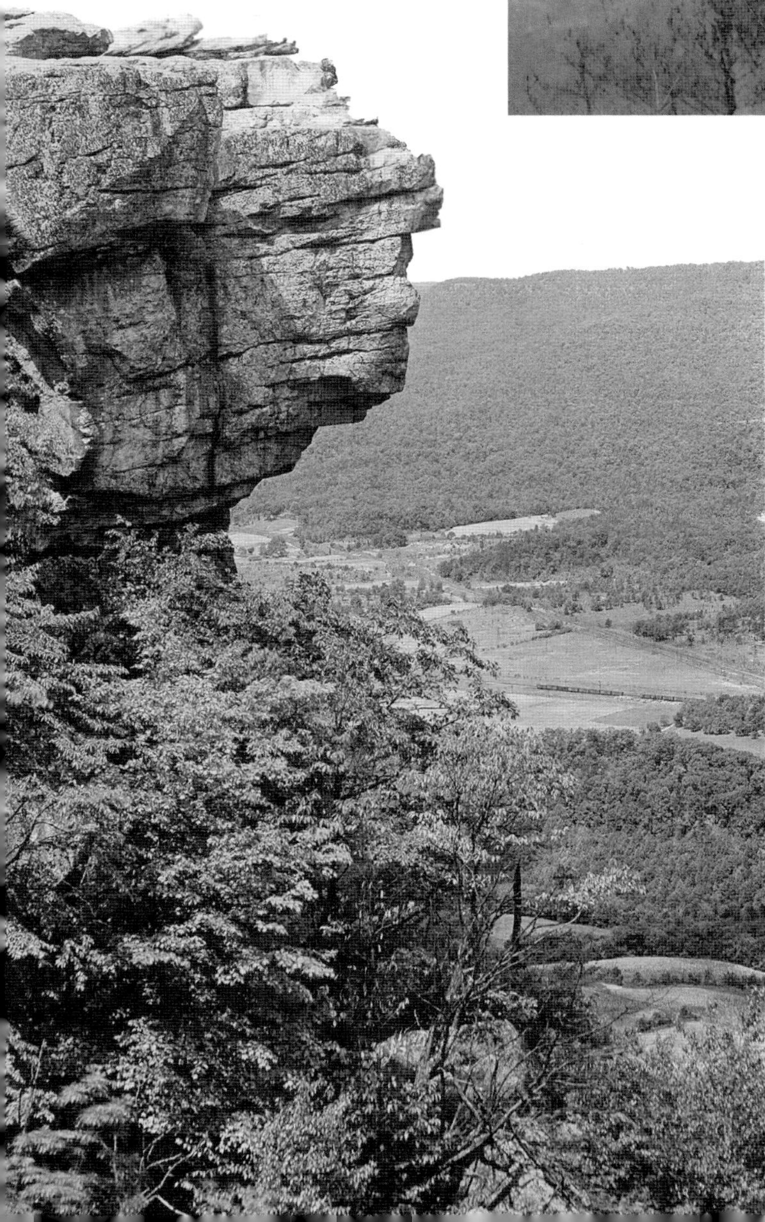

Lookout Mountain Profile
This human profile in stone has long been the source of a local legend about an Indian chief who lived in the valley. In failing health and knowing his people were dying, he asked the gods to remember them. That night, a storm came and lightning struck the stone, carving the visage. The fanciful story seems to be a way to give the Cherokee's suffering some romance and nobility. (Courtesy Chattanooga Public Library.)

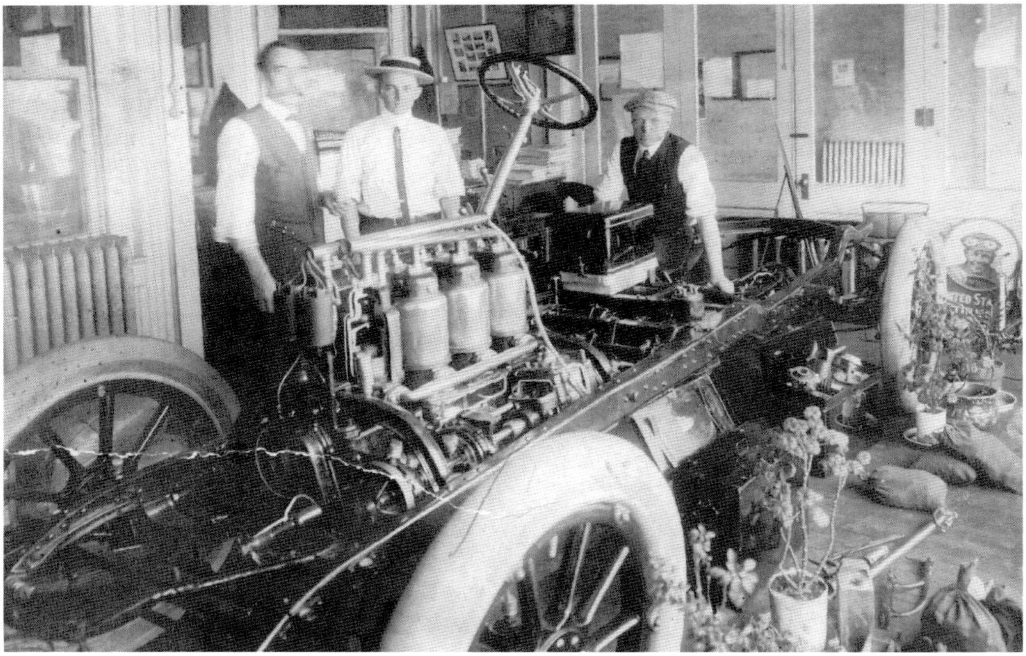

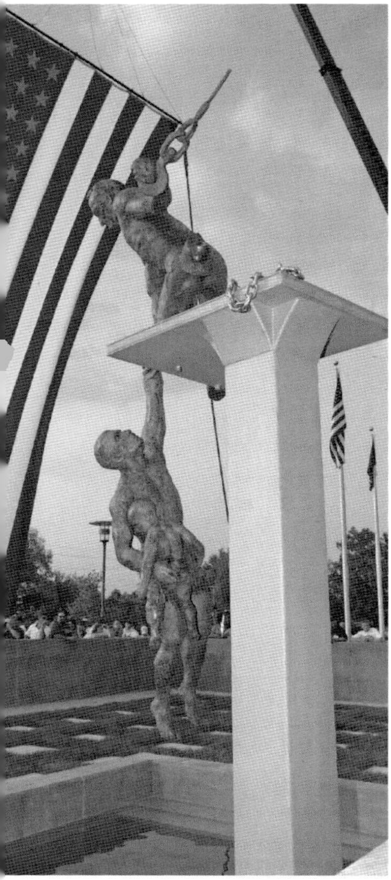

Ernest Holmes in His Shop

The author's grandfather John G. Fulmer would often intone, "Necessity is the mother of invention." Ernest Holmes, Fulmer's neighbor on Hixson Pike, saw a situation that needed a remedy—automobiles in distress. At the beginning of the automobile age, a car stranded off the road had to be rescued with ropes, many human hands, and hours of labor. As the roads of America began to fill with early model cars, Holmes put together a vehicle in 1916 from a used 1913 Cadillac with a platform containing pulleys and cables in 1916, specifically a "twin boomer" that could wrench a wrecked auto up an embankment. As the business, Holmes Wrecker, on Market Street grew, he added outriggers or anchors to the side of the trucks and installed a pivoting boom that had greater range of motion. This photograph shows him at his shop in the process of creating a new industry. The whole story of his business acumen, his service to others, and the many people who worked in the profession is told at the International Towing and Recovery Hall of Fame and Museum on Broad Street near the foot of Lookout Mountain. (Courtesy International Towing and Recovery Museum.)

International Towing and Recovery Museum

The gripping sculpture of the figure reaching down to rescue another is the work of Cessna Decosimo. Rooted firmly in the figurative tradition, Decosimo's emphasis on the power and musculature of the torso is born out here in these carefully limned figures and their intense life and death connection. With a master's degree in fine art from the New York Academy of Fine Art and considerable time abroad, he has created a captivating piece of art that stands on South Broad Street depicting a real-life instance of a tow rescue operator in an act of selfless heroism. (Courtesy International Towing and Recovery Hall of Fame and Museum.)

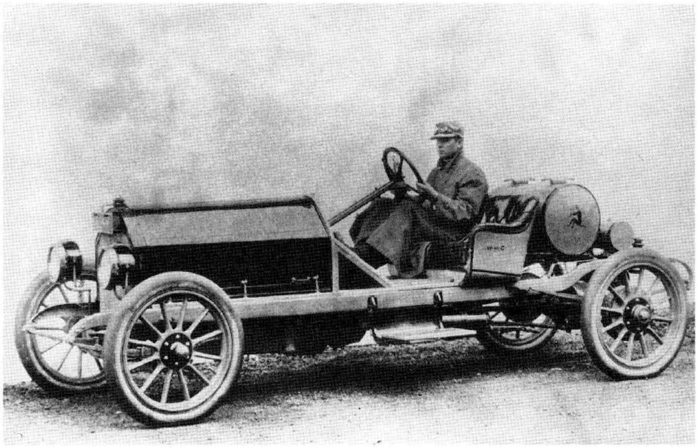

Nyberg Car

Henry Nyberg was a Chicagoan, who built a plant in Chattanooga (he had another in Indiana) to make the Nyberg in 1911. He built powerful long-stroke motors and luxury cars in 22 styles—the Dixie Special being one of those constructed here. Whereas Ford Model Ts might run $400, a Nyberg cost $1,900. They featured sturdy V-6 engines, were large, roomy, and very comfortable to ride in, with notably "soft cushions." The varnish was even unusually high quality—billed as "dust, water, and soap proof." One truck the plant produced even had a musical organ in the front seat that was operated by the driver and powered by the engine. The Nyberg became well known for a local endurance race that went from Chattanooga to Knoxville. Only two Nybergs survive today. (Courtesy Chattanooga Public Library.)

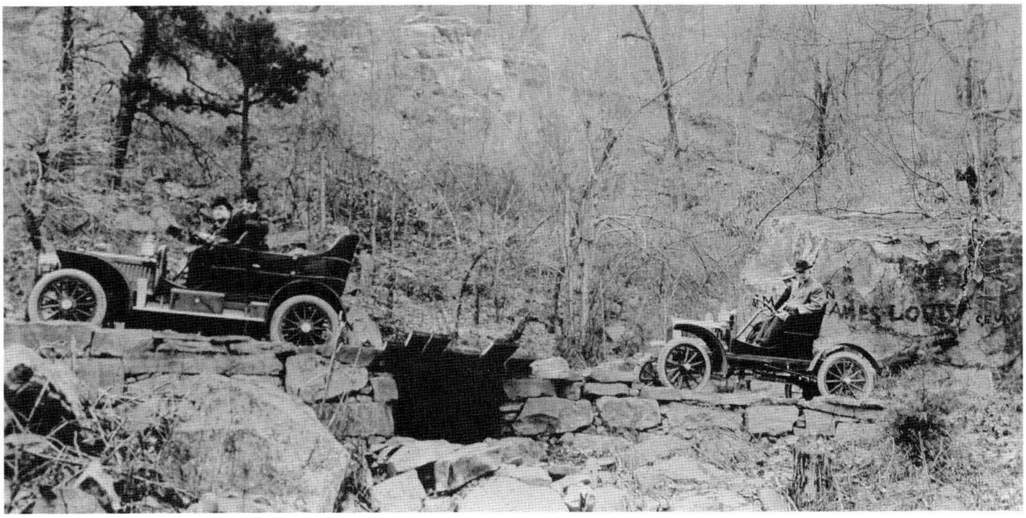

Driver up Lookout Mountain

Erwin "Cannonball" Baker was a man in a hurry. Originally an unmatched motorcyclist, he became famous for his transcontinental runs, the first of which was in 1914 over some rough and rugged terrain. A New York writer named him "Cannonball," making a comparison to Casey Jones's famous train. In 1915, he went from Los Angeles to New York City in 11 days in a Stutz Bearcat and then, the next year, smashed his own record in a Cadillac 8 doing the long trip in an amazing seven days. So famous was he that thousands of people came to Chattanooga to see him compete—and win—the 1909 race up and down Lookout Mountain at a fast and furious 36 miles per hour, beating among others, auto-lover Louis Chevrolet. (Courtesy Chattanooga Public Library.)

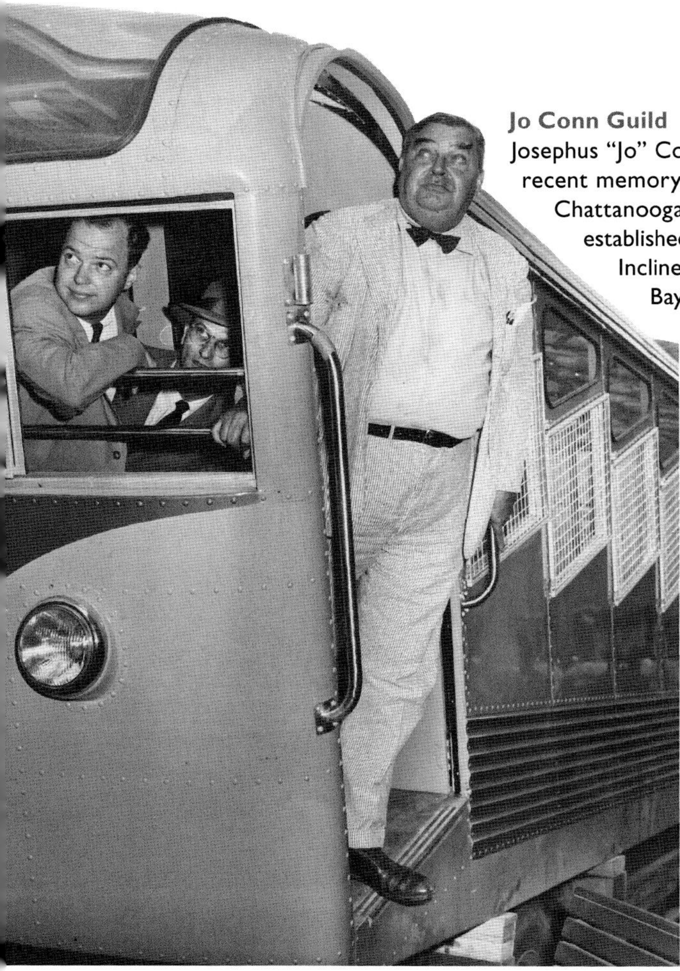

Jo Conn Guild

Josephus "Jo" Conn Guild Jr. is a name that has receded from recent memory, but his work was significant in establishing Chattanooga as an electrical powerhouse. The son of an established engineer who designed the Lookout Mountain Incline Railway, Guild was born in 1887 and attended Baylor School. Studying at the University of Virginia and Vanderbilt University, he worked with his father's company to complete Hales Bar Dam, a huge undertaking that was just south of Chattanooga. After the operation of the dam began, he rose to the rank of general manager and started to buy smaller power operations on neighboring rivers, eventually creating the Tennessee Electric Power Company (TEPCO) of which he became president in 1933. By this time, he had absorbed or controlled 45 different utility companies in the mountain regions. But Pres. Franklin Roosevelt's creation of the Tennessee Valley Authority (TVA) threatened his business, and he fought the federal program tooth and nail, resulting in a Supreme Court decision against him. He spent his remaining years operating the local streetcars of which the Lookout Mountain Incline (seen here) was a part. (Courtesy Chattanooga Public Library.)

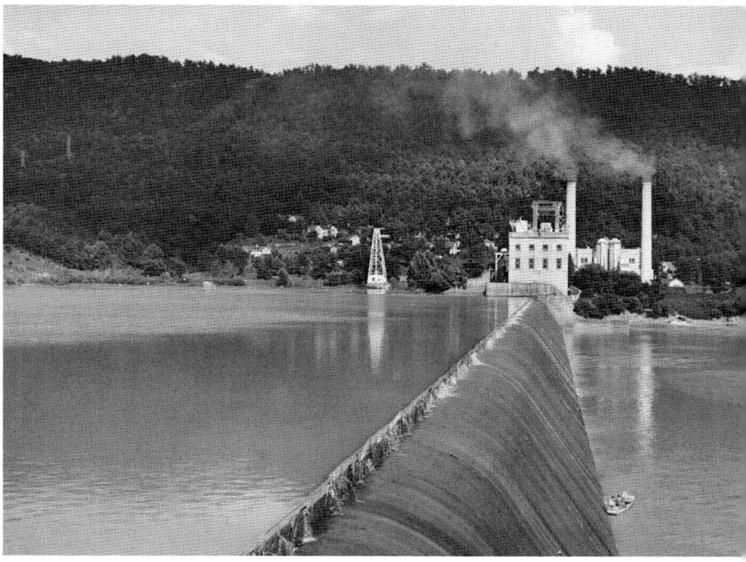

Hales Bar

Little remains of Hales Bar, the first hydroelectric dam built in the South. Begun in 1905 it was difficult to build and took eight years to complete. Spanning a wide, navigable channel in the gorge of the river, it constantly leaked from the beginning. Eventually, TVA found it too expensive to repair and ceased operation there in 1968. (Courtesy Chattanooga Public Library.)

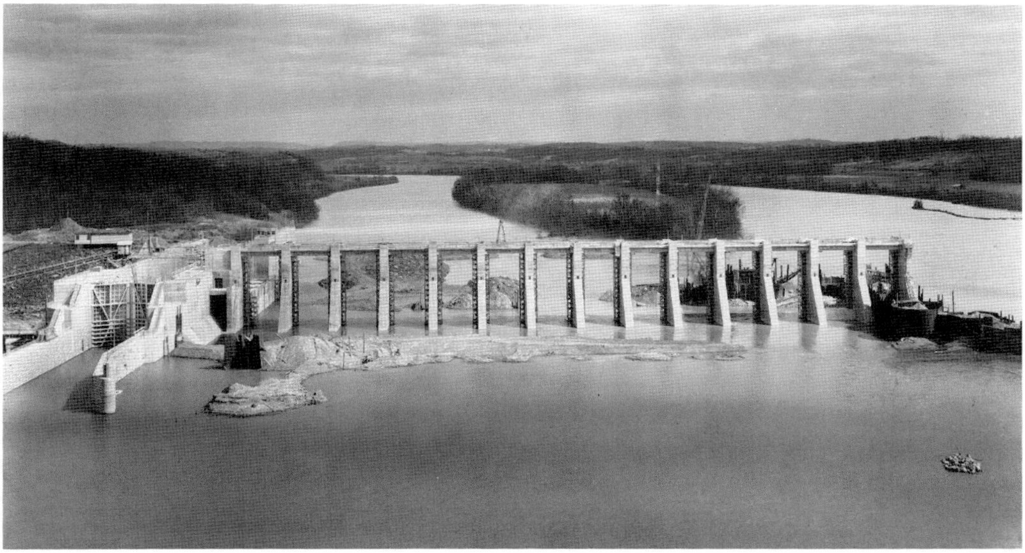

Chickamauga Dam

The New Deal of Franklin D. Roosevelt had an enormous impact on Chattanooga, the most visible of which is the Chickamauga Dam. Begun in 1936, it required moving 903 families and a number of cemeteries and was so named because it was near the Chickamauga Indians' home. Over a mile long, the dam was finished in 1940 as a way to control the horrible flooding that had devastated the city several times. (Courtesy Chattanooga Public Library.)

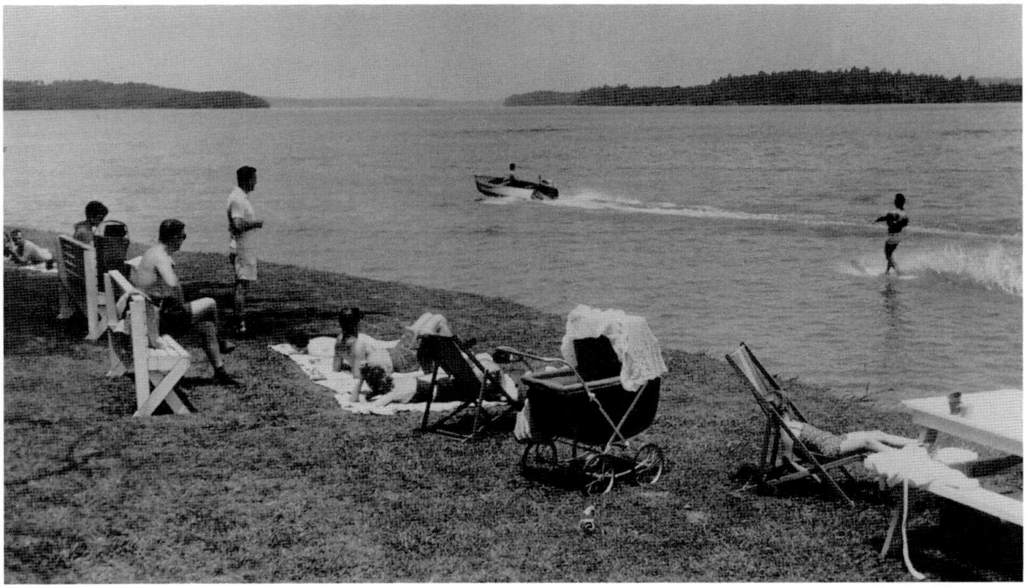

TVA Lake

Though public opinion was divided about the changes that TVA brought to the land, there is little doubt that the lakes that were created were extremely popular. For fishermen, it was heaven. For ordinary people who just wanted to swim or relax by the water, it was a boon. For the family that enjoyed cooking out, it was ideal. And when motorboats and there new cousins, the jet ski, came along, it was pure pleasure. (Courtesy Chattanooga Public Library.)

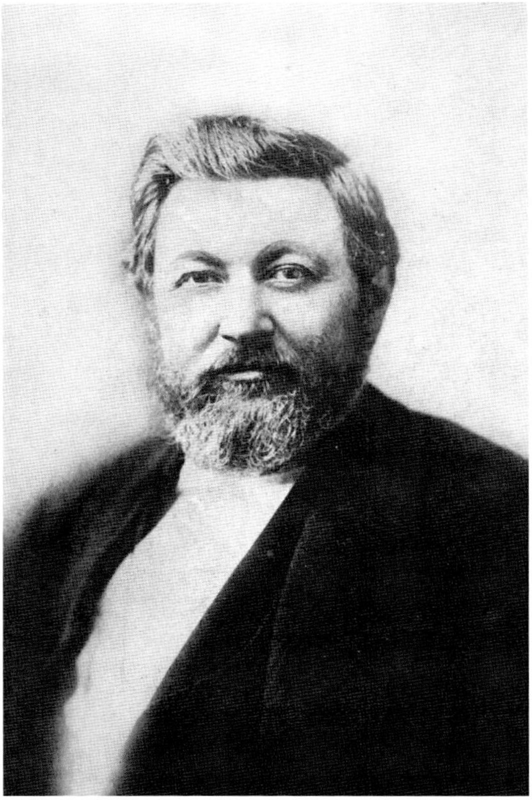

Tom Crutchfield

Tom Crutchfield owned and managed the Crutchfield House and made a good living at it but sold it before the war in anticipation of the forthcoming hostilities. In a famous scene, he and brother William went to the hotel to see Jefferson Davis, the new president of the confederacy make a speech. William berated him and called him a traitor to which Davis responded with a challenge. Fortunately, cooler heads prevailed and no blood was shed. (Courtesy Chattanooga Public Library.)

Crutchfield House

The Crutchfield House sat directly across from the first railroad depot and for years, was the finest hotel in the city after it was built in 1847. A piece of elegance in what was essentially a frontier town with muddy streets, it was a haven for well-heeled travelers and incorporated a porch for relaxation as well as some other simple amenities. (Courtesy Chattanooga Public Library.)

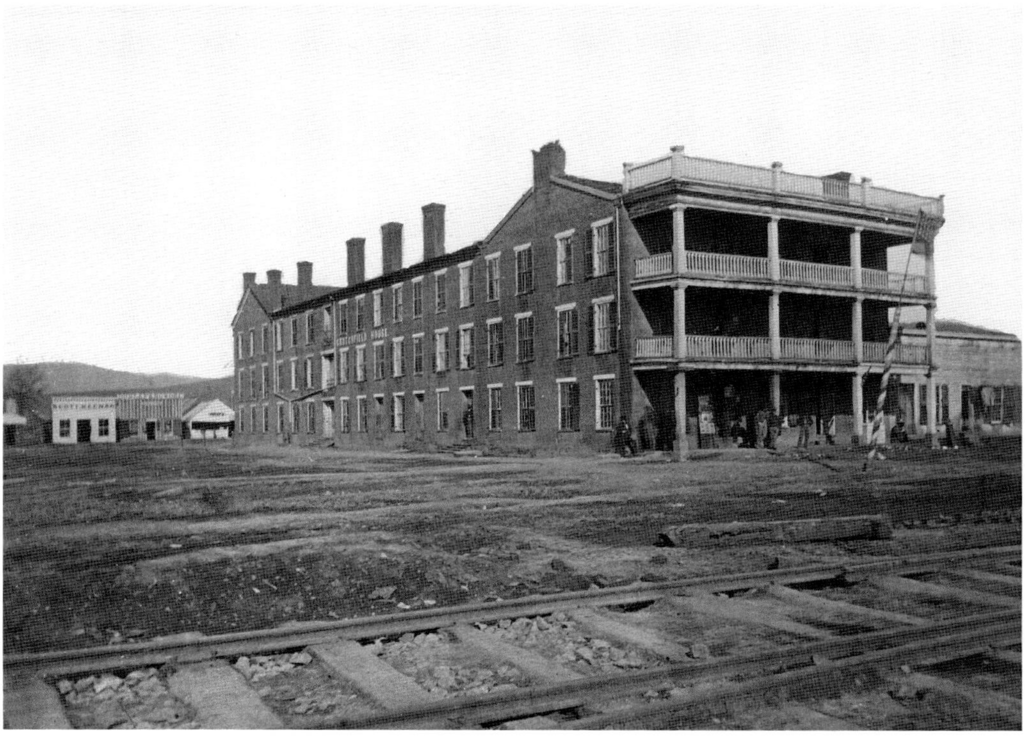

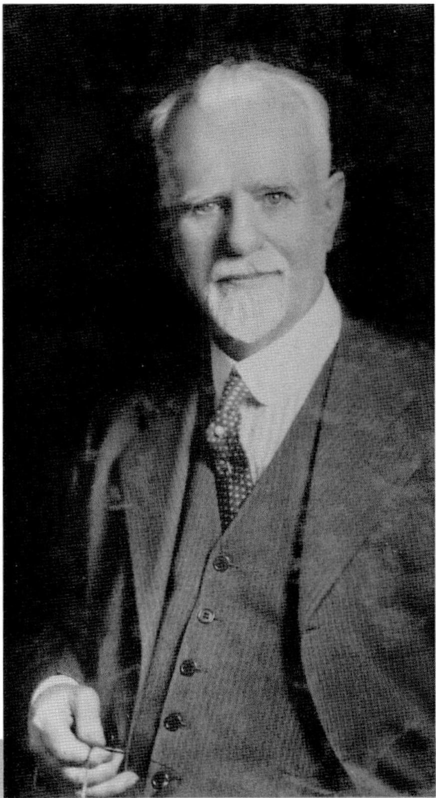

Samuel Read
Samuel Read felt like he had a chance to make a success in the hotel business and took over the Crutchfield House site. Even though things were slow for years after the Civil War, the fact that his property was across the street from the depot was all he needed to prosper. In 1927, he replaced the older hotel with the one seen currently, a handsome Georgian-style building that reflected the prosperity of the Roaring 20s. (Courtesy Chattanooga Public Library.)

Read House
This 10-story beauty of a hotel was placed in the National Register of Historic Places in 1977. With intricate brickwork, the handsome facade welcomes the visitor to a lobby with terrazzo floors inlaid with marble, gilded woodwork, and beautiful, fine-grained walnut paneling. The silver ballroom features a Waterford crystal chandelier and sconces of silver. Famous guests have included Gary Cooper, Winston Churchill, and Tallulah Bankhead. (Courtesy Chattanooga Public Library.)

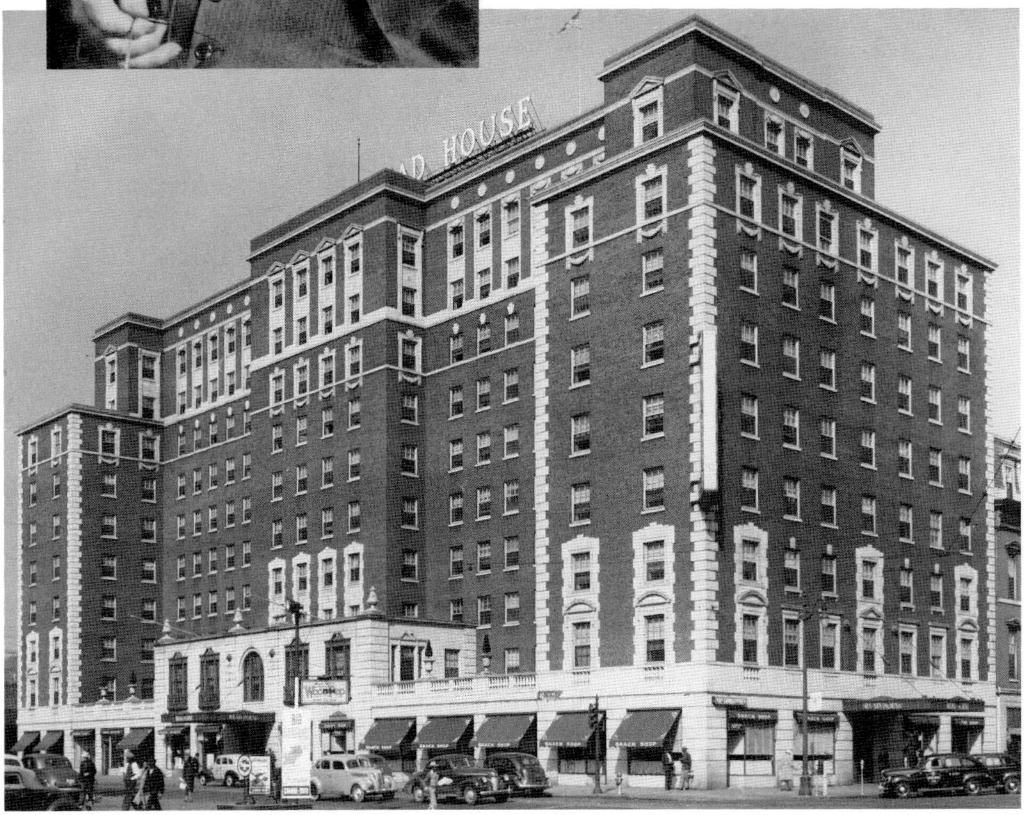

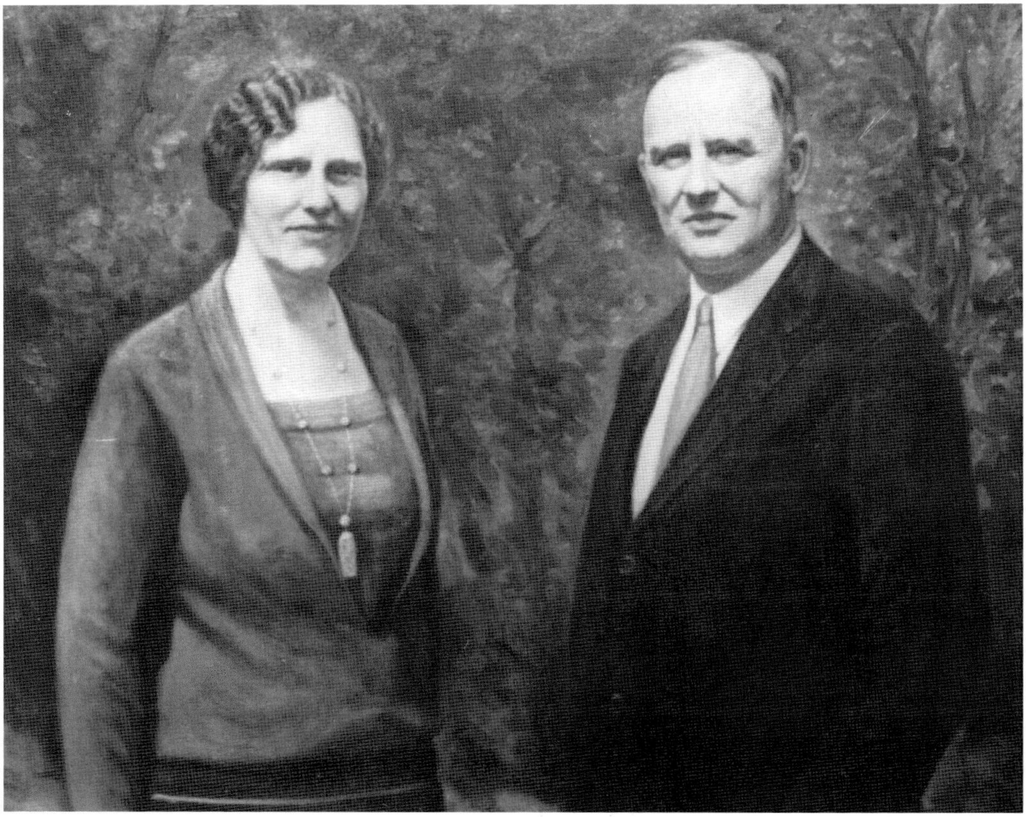

Garnet and Frieda Carter
Garnet Carter was not afraid to take a risk and try something new. Born in Sweetwater, Tennessee, his family moved to Lookout Mountain when he was 11. As a young man, he tried his hand at several occupations and did well. A trip to Florida during the boom of the 1920s—where real estate fortunes were being made—gave him the idea to start his own venture by building a modern residential community on Lookout Mountain. After purchasing and clearing the land, he opened the development with lots and roads in 1924. On the property, he constructed the handsome, stone Fairyland Inn, a clubhouse for the future residents that today is the private Fairyland Club. The name was inspired by his wife, Frieda, who designed some of the homes and named the streets and whose interest in European folklore was a consuming passion. One of the attractions to the area was a modern golf course, something quite popular in the era of golfer Bobby Jones. Because of delays in the course's completion, Carter assembled a small or miniature golf course out of drain tiles and building materials almost for fun as much as anything. Unexpectedly, the public became fascinated with this game that any man, woman, boy, or girl could play. Carter named the game "Tom Thumb Golf" and began licensing the new attraction to other entrepreneurs, eventually selling it for a tidy profit. Adjacent to the Fairyland development was an intriguing wild landscape of large boulders with winding paths known locally as the city of rocks. The idea of a recreational area for travelers built around this "rock city" appealed to both Garnet and Frieda, and the idea of Rock City came to fruition, populated with gnomes and fairies of all stripes. While the Great Depression quashed the full development of Fairyland, Rock City opened in 1932 and slowly gained traction. Eager to see more visitors, Carter hired Clark Byers, a sign painter, to find farmers that would let him paint "See Rock City" on their barn roofs in exchange for painting the farmer's entire barn for free. It worked, and an American icon was born. Today, Rock City is 80 years old, going strong, and still a stop on the great American highway for over 250,000 visitors a year. (Courtesy Chattanooga Public Library.)

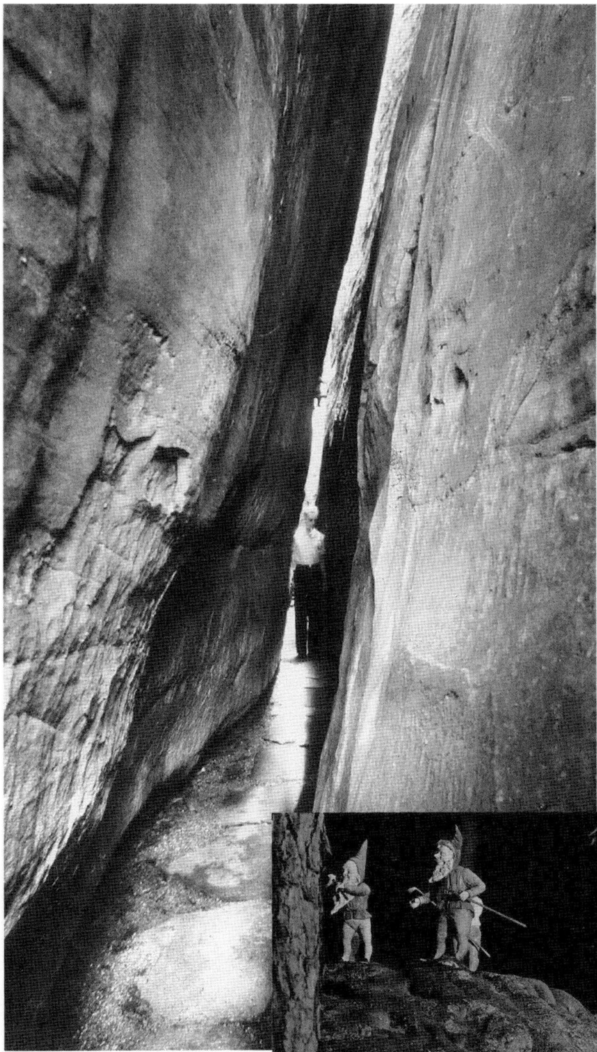

Rock City

The fascinating variety of rocks that reside at Rock City are amusing in themselves and succeed in taking the visitor into another world of careful walking if just for a while. Fat Man's Squeeze would probably be named something else in today's politically correct world, but still, the challenge of sidling through the opening would remain. (Courtesy Chattanooga Public Library.)

Tom Thumb Golf

Tom Thumb golf was born out of Carter trying to provide some golfing fun for his visitors while his real golf course was being completed. He scratched around his property and took drainpipe, cups, and boards to make a child's-size imitation game of golf. It caught on with the public in a big way. Here, some folks try their hand at the small game that must have been such a novelty then. (Courtesy Chattanooga Public Library.)

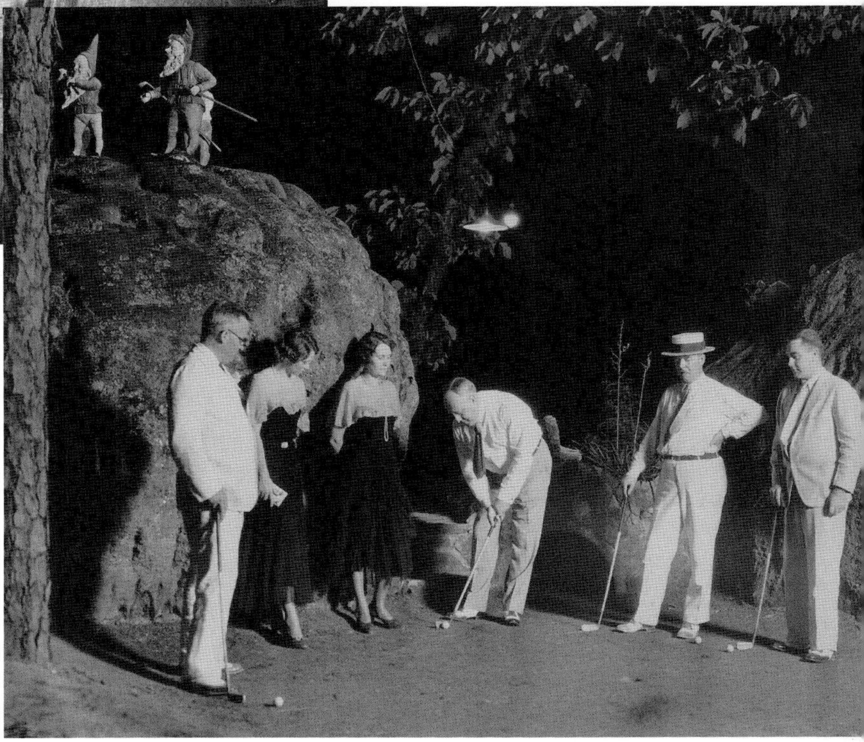

Leo Lambert

Leo Lambert was a chemist by trade but a spelunker at heart. An adventurous man, he purchased land in 1928 on Lookout Mountain in order to create a new opening into the Lookout Mountain Cave below by drilling down from far above the cave. But in doing so, he found another cave with a waterfall. With his companions, he descended into the cave for 17 hours, enthralled by what they had found. On his next trip into the beautiful cavern, Lambert took his wife, Ruby, and told her that he would name the falls for her. Determined to bring this wonder to life, Lambert built an entrance of cave limestone, installed an elevator, and opened it to the public. Opened in 1930, Ruby Falls was equipped with electric lights, a novelty in the 1930s, and was on its way to becoming one of America's great roadside tourist attractions. "See Ruby Falls" signs are common in the tristate area and the famous natural wonder is now a registered National Historic Landmark. (Courtesy Chattanooga Public Library.)

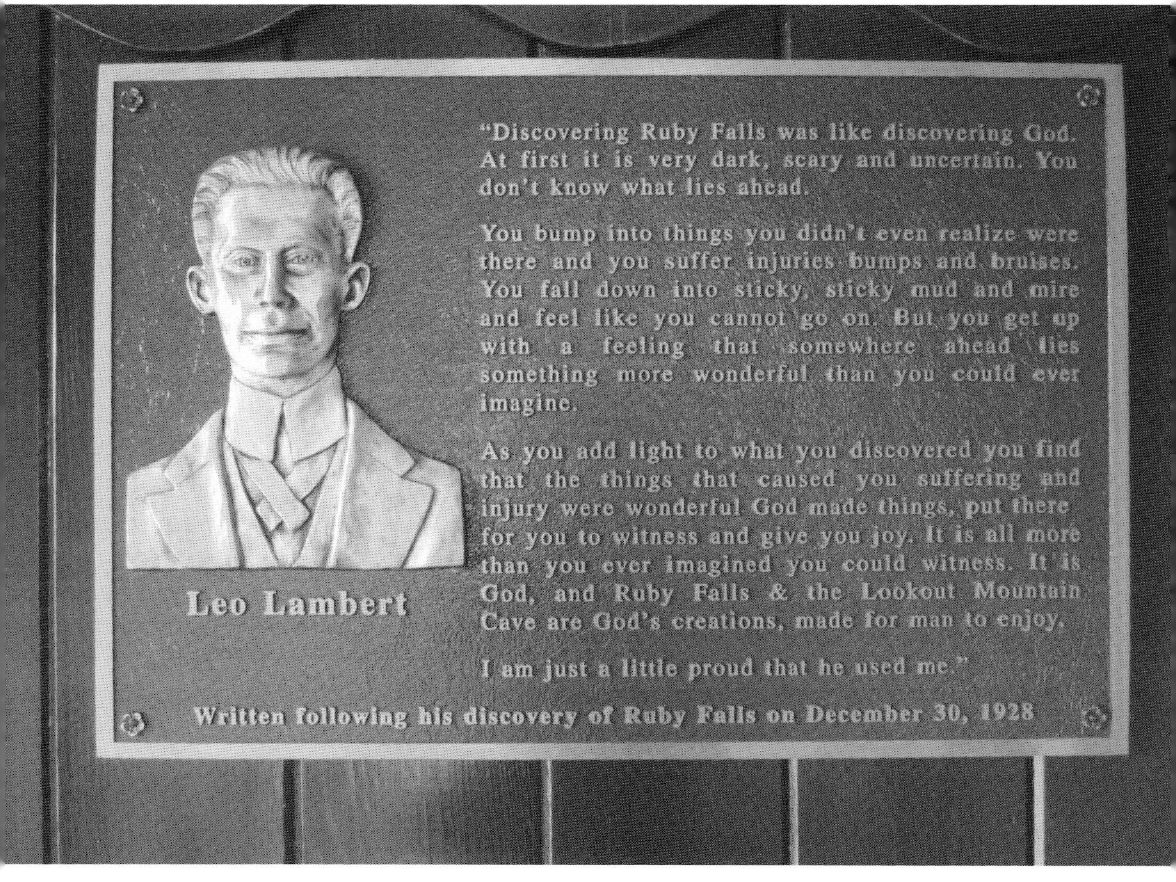

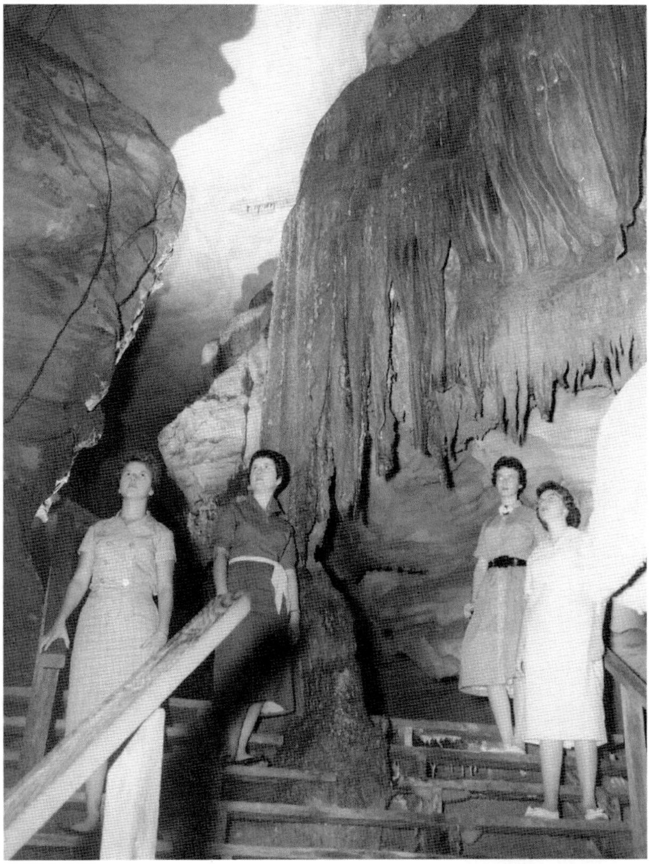

Ruby Falls
Ruby Falls is a true wonder of nature. Deep within a mountain, the path winds down to the waterfall, which drops from 145 feet on high to a dark pool illuminated with colored lights. Could it be that these young women with their bobby socks are posing for a 1950s movie poster for "Creature from the Cave"? (Courtesy Chattanooga Public Library.)

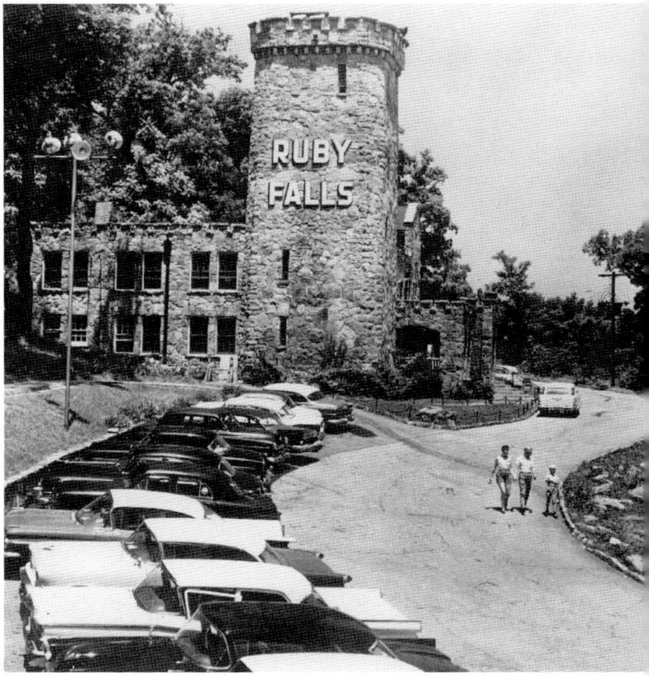

Ruby Falls Tower
This castle-like tower at Ruby Falls was built by Chattanooga architect Reuben Harrison Hunt, a prolific builder in the region. The proto-medieval edifice is an example of his signature ability to construct any style of architecture demanded of him. Hunt was born in Elbert County, Georgia, in 1862 and began a career as a carpenter at the age of 14, eventually coming to Chattanooga at the age of 20. Astonishingly, he was part of the firm of Hunt and McDaniel four years later. From the 1890s to the 1930s, he built every major building in the city and ranged across the South, especially in Mississippi, as a designer of large public works, specifically churches, schools, and commercial buildings. His services were in such demand that Hunt's designs were disseminated through the South via his firm's pattern book. (Courtesy Chattanooga Public Library.)

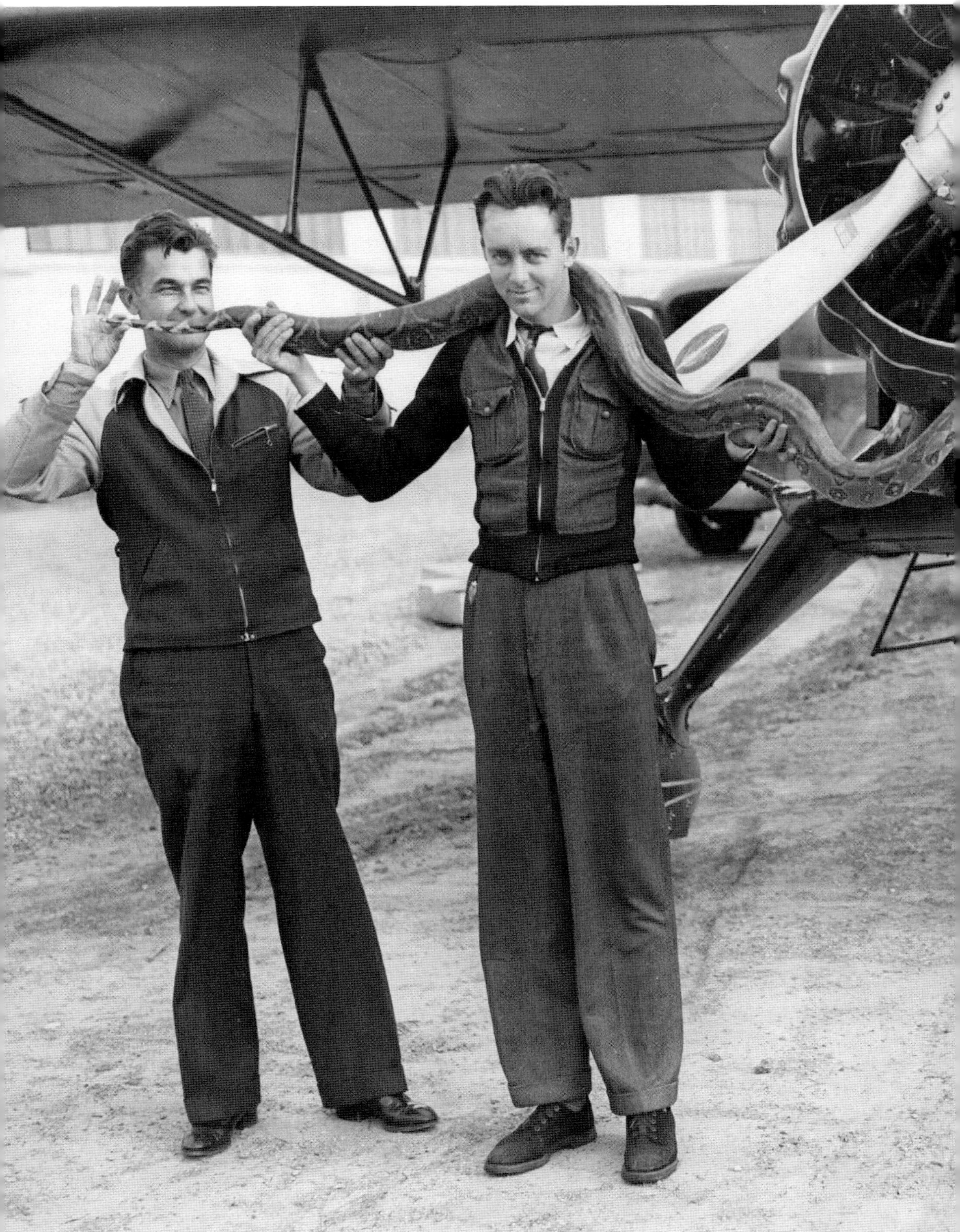

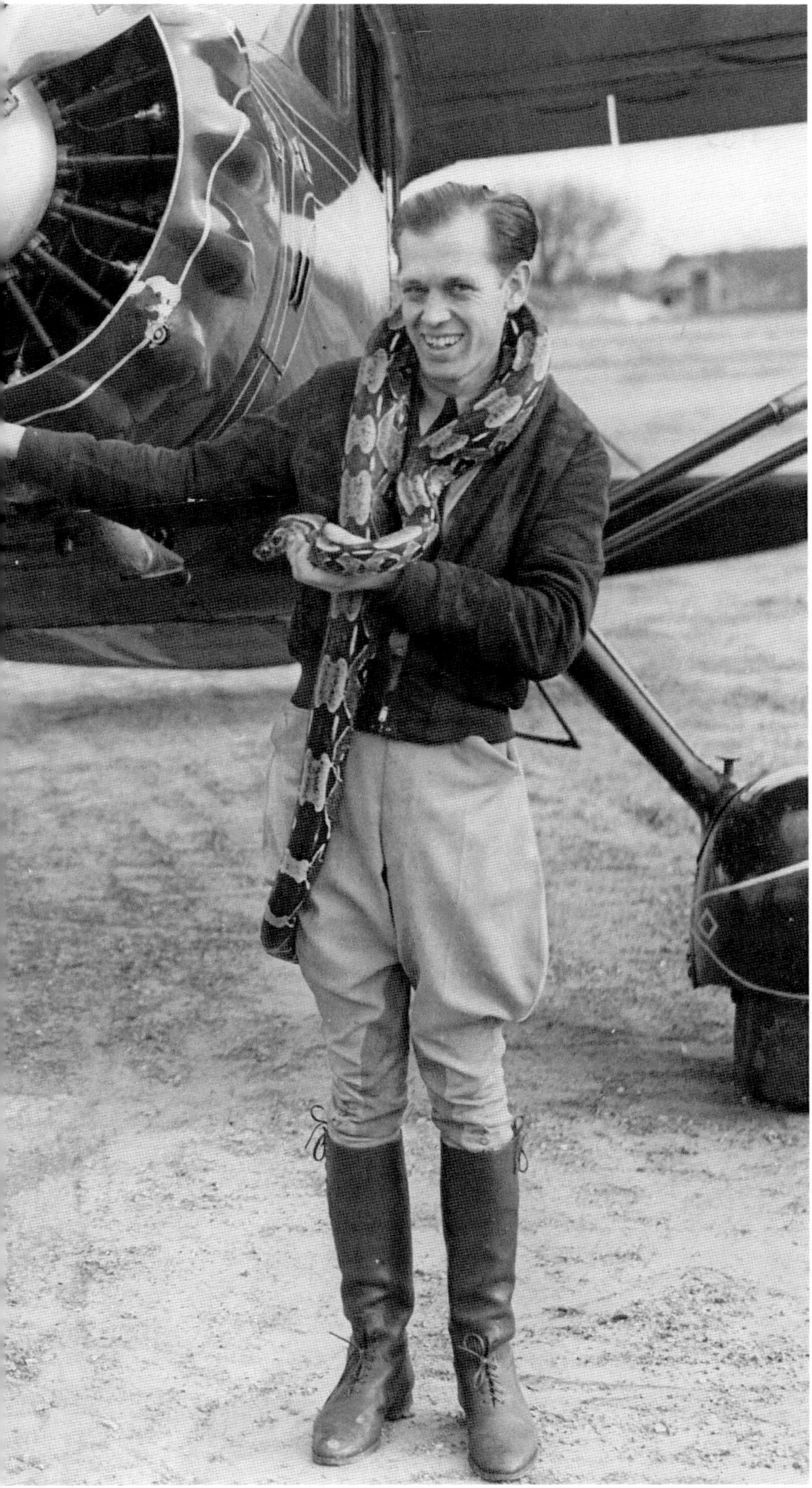

Harry Porter with Snake
Harry Porter (far left) holds part of a long cobra snake as he and two flying comrades stand in front of a classic propeller plane at Lovell Field. Porter was a fixture at the airport and ran a flying school for many years. He first flew a plane in 1923 and was an active aviator for 64 years. At the age of 90, he was recognized as the oldest active pilot in the United States. (Courtesy Chattanooga Public Library.)

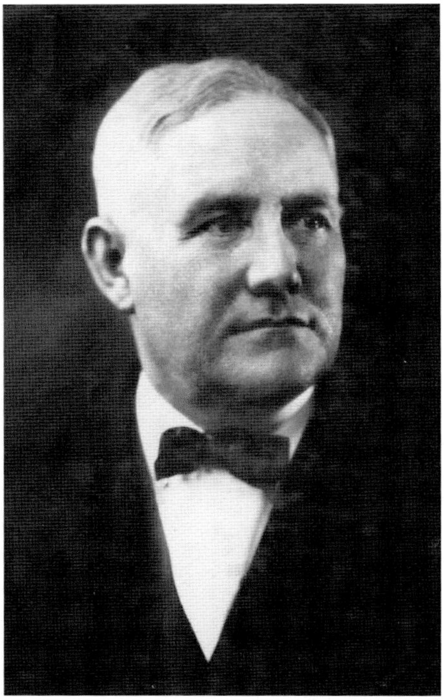

Judge Cummings
Judge Will Cummings was active in a number of political causes in Chattanooga. A mover and shaker, he was known especially as a promoter of "good roads" in the early days of the automobile. Promoting a highway route across from the Moccasin Bend was a major project that resulted in the state naming the road Cummings Highway. (Courtesy Chattanooga Public Library.)

Judge Cummings with FDR
A classic New Deal democrat who believed in the power of federal spending for the betterment of the community, Cummings was adamant in his support of a dam for flood control. Here, he (left) is seen talking to Pres. Franklin Delano Roosevelt (right) at the dedication of the Chickamauga Dam in 1940. Roosevelt was here on Labor Day in a nationally broadcast speech and ceremony as he campaigned for his fourth term. (Courtesy Chattanooga Public Library.)

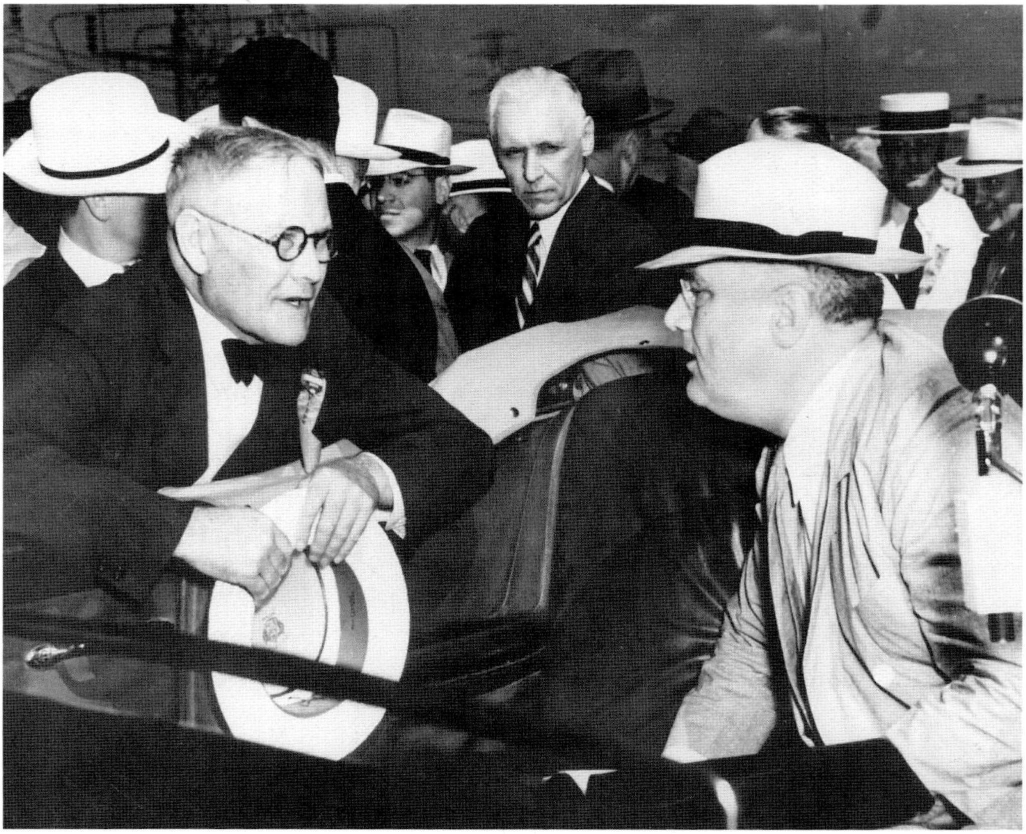

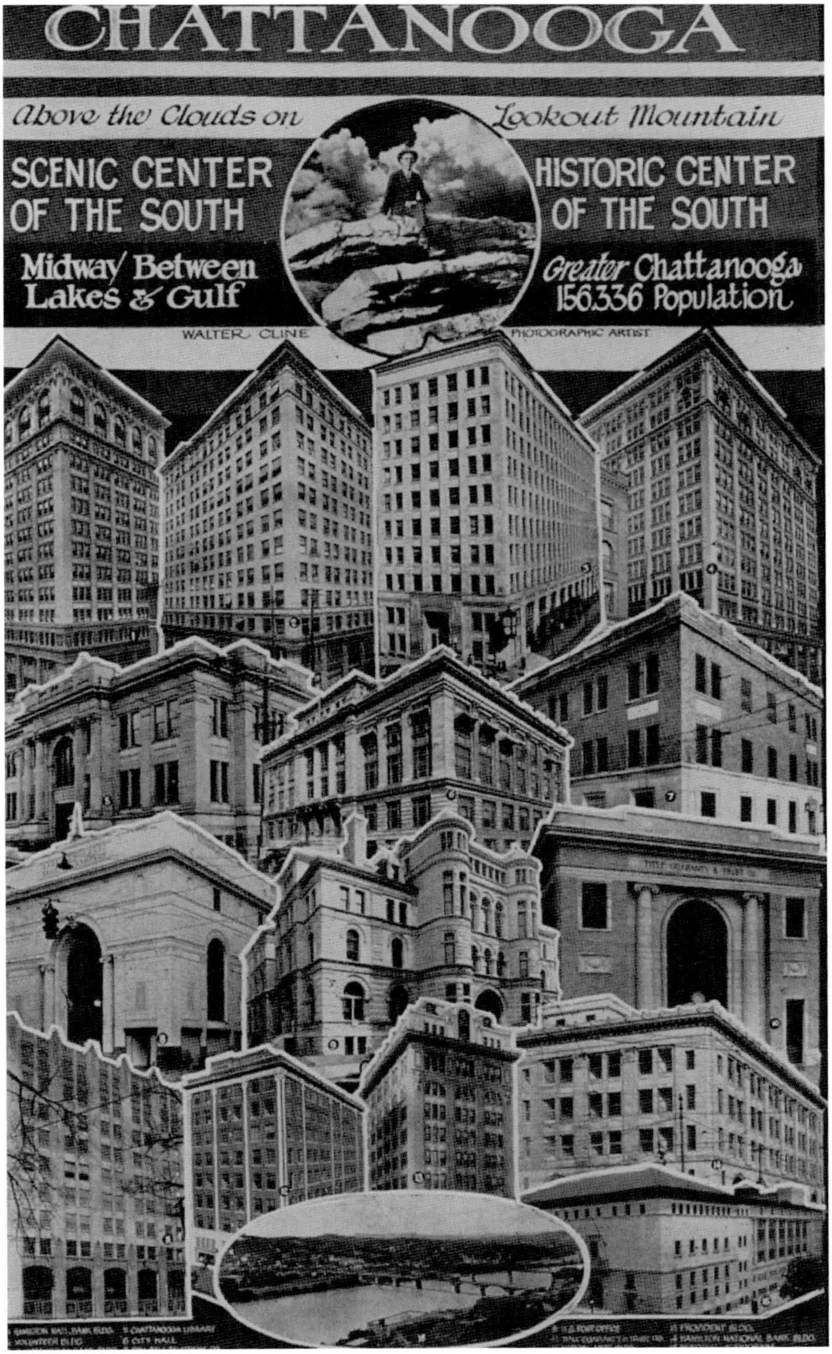

Big Page with Buildings

A splendid collage of downtown's panoply of buildings is pictured in the 1920s. Chattanooga was economically bursting at the seams, and the city center was in full swing. Since Chattanooga's business district was small, this promotional piece used a couple of buildings twice. Nevertheless, included are the James Building and Municipal Auditorium, two of local architect R.H. Hunt's fine designs. (Courtesy Chattanooga Public Library.)

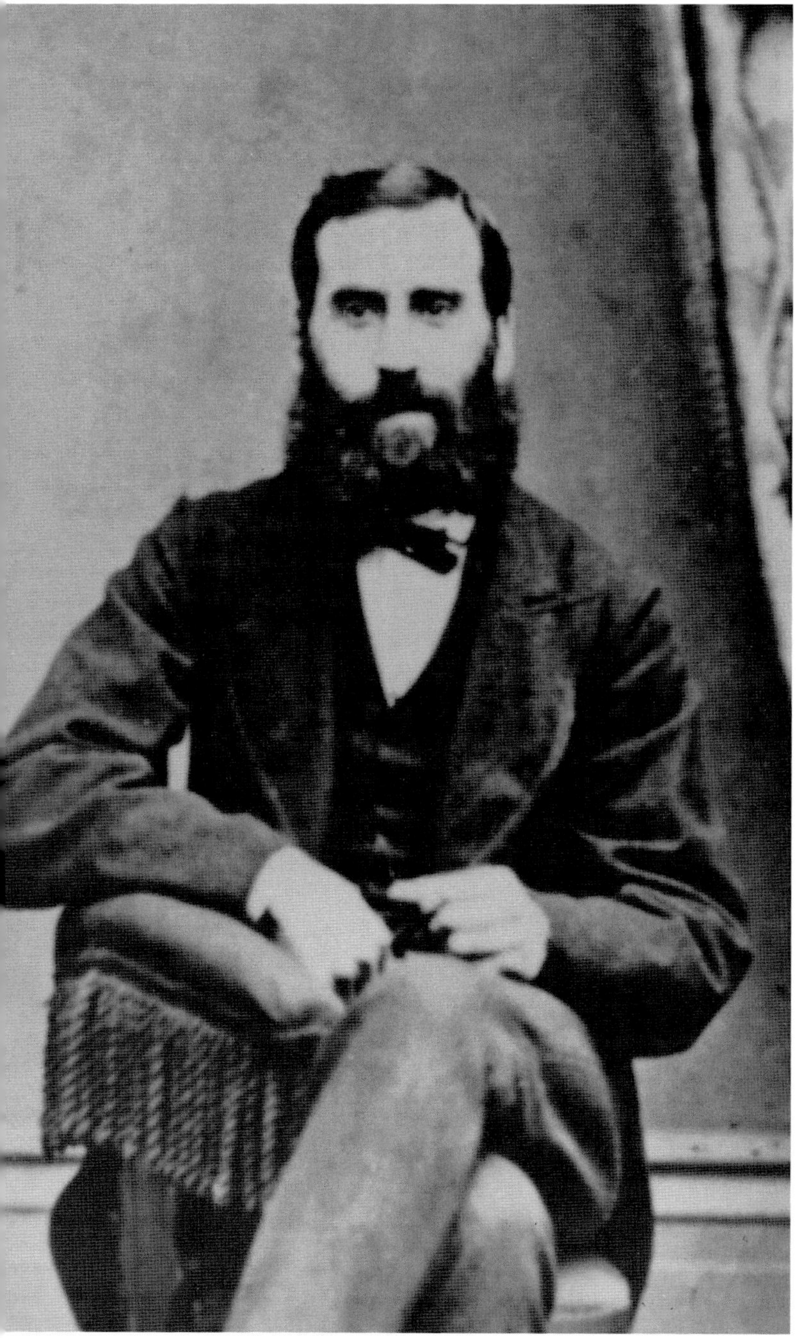

Thomas Maclellan
Thomas Maclellan, a Scotsman, settled in Chattanooga in the 1890s and became the president of the Provident Life and Accident Insurance Company. A devout covenant Presbyterian, he was a man of modest means but a focused entrepreneur, who sold policies to the "uninsurables"—people who worked in dangerous places like coal mines or blast furnaces. His family, over the course of a century, enlarged the business until it became the biggest disability insurer in the world, known as Unum Provident. (Courtesy Chattanooga Public Library.)

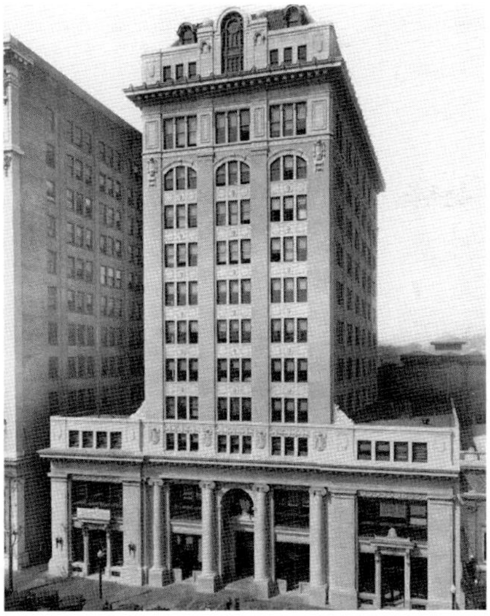

Maclellan Building
R.H. Hunt was a master of diversity. He built in the Romanesque style (Second Presbyterian Church), the Neo-classical style (Hamilton County Courthouse), and the Art Moderne style (Solomon Federal Building). Or, he could design a handsome commercial structure such as the Maclellan Building, shown here, as he did in the late 1920s—a beautiful early 20th–century skyscraper that features finely detailed work on the facade and a mansard roof at the apex. All these buildings still stand—a testament to the quality of his work and the beauty they bring to Chattanooga. (Courtesy Chattanooga Public Library.)

Scott L. Probasco Jr. and Rodi Davenport
Scott Probasco (left) and Rodi Davenport (right) are two men who have had a profound impact on Chattanooga. Probasco is a true believer in the power of giving and has been a major donor to many facets of urban life working with the Community Foundation of Greater Chattanooga, the United Way, and the Bethel Bible Village just to name a few. More often than not, his donations are made in a quiet manner. A banker by trade, his father began the local American National Bank, which today is part of SunTrust Bank; fittingly the Probasco Chair of Free Enterprise at UTC was named in his honor. Davenport and his family have served Chattanooga as well setting up the Lula Lake Land Trust and acting as early supporters of the Tennessee Aquarium and the Tennessee Riverwalk. Davenport began Krystal Hamburgers in the grip of the Great Depression. The first Krystal restaurant opened at the corner of Cherry and Seventh Streets in a sparkling clean restaurant outfitted in chrome and tile, with friendly service, and low-cost, hot food. The steam-cooked burgers were 5¢, square, small, and could be easily bagged together so that folks could "take home a sack full." A Chattanooga late-night tradition, Krystal has been a Southern favorite for 75 years. (Courtesy Chattanooga History Center.)

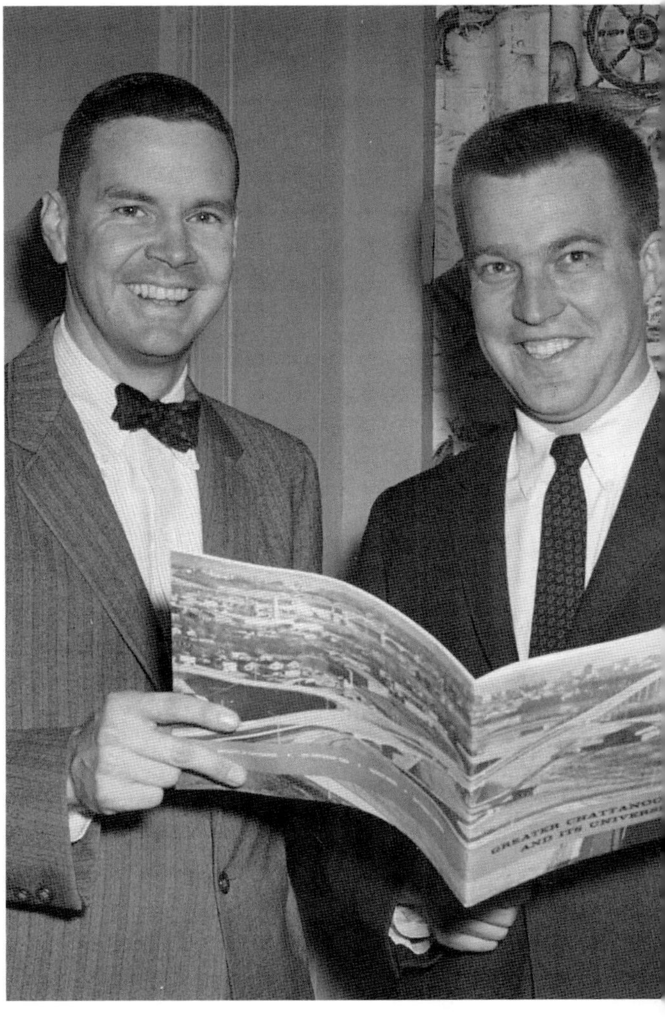

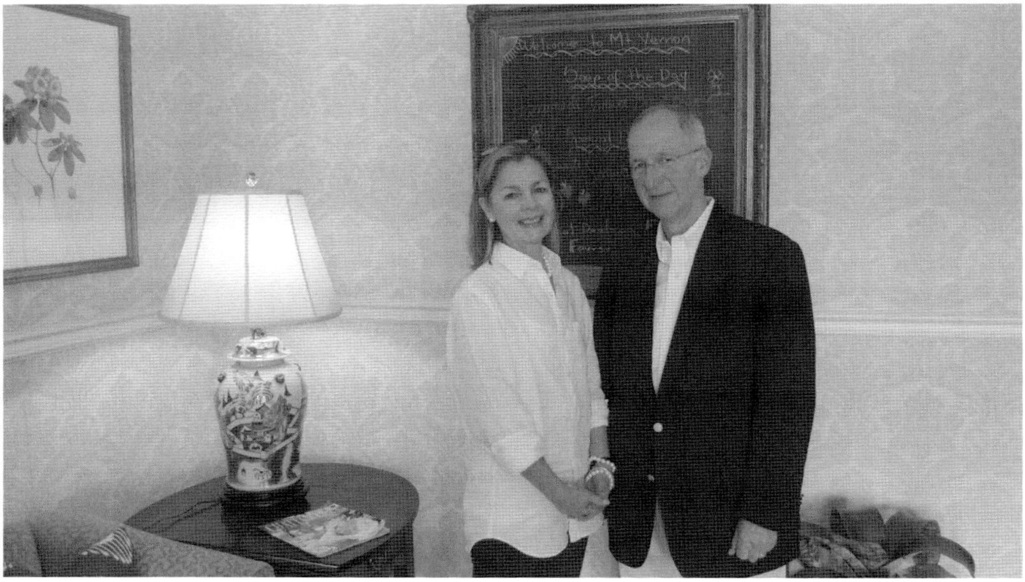

Mount Vernon

In today's world of fast food and takeout, it is a singular pleasure to eat at an established restaurant like Mount Vernon. With an atmosphere of gentle elegance, tasty cooking, and homemade desserts of the first rank, this family-owned restaurant is the epitome of good Southern cooking. Its origin lies in the story of Gus Tombras, a Greek immigrant who worked in the family grocery and saved for five years in order to buy passage to New York City, where he landed with his brother in 1898 at the age of 19. His first job was working in a restaurant where he ate apple pie for a week. Since then, all his restaurants have specialized in that dessert. He and his brother moved to Chattanooga in 1905 and soon opened two restaurants, the Manhattan and the Farmers Market. Eventually, Mount Vernon took shape in 1953 and has been a favorite of generations at its home on Broad Street at the foot of Lookout Mountain. The family still runs the restaurant as Jeff and Cindy Messinger continue the tradition of fine dining with such classic offerings as turkey and dressing, fried chicken, and fresh vegetables. And, of course, a slice of apple pie continues to bring daily satisfaction to customers from around the city. (Courtesy Chattanooga Public Library.)

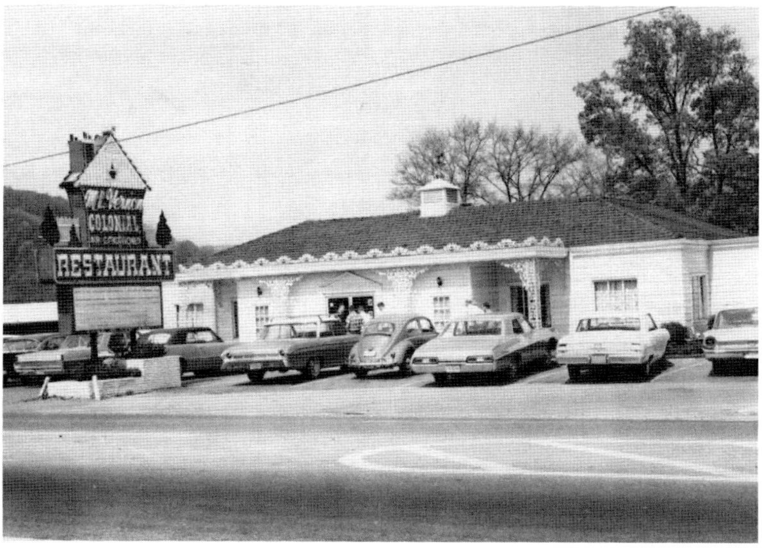

View of Restaurant

The facade of the restaurant purposefully replicates George Washington's home. (Courtesy Jeff and Cindy Messinger.)

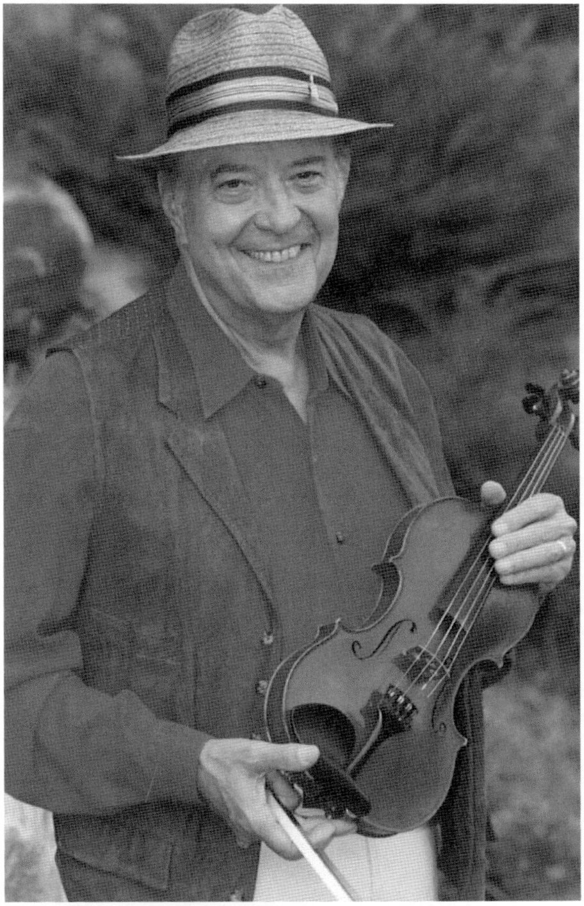

Fletcher Bright

Fletcher Bright has been making a living in real estate so he can have time to fiddle around. A lifelong Chattanoogan, Bright is known as a first-class bluegrass fiddler. But to make ends meet, he has been selling houses and properties since 1953 and has since expanded his family's business into a sizable regional firm that manages more than 100 shopping centers. As a child, he was given music lessons at Cadek conservatory, but his love of hill music bloomed while a student at McCallie School. In the days before taped radio, he and his band would play live segments on local radio station WDXB ("WDXB in Dixie") in the summertime. His band, The Dismembered Tennesseans, plays regularly all over town as they have for decades. One of his great gifts to the city is The 3 Sisters Bluegrass Music Festival, now in its fifth year. The festivities are a fall weekend event held downtown on the banks of the river with top-name groups, and it is completely free, underwritten by Fletcher Bright. A great booster of all things Chattanooga, Bright defines the term local tradition; he lives next door to the home he grew up in. (Courtesy Fletcher Bright.)

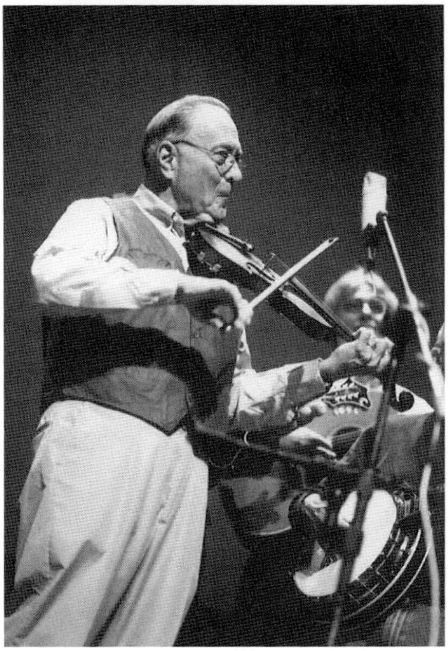

Fletcher Bright Fiddling

Fletcher Bright saws on a fiddle as the band plays on. (Courtesy Fletcher Bright.)

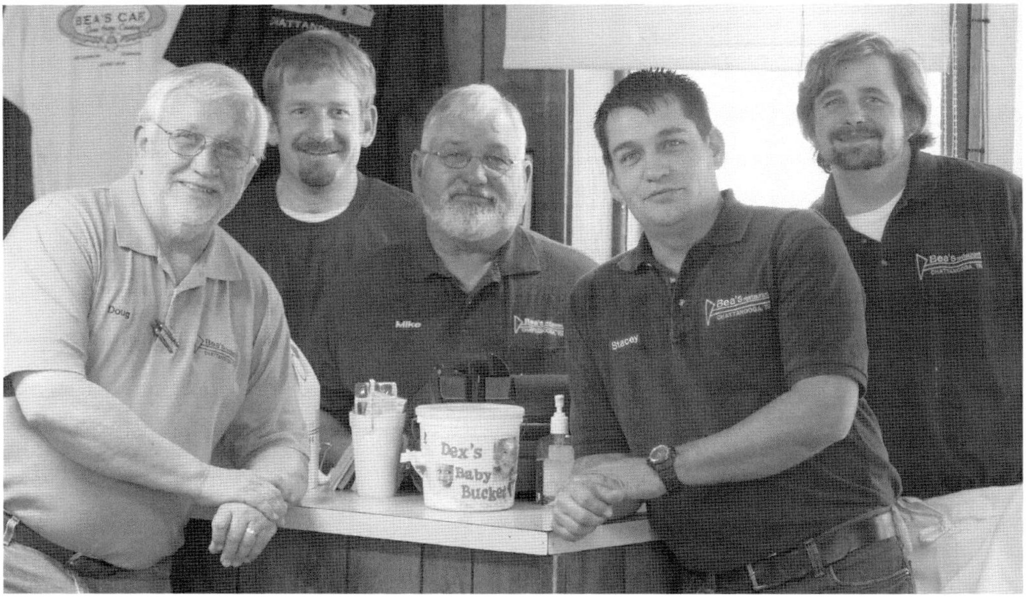

The Bradshaws of Bea's

"Don't mess with a good thing, y'all" is an old Southern saying. Bea's Restaurant in East Lake on Dodds Avenue has lived by that maxim for 60 years now. Begun in 1950 by Bill and Beatrice Steele, Bea's fits to a tee the definition of a Southern, family-style restaurant. For decades, the neighborhood was humming constantly with factories, such as Chris-Craft, and workers needed a quick 30-minute lunch. Originally, food was served family style, with patrons passing the food back and forth. But to allow folks to get in and get out quickly they added big Lazy Susans on each table so a diner could sit right down and eat expeditiously. And in the early years, Bea's operated on the slogan "Get your fill for a dollar bill." Beatrice Steele ran the kitchen and soon became known for the down-home goodness of her fried chicken, a tasty mouthful that kept people coming back for more. Add in fresh vegetables and soft, flavorful yeast rolls and it is easy to see why many of their customers are lifetime patrons. Not to mention that a number of today's diners first came to eat with their grandparents. As always, the cook is in the kitchen by 5:00 a.m., starting from scratch, and in a typical week, the restaurant will serve an estimated 4,000 pounds of chicken and pour about 150 gallons of tea a day. With the third-generation family running the show, in 2013, Bea's Restaurant shows no sign of slowing down, and hungry folks are glad of it. (Photograph by Chris Villines, Tennessee Farmers Co-op.)

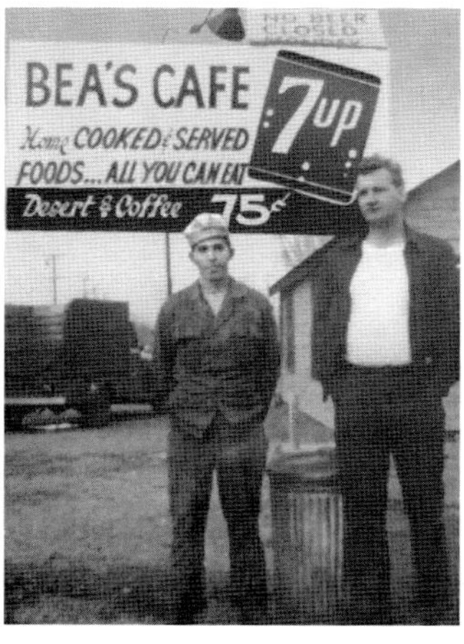

Bea's

Notice the old sign behind the young, hungry patrons who stand outside the restaurant. (Courtesy Bea's Restaurant.)

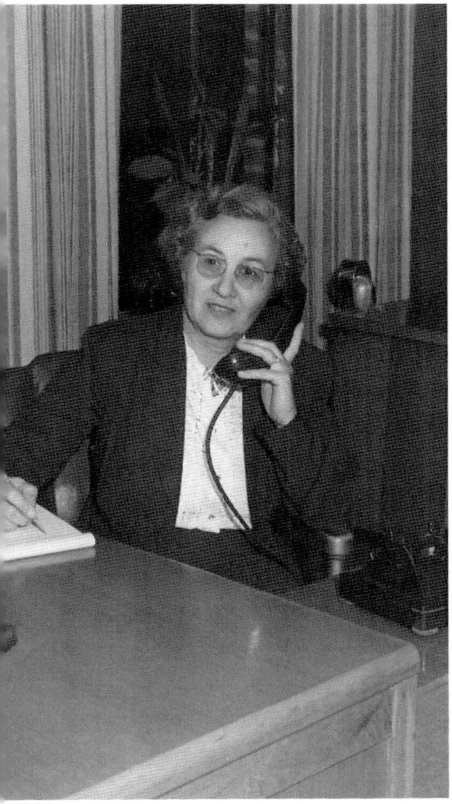

Lake Winnie

The amusement park at Lake Winnepesaukah is a true piece of Americana, and a perfect way to spend a summer day. Begun in 1925 by Carl and Minette Dixon, it has been under the guidance of the same family for over 85 years. Originally an attraction because of its lake for swimming, boating, and picnicking, the park added a boat chute in 1927, designed and built by Carl Dixon; it is the oldest "dark ride" in the United States. When he passed away a few years later, the operation was managed successfully by his widow, Minette (left), for over 20 years, especially through the difficult years of the Depression. She was able to sustain attendance even though she lost a skating rink to fire along the way. With over 33 rides to choose from, Lake Winnie today is a mix of the old and the new. A beautiful carousel built in 1916 from the old Lakewood Fairgrounds in Georgia is one of the lake's beloved treasures. The Cannon Ball, a wooden roller-coaster, is one of the park's most famous draws, built by the Philadelphia Toboggan Company in 1967 with an initial drop of 70 feet and some tight turns. A band shell for concerts, Jukebox Junction has featured a number of local and regional entertainers over the years from Archie Campbell to the Charlie Daniels Band. Lake Winnepesaukah also offers an ambiance that is hard to match, with its timeless rides, carnival games, picnic tables under spreading oaks, and wide lake with paddleboats. It is truly a Southern classic.

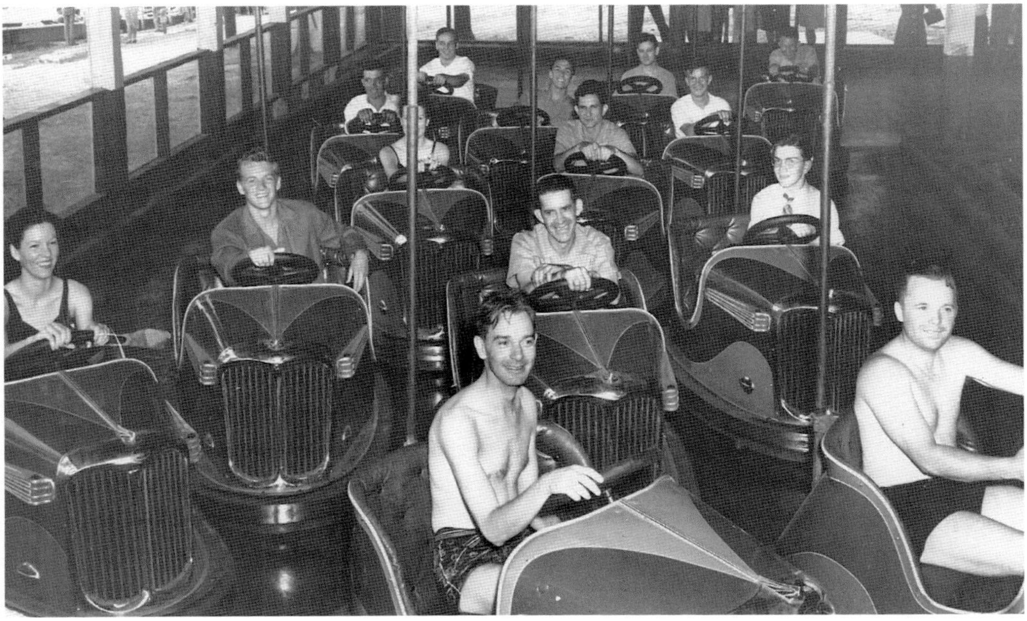

Bumper Car Riders

Bumper car riders during the 1940s were often servicemen who were training at nearby Fort Oglethorpe. They would often march from the grounds of the camp on a footpath to the park for a little R and R.

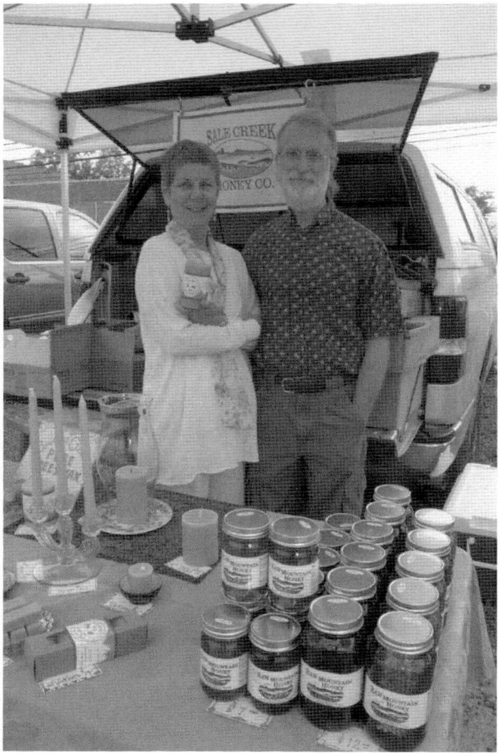

Eddie and Lou McKenzie

North of town in Sale Creek is a good deal of forestland, and for beekeeper Eddie McKenzie, that is exactly what he wants. A producer of premium honey since the 1970s, his bees seek the nectar of the Southern sourwood trees that grow primarily in the Southern Appalachians. With guidance from Hoyt Bond at the beginning of his work, McKenzie and his wife, Lou, have developed a sustainable, holistic approach to the bees, shunning antibiotics and manufactured foods, respecting the "biology of the creature." The result: disease-free insects and smooth, delicious sourwood honey that is healthy and clean. The careful management of the colonies also includes a useful by-product, Lou McKenzie's long-burning, traditional beeswax candles. (Author's collection.)

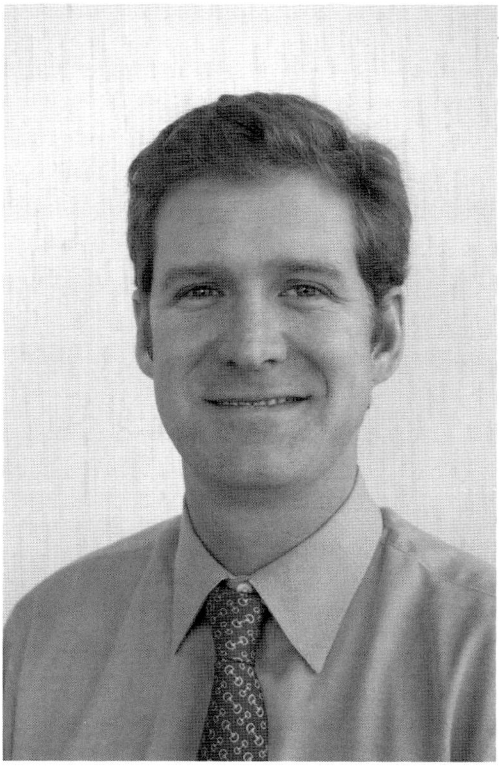

Tim Kelly

Tim Kelly's grandfather, Jim Ayers, was a Sand Mountain native who set up a General Motors dealership on Broad Street in 1939. With close attention to customer service and pride in making a fair deal Tim is a third generation automobile dealer. Always maintaining a presence downtown, the dealership that thrived on American cars moved into the import arena in 1980 with Saabs and then Hummers in the new century. In the last 10 years, Kelly has scored a coup by taking his Southern Honda Powersports business and making it impressively the No. 1 dealership of its kind in the United States. (Courtesy Tim Kelly.)

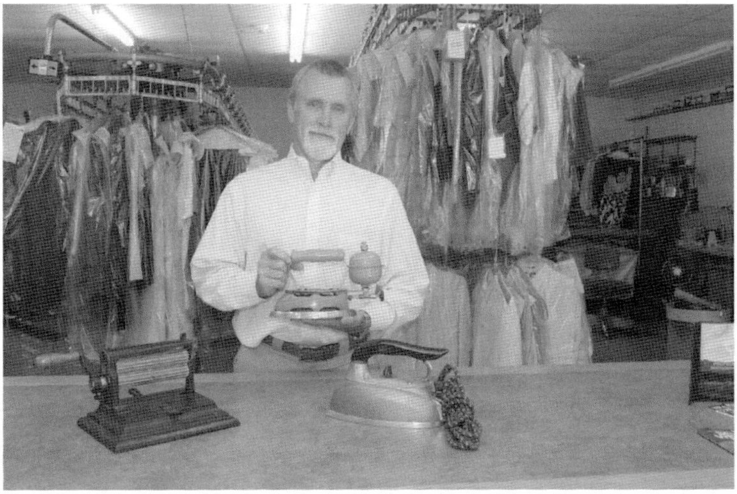

Gordon's Cleaners

Little rivals the look of a freshly starched shirt and a pressed pair of pants. Founded in 1952 by Gordon Ledbetter, his store on McCallie Avenue has been doing a brisk business for 60 years. Gordon, known for his good-natured friendliness, also had a passion for collecting the many varieties of irons that were used for pressing clothes. Over 1,000 irons are handsomely displayed in finished cabinets at their three stores along with a display of washboards from the dreadful days of hand scrubbing. Son Jim Ledbetter, who now runs the business, remembers family trips that were frequently punctuated with stops at country antique stores in search of unusual irons. Because of their interest in the history of commercial cleaning, the family has graciously donated a number of irons to the Chattanooga History Museum as well as several pieces that were accepted by the Smithsonian Institute. (Author's collection.)

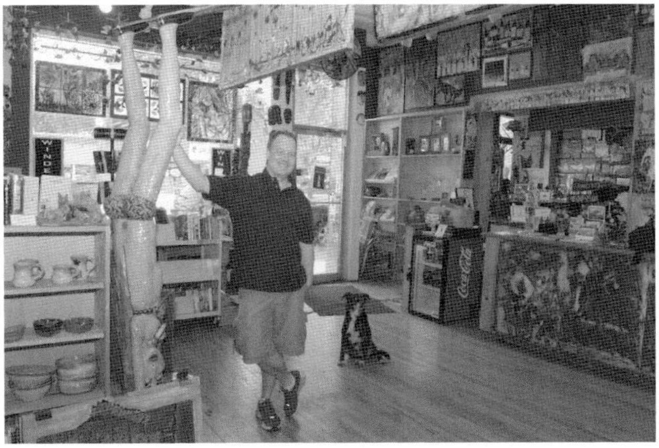

Winderbinder

Walking into David Smotherman's shop, WinderBinder, one realizes that this store is alive. That may be because one day on a trip to New Orleans, he came across a unique antique shop that seemed to have a pulse of its own; it became the inspiration for his own place. As a child, he played with windup tin toys at his grandparents' and as a collector, featured them in his store. Now, the walls are literally covered in local art with a decided tilt towards bold outsider and self-taught work; a decided emphasis on regional artists using recycled materials is key. Another side of the store features handmade tee shirts mixed in with collectibles of all sizes and shapes—and of course, books. With a space in Winderbinder for live performances, Smotherman also promotes parking lot art shows monthly as well as the annual WhoFest and Faux Arts Bridge Fest to promote Southern artisans. (Author's collection.)

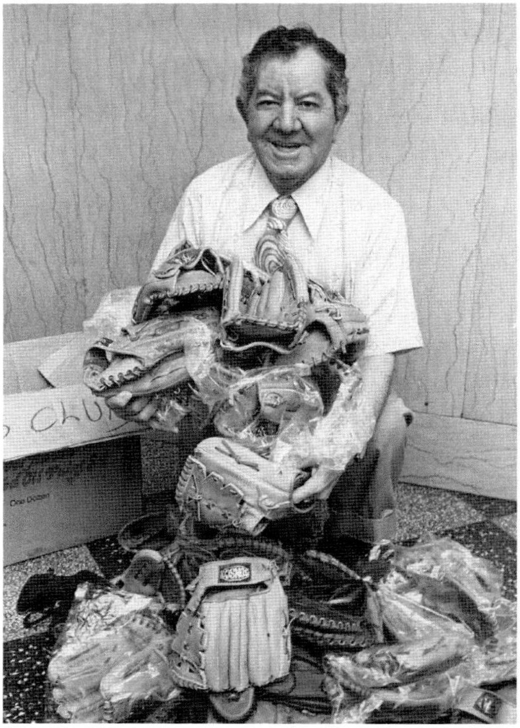

Abe Zarzour
Abe Zarzour loved baseball. He played summer ball as a boy and some semiprofessional as a man; he was a fixture at Engel Stadium in the days when minor league baseball and the Lookouts were king. More than anything, though, he wanted to make sure that youngsters had the chance to play baseball and to that end established the Abe Zarzour Baseball School where he was known for donating baseball equipment to underprivileged kids. He was given the Distinguished Citizen Award for his good work in the city. Frank Burke, the owner of the Lookouts baseball team, eulogized him, calling Zarzour the "Mayor of Main Street." (Courtesy Chattanooga Public Library.)

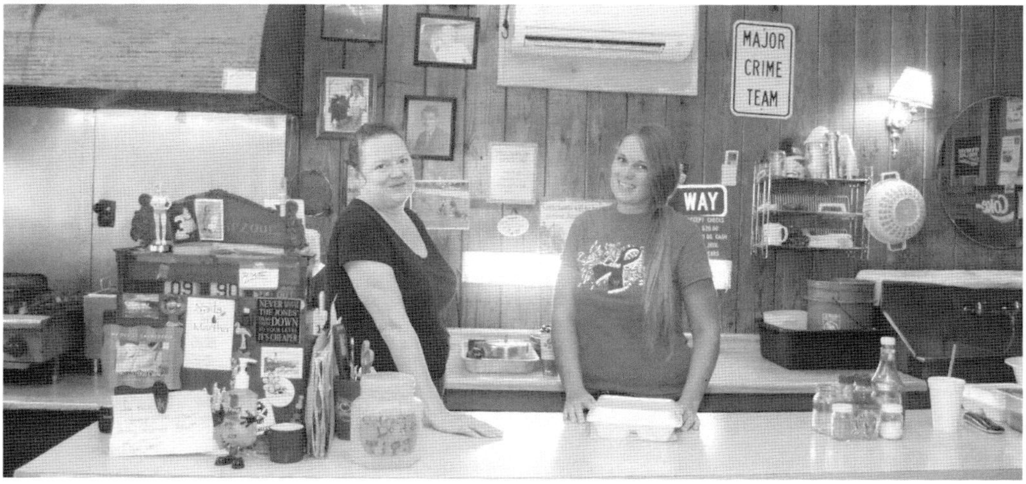

Zarzours
Charley and George Zarzour are examples of the American immigrant success story. They came to Chattanooga in 1918 from Lebanon and started a restaurant in the working-class neighborhood off Main Street on Rossville Avenue. Originally, Charley, who raised five children by himself after his wife died, sold Coca-Cola and hamburgers from the house before becoming a Southern-style eatery. Ninety-five years later, Shirley Zarzour Fuller (left) keeps the family tradition alive at the classic "meat and three" that sits in an old shotgun house. It is quite possible that Zarzour's Café is the oldest continuously running family-owned restaurant in Tennessee. With "y'all sit down" service and tasty butterbeans and collards, the restaurant has stayed true to savory, home-cooked food. Along with a good dose of neighborliness, a hot lunch is what the restaurant serves—and all that it serves—Monday through Friday. (Author's collection.)

CHAPTER THREE

Public Service

Chattanooga's residents have been bountiful in their giving and service over the years. It is difficult to recognize all the teachers, pastors, law enforcement members, youth organizations, and volunteers who have served this community in these few pages. Rev. T.H. McCallie was a force for good and caring during the early years of the city. One man who fought for African American livelihoods and dignity was Randolph Miller, who was born into slavery, yet who published his own newspaper and spoke out boldly for equal treatment under the law. Zella Armstrong was a historian and community leader who was one of the early historic preservationists in the city. E.Y. Chapin left his mark on a number of public institutions around town such as the Chattanooga Public Library. Adolph Ochs, the publisher of the *Chattanooga Times*, was not only an outspoken proponent of worthy causes but also a generous philanthropist who left his mark on Chattanooga. Orange Grove, a center for treatment for persons with developmental disabilities, was started by a group of motivated, local families seeking a better life for their children. Servicemen like Charles Coolidge, winner of the Medal of Honor, have brought honor to the community and the town has responded naming its newest, brightest park for him. The spirit and commitment of these citizens and so many giving souls like them has unquestioningly raised the quality of life for everyone in the city.

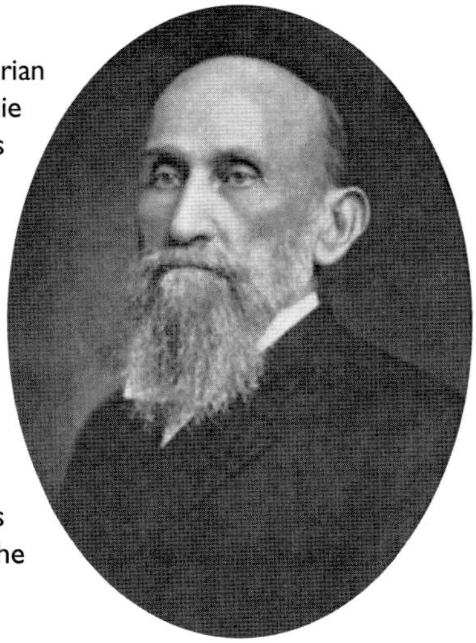

Thomas Hooke McCallie

Thomas Hooke McCallie became pastor of the First Presbyterian Church in 1862. The son of an early pioneer, Thomas McCallie served the church 10 years, becoming active in many phases of Chattanooga's civic life. The comfort and care he extended to all the citizens of the city—and soldiers on both sides—during wartime was legendary. His family's first home stood across from the Soldiers and Sailors Memorial Auditorium near Memorial Auditorium on, of course, McCallie Avenue. Desirous of a legacy, he made an offer of 40 acres and $2,500 to his sons to start a boys' preparatory school on the family farm on the western side of Missionary Ridge. The result was the McCallie School, which was founded in 1905, and continues to thrive as one of the top-notch college prep schools in the South. (Courtesy Chattanooga Public Library.)

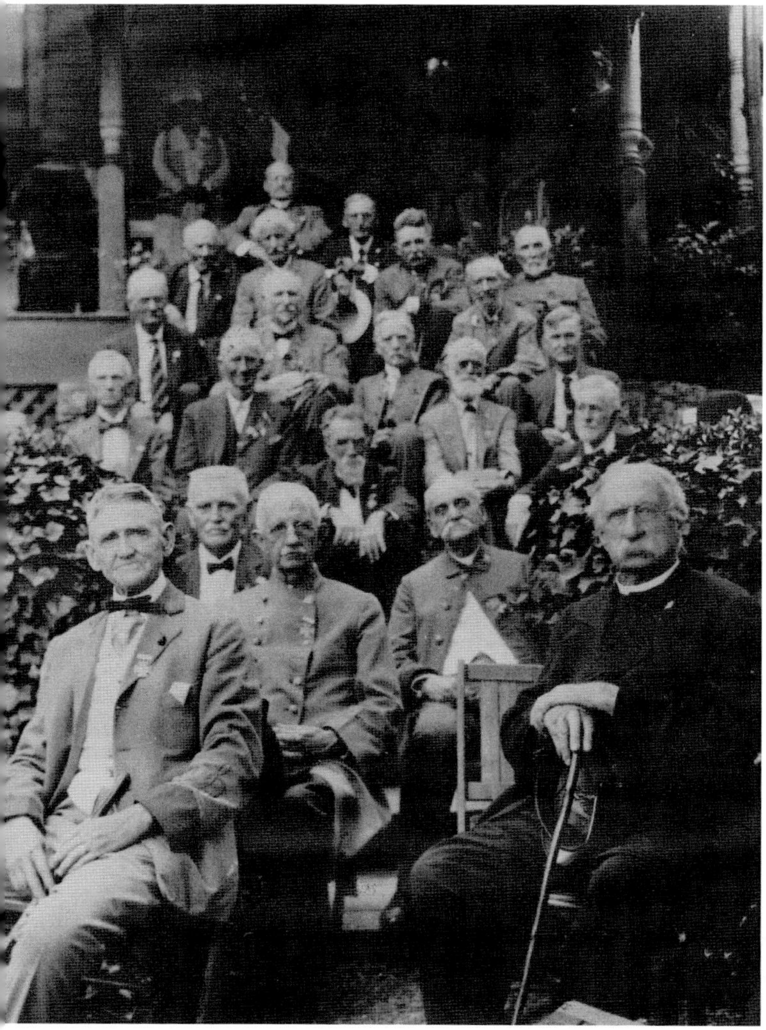

Dr. Jonathan Waverly Bachman

When Dr. Jonathan Waverly Bachman was 35 years old, he accepted the call to become pastor at the First Presbyterian Church and ministered there for 50 years. A Confederate army veteran who had served with Gen. Robert E. Lee, he understood the condition of the town struggling to overcome its recent devastation and became a tireless worker for the betterment of the lives of its citizens. So respected was he that he was asked to read the prayer at the dedication of the Walnut Street Bridge in 1891 and again at the Market Street Bridge opening in 1917. His funeral was attended by 5,000 people. Today, a pair of traffic tunnels running through Missionary Ridge, the Bachman Tubes, bear his name. (Courtesy Chattanooga Public Library.)

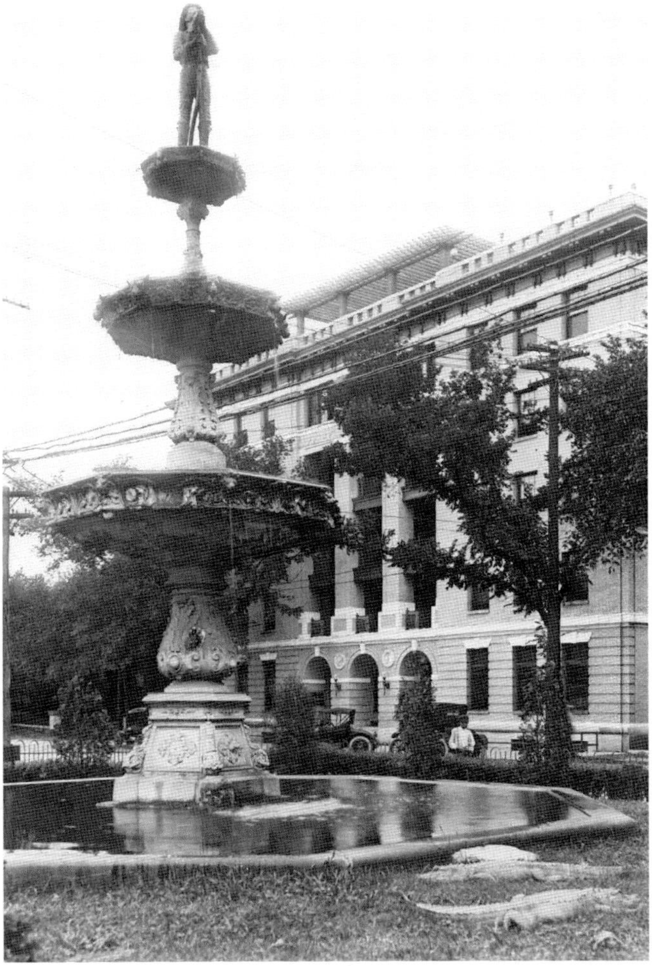

Fireman's Fountain
The fireman's memorial fountain on Georgia Avenue was dedicated in 1888. The memorial reflects the citizens' respect for two firemen—Iler and Peak—at a time of civic unity when Chattanooga was really experiencing its first real economic boom after the Civil War. Strangely enough, alligators are visible crawling around inside the iron fence. The statue has something of a thoughtful air and is striking when the water turns into a frozen cascade during icy weather. (Courtesy Chattanooga Public Library.)

Firemen
Henry Iler (standing, far right), William Peak (standing, behind dog), and their fellow firefighters are pictured on a hose reel wagon for this photograph. They answered a daytime call to a fire on Market Street and never returned. The blazing store collapsed on the men while they were inside. (Courtesy Chattanooga Public Library.)

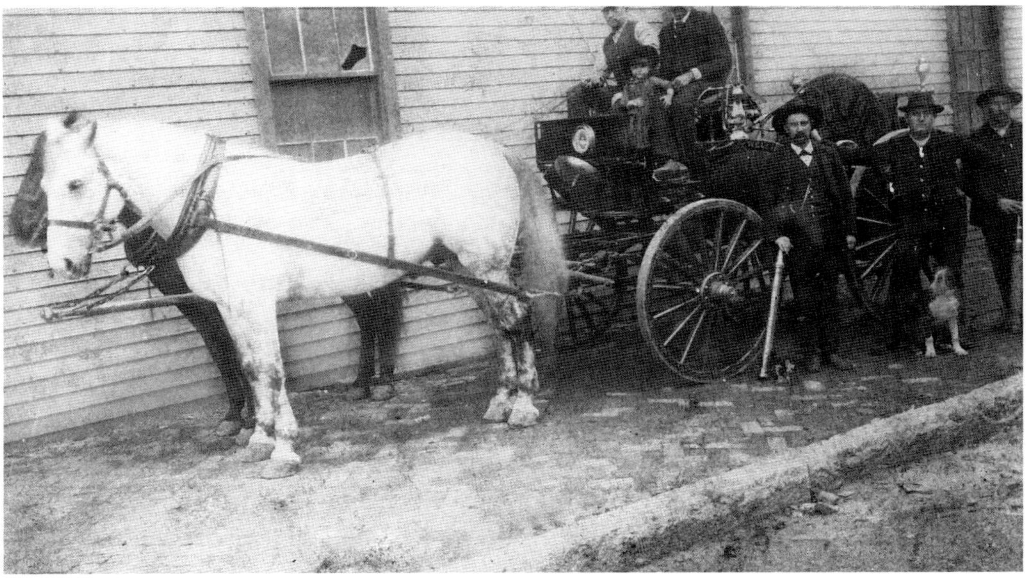

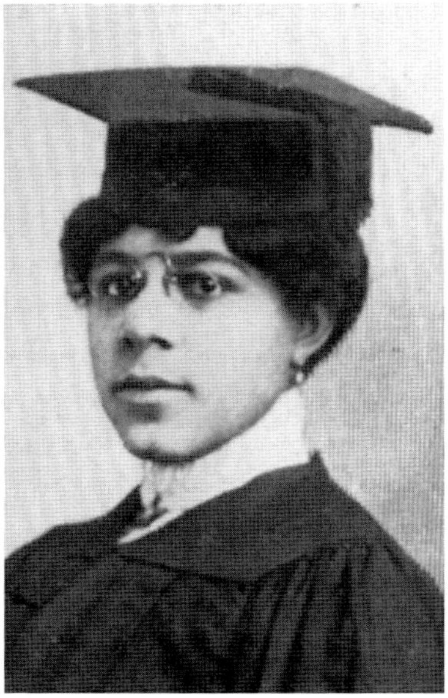

O.L. Davis

Dr. O.L. Davis was born on Lookout Mountain and was an anomaly for her time. In an era when women rarely went to college, she managed to attend Spellman Seminary in Atlanta and graduate. Following that, she moved to Nashville to attend Meharry Medical College, obtaining her graduate degree in 1902 and returning home to open an office. Remarkably at the time, she was "the first and only colored lady dentist to graduate in the South and the first to enter into practice," according to *A History of Hamilton County, Tennessee*. (Courtesy Chattanooga Public Library.)

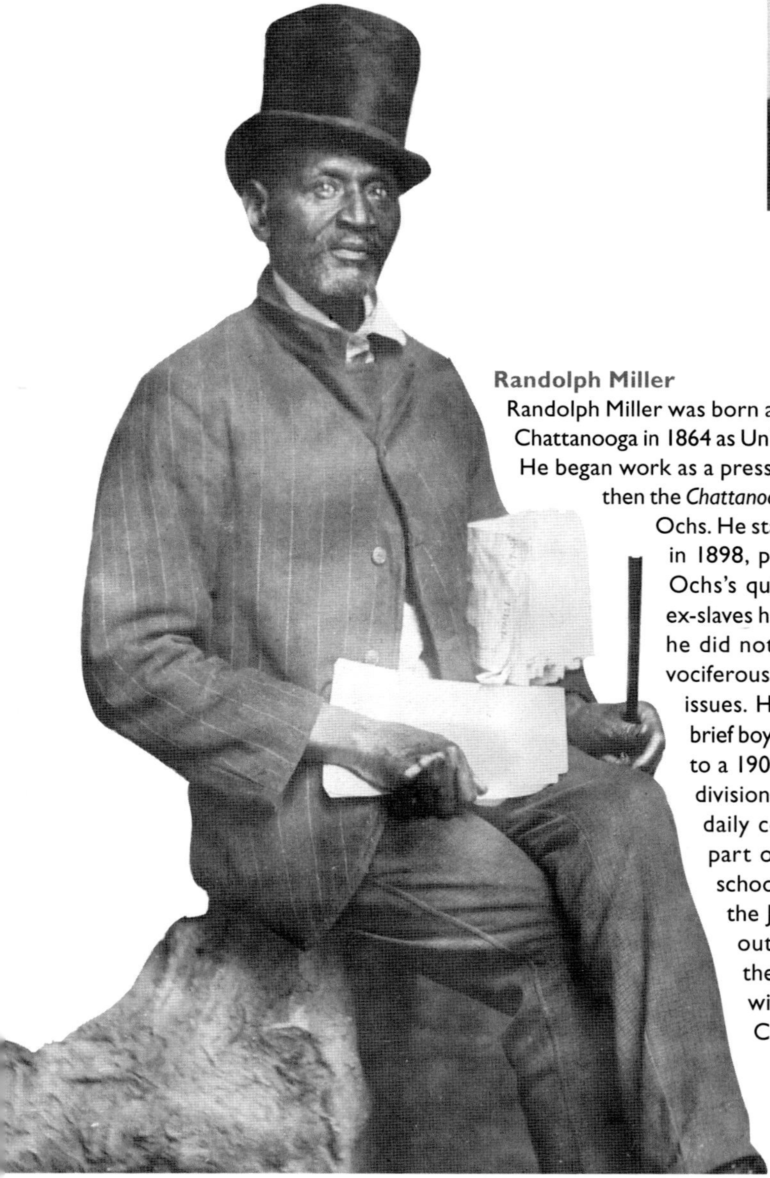

Randolph Miller

Randolph Miller was born a slave in middle Georgia and came to Chattanooga in 1864 as Union forces marched through the South. He began work as a pressman for the *Chattanooga Gazette* and then the *Chattanooga Times,* which was owned by Adolph Ochs. He started his own paper, the *Weekly Blade*, in 1898, possibly with newspaperman Adolph Ochs's quiet backing—something only a few ex-slaves had done. As a community spokesman, he did not shrink from controversy and was vociferous in his support of African American issues. He fought racial segregation and led a brief boycott of the local streetcars in response to a 1905 Tennessee law that enforced racial divisions on public conveyances. One of his daily columns said: "They have taken our part of the library; they have moved our school to the frog pond; they have passed the Jim Crow law; they have knocked us out of the jury box; they have played the devil generally; and what in thunder will they do no one knows." (Courtesy Chattanooga Public Library.)

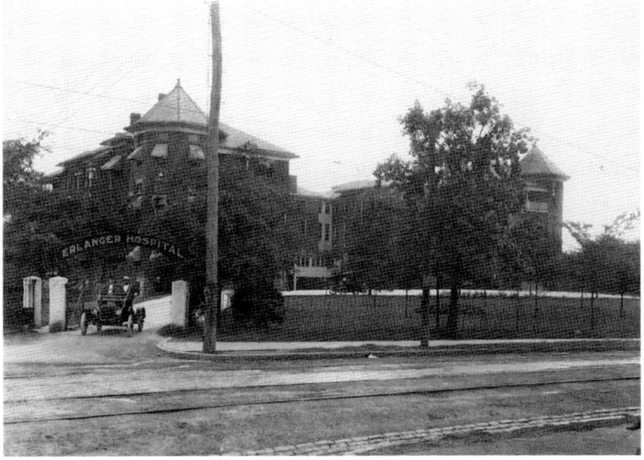

Frederic Emile d'Erlanger
Frederic Emile d'Erlanger, a European investor, bought into the railroads in Tennessee after the Civil War. Realizing there was no care for injured workers, he offered a hefty $5,000 for a fund to build a hospital in Chattanooga. Citizens got behind the effort, and Erlanger Hospital was opened in 1899 with 72 beds, east of the old Gardenhire home on East Third Street. Parts of this building still exist within the current modern complex. (Courtesy Chattanooga Public Library.)

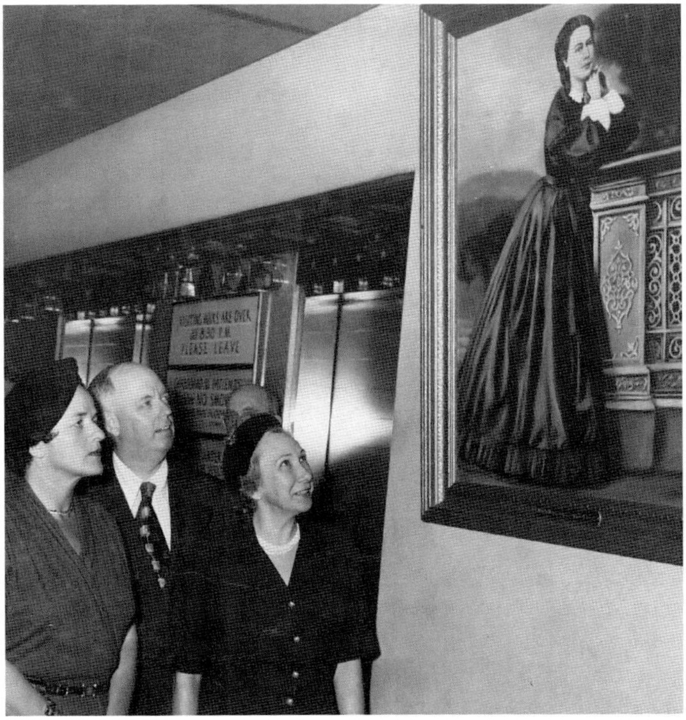

Erlanger Portrait
The Baroness Marguerite Mathilde Slidell d'Erlanger is the namesake of Chattanooga's oldest hospital. Raised on the Slidell plantation north of New Orleans, her father, US senator John Slidell, was prominent in Southern political affairs. As a diplomat to France for the Confederacy, he and his daughter Mathilde were onboard the British ship during the Trent Affair and were taken captive illegally by the Union navy in an international dispute. She later married Frederic d'Erlanger and lived the good life in Europe, where she was known for her beauty. The baroness made the first call on the French transatlantic telephone cable in 1869. This painting of the Baroness Marguerite Mathilde Slidell continues to hang in the lobby. Admiring the portrait of the baroness in 1950 are, from left to right, Mrs. Garrison Elder, Roy McDonald, and Mrs. Earl Hale. (Courtesy Chattanooga Public Library.)

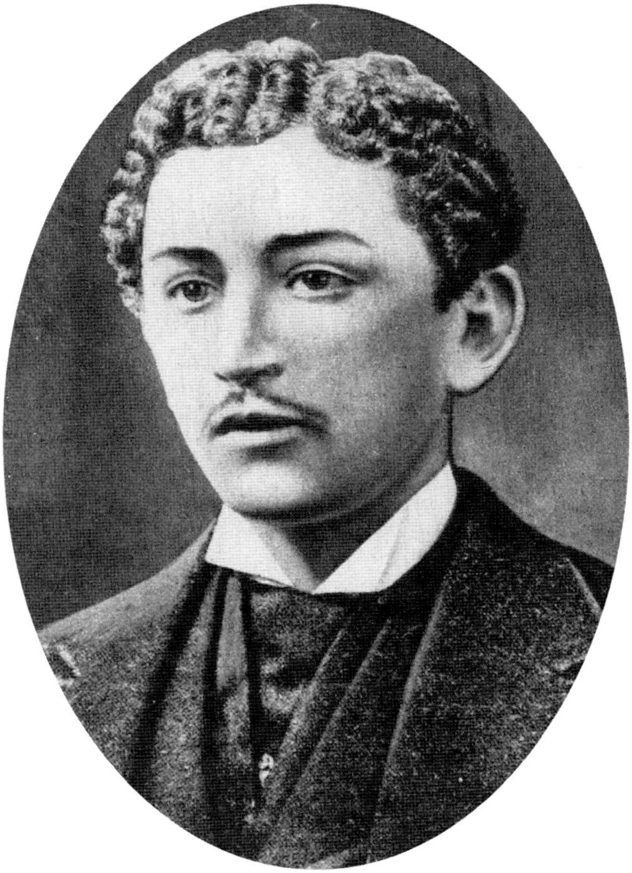

Adolph S. Ochs
Adolph S. Ochs was an ambitious young man who had minimal schooling but had a father who spoke six languages and instructed his gifted son. Born in 1858, he became a newspaper office boy at 11 and at the age of 19 borrowed money to buy the *Chattanooga Times* in 1878. By 1880, the newspaper flourished as the city underwent an economic boom some 20 years after the Civil War ended. In 1892, the paper had its own newspaper building, the Ochs Building (or Dome Building), a handsome Italianate commercial structure on Georgia Avenue that is still standing. The Mizpah Congregation Temple on McCallie Avenue was built in 1928 by Ochs as well. And part of the national military park on Lookout Mountain is land that he donated. A son of Jewish immigrants from Bavaria, he was continuously active in numerous civic and philanthropic affairs in the city, a staunch believer in building community. But his name will long be remembered for his acquisition (on loaned money) of a struggling paper in 1896—the *New York Times*. He was intent on creating "a high standard newspaper, clean, dignified, and trustworthy." As owner and publisher, he transformed it into one of the leading newspapers in the world. (Courtesy Chattanooga Public Library.)

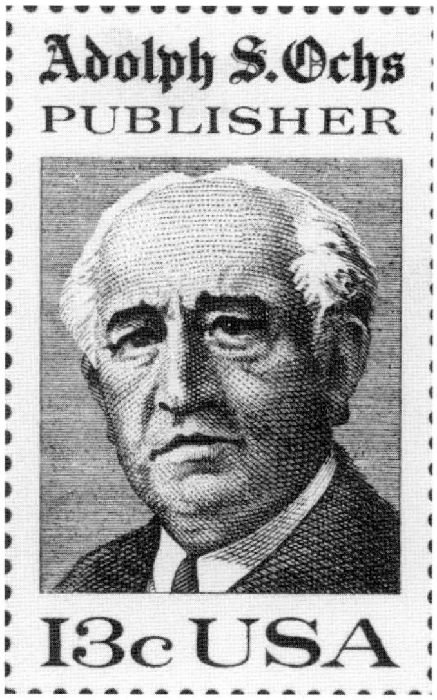

Ochs Stamp
Little needs be said of a man's impact if he has a US stamp featuring him. The importance of the *New York Times*, 80 years after his leadership began, made him a legendary figure. In America's bicentennial year, this postage stamp was issued at a face value of 13¢. (Author's collection.)

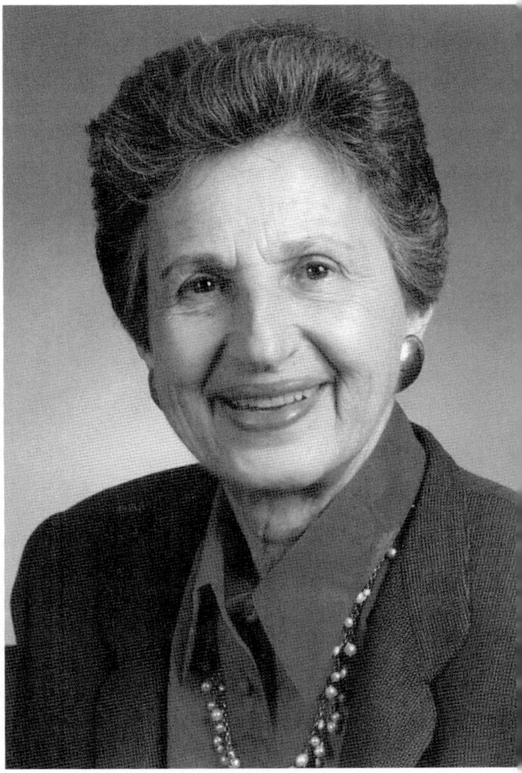

Ruth Sulzberger Holmberg
When it comes to civic contribution, Ruth Sulzberger Holmberg is a shining example of commitment. The granddaughter of newspaper publisher, Adolph Ochs, she served as publisher of the *Chattanooga Times* from 1964 to 1992, a famously liberal paper in the conservative South. A stalwart defender of issues such as racial integration in the 1950s and 1960s, Holmberg has never been afraid to support her beliefs in action as well as in writing. Her acumen in business led Holmberg to become the first woman to serve as president of the Chattanooga Area Chamber of Commerce and for that matter, to run a major Chattanooga business. She has served as the director of the Chattanooga Symphony and Opera Association and was chair of the Hunter Museum of American Art Board of Directors from 1979 to 1983. Her many years of work as chair of the local Public Education Foundation reflect her desire to expand opportunity for minorities' access to higher education. Known as a generous donor to numerous causes throughout the years, she has received the Tennessee Woman of the Year Award and the Kiwanis Distinguished Service Award. Most recently, a beautiful glass walkway connecting the Walnut Street Bridge to the Hunter Museum of American Art was named in her honor. (Courtesy Ruth S. Holmberg.)

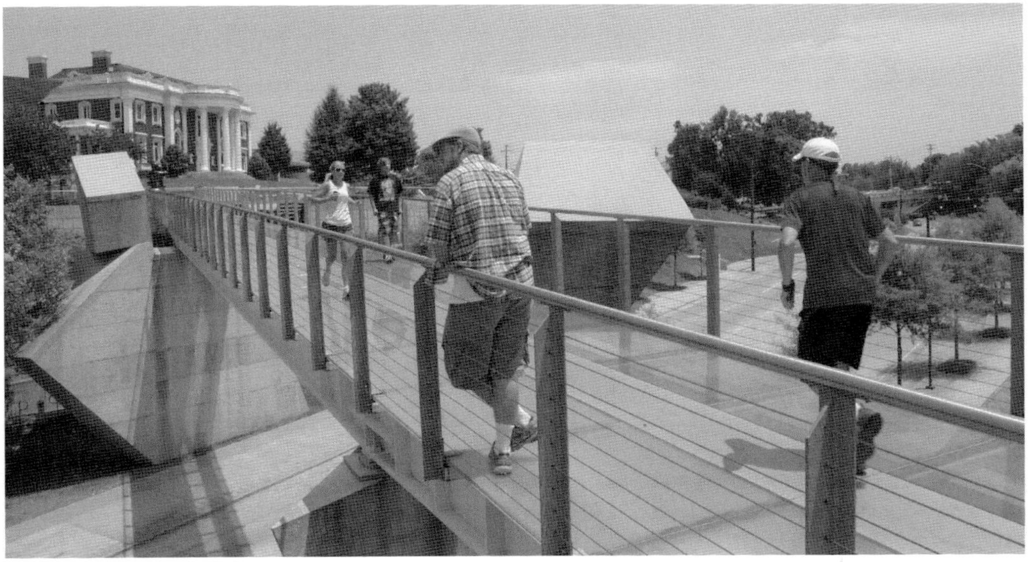

Holmberg Bridge
In 2005, the Holmberg Bridge was completed, connecting the Hunter Museum with the Walnut Street Bridge. Dedicated to the memory of Bill Holmberg, it is a uniquely formed symbol of the bridges that Ruth and Bill Holmberg built between people in Chattanooga. Not only are the supports unusual geometric shapes, but also the bridge floor is made of laminated glass that is gently lit from below in the evening. (Author's collection.)

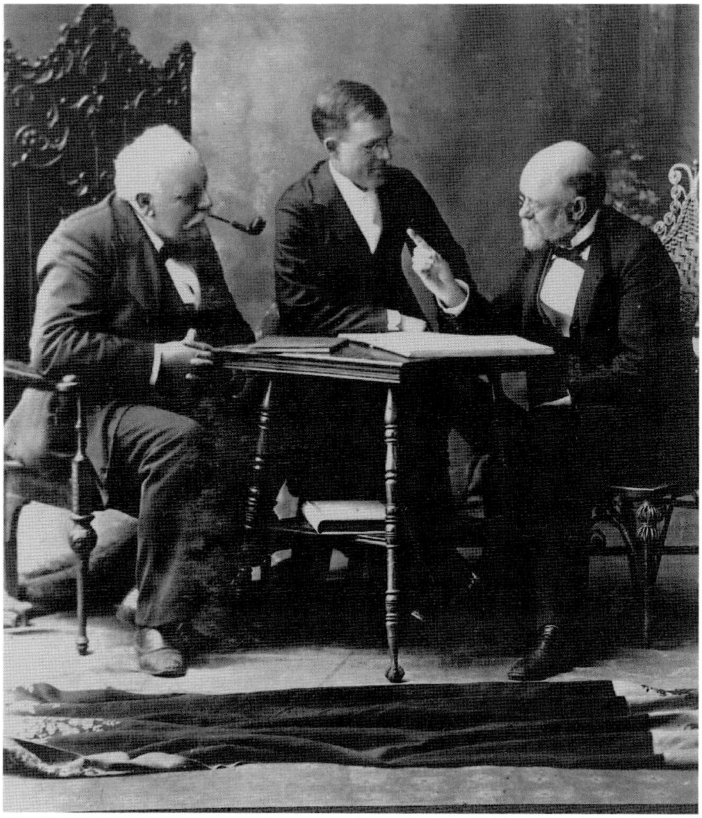

E.Y. Chapin

E.Y. Chapin (center) was a smart lawyer who became quite a successful banker. On numerous company boards, he turned his energy to philanthropy in the community, beginning with Erlanger Hospital at the turn of the last century. He was a force behind organizing the tuberculosis sanitarium, an important public health initiative. He helped found the Little Theater, still active today. Most notably, Chapin left a solid legacy in support of the public library and as a donor to different school libraries all over town, driven by his belief in the value of reading for all. To his right is former mayor Dr. Philander Sims. (Courtesy Chattanooga Public Library.)

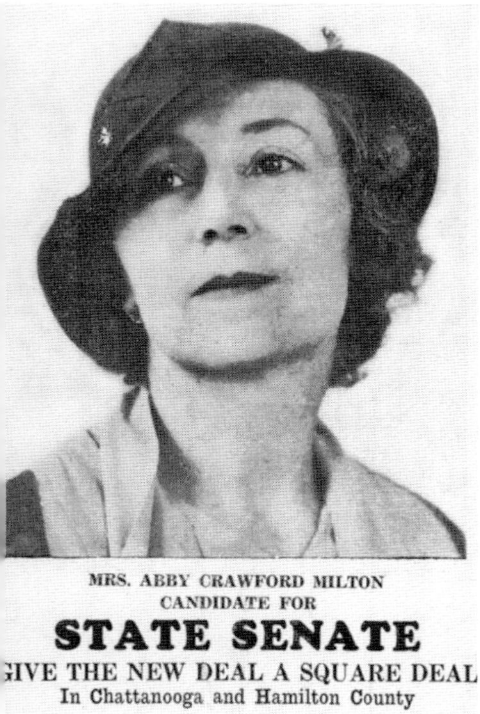

Abby C. Milton

It has been almost 100 years since women won the right to cast a vote, and it was the State of Tennessee that was the 36th and final state to approve the measure. In the forefront of that movement was Abby Crawford Milton of Chattanooga. Daughter of a well-known political family in Georgia, she married George Fort Milton, a newspaper executive, and was a tireless organizer of meetings for the suffrage cause. In the summer of 1920 when the nation focused on the ultimate passage of that amendment, she lived in Nashville, promoting her ideas in the state house halls during that tense political situation. During this time, Milton, age 38, was the leader of the Tennessee Equal Suffrage Association; subsequently, she became the first state president of the League of Women Voters when it came into existence. Milton remained active, later campaigning for the creation of the Great Smoky Mountain Parks and then the Tennessee Valley Authority, a controversial project that was trying to gain traction in the region. Besides being a mother of three, she obtained a degree from the Chattanooga College of Law and was a published poet during her busy 110 years of living. (Courtesy Chattanooga Public Library.)

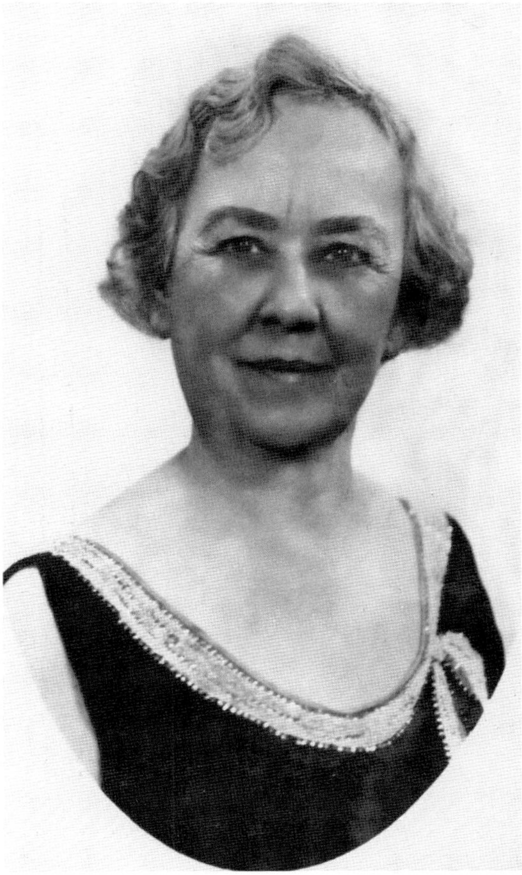

Zella Armstrong
Zella Armstrong can be seen as the quintessential blue blood who loved her town and its history and worked in many ways to make it count. One of her legacies is the *Lookout*, a periodical that centered around stories about "society," particularly that of Lookout Mountain. She wrote *The History of Hamilton County and Chattanooga Tennessee*, *Notable Southern Families*, and even a book about the Madoc. She led an early group of preservationists in the 1950s in a gallant effort to save Cameron Hill, an old section of town, before the local government destroyed it in the name of urban renewal. They raised a ruckus but were no match for city and state legislators. Perhaps her most long-lived contribution was the Cotton Ball, an annual social affair that brings young women of note to wider notice. (Courtesy Chattanooga Public Library.)

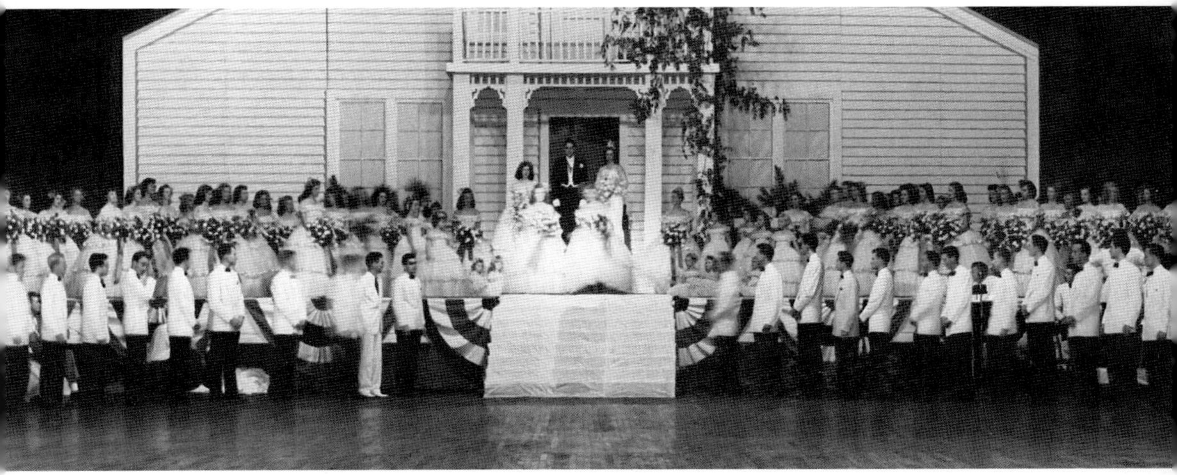

Cotton Ball
The Cotton Ball is the creation of Zella Armstrong, who began an annual social affair to recognize certain Chattanooga young women who were "coming out" into society and to raise money for the hospital's charity ward as well. An invitation-only event, the Cotton Ball crowns a young lady in a floor-length dress as queen; the king is usually an older, established, well-connected gentleman. Seventy-five years after its inaugural festivities, it continues in full swing each August. (Courtesy Chattanooga Public Library.)

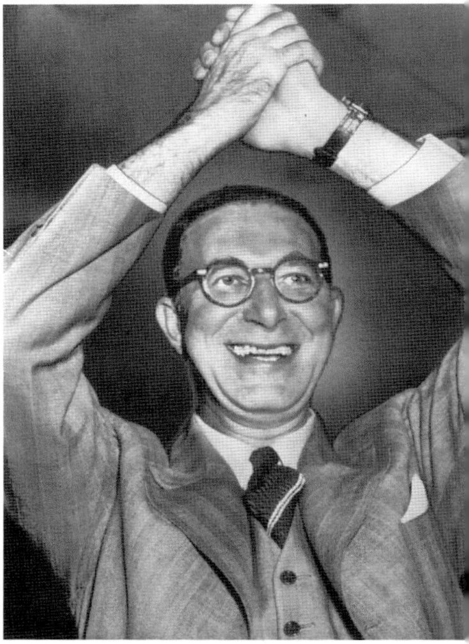

Estes Kefauver

The closest brush with the presidency of the United States ever had by a Chattanoogan came in the person of Estes Kefauver. Kefauver ran as vice president with Adlai Stevenson on the Democratic ticket in 1956, losing to incumbent president Dwight Eisenhower. An East Tennessee native who graduated from Yale Law School, Kefauver began practicing law in Chattanooga in 1927 and was elected as the district's congressman in 1939. A liberal Roosevelt Democrat in the South, he became famous for his trademark coonskin cap and his activist approach, which he brandished as a US senator beginning in 1949. His hearing on interstate crime was one of the first televised congressional hearings and helped to make him a national figure. Something of a maverick, he championed many causes such as supporting the TVA, pushing antimonopoly legislation, legislating against large drug companies, and investigating pin-up magazines. Always outspoken in his views, he suffered a heart attack on the Senate floor in 1963 and died several days later. (Author's collection.)

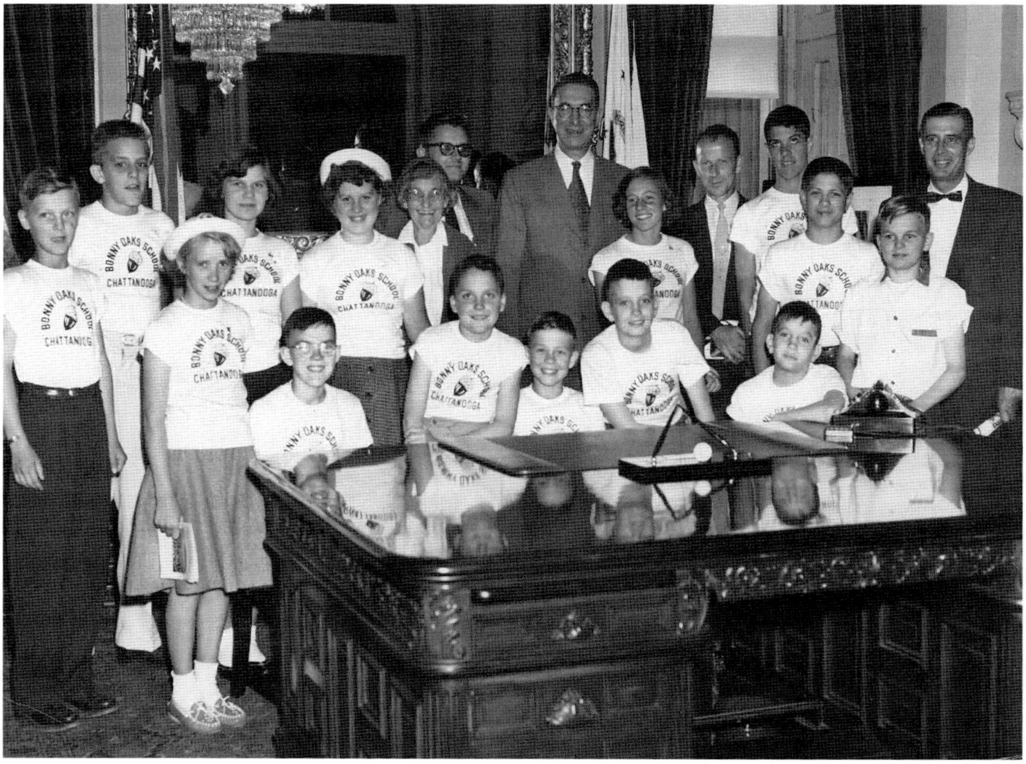

Kefauver with Children

A group of 14 students from the Bonny Oaks School, an orphanage in Chattanooga, are on a field trip to Washington, DC, to see Sen. Estes Kefauver in 1954. The senator highlighted their day by taking them to see Vice Pres. Richard Nixon's office as seen here. (Courtesy Chattanooga Public Library.)

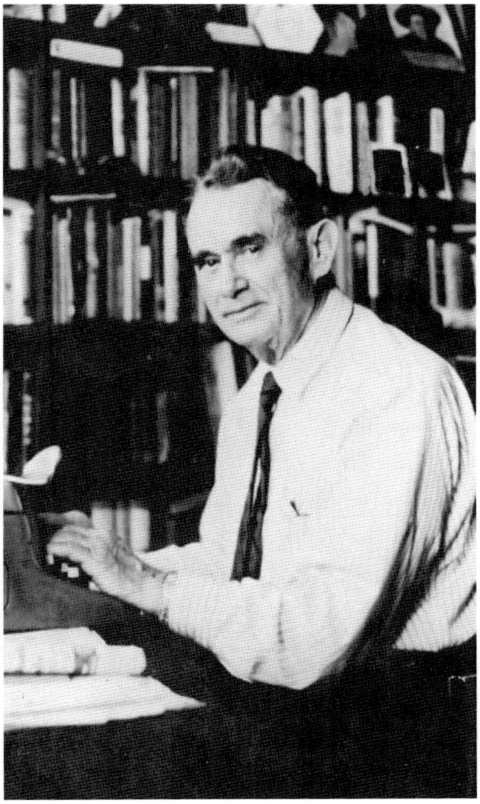

Ralph McGill

From humble beginnings in the small community of Soddy Daisy, Ralph McGill became one of the most widely read southern newspaper columnists of his day. Born in 1898, he grew up in Chattanooga and once remarked, "I lived in history," referring to the area battlefields and the intense feelings about the War Between the States that pervaded the city then. He enrolled locally at the McCallie School and went to college at Vanderbilt University. In 1929, he landed a job as a sportswriter at the *Atlanta Constitution,* but social issues were what interested him, and he gradually became a vociferous opponent of segregation. He became editor and publisher of the paper; in Georgia, his front-page editorials became famous for their outspokenness and he incurred the wrath of old-time Southerners who intimidated him and his family. In 1959, McGill won the Pulitzer Prize for editorial writing and became a nationally syndicated columnist and, as a longtime Democrat, a friend of Presidents Kennedy and Johnson. Hailed by many for his courage, his fluid writing skill, and his vision for a better South, McGill's contribution to the civil rights movement will not be forgotten. (Courtesy Chattanooga Public Library.)

John Popham

The *Chattanooga Times* newspaper had an umbilical connection with the *New York Times* for a century because both papers were owned by Chattanoogan Adolph Ochs. Because of this connection, young *New York Times* reporters from the North often spent time working in Chattanooga in order to get a taste of small-town life. John Popham was one of those people, becoming the first correspondent from the North to regularly report on Southern life and politics. Known for a green Buick that he drove tens of thousands of miles a year, Popham had a rare gift for reporting with insight into many aspects of life especially in the burgeoning years of the civil rights movement. Race relations were something he was especially keen on since he was witnessing the daily upheavals that were occurring in the 1950s. In 1958, he came off the road to become an editor for the *Chattanooga Times* for 20 years until 1977. Never one to sit still, he then commuted to Atlanta weekly to attend law school, garnering his law degree at the age of 72. A witty, thoughtful, and persuasive writer, he is remembered at the Popham Seminars, a gathering of Southern journalists held regularly to discuss topical issues affecting the South. (Courtesy Southern Regional Council.)

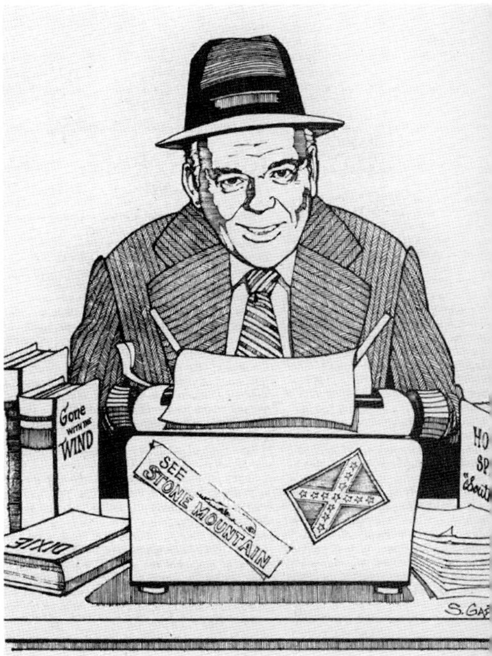

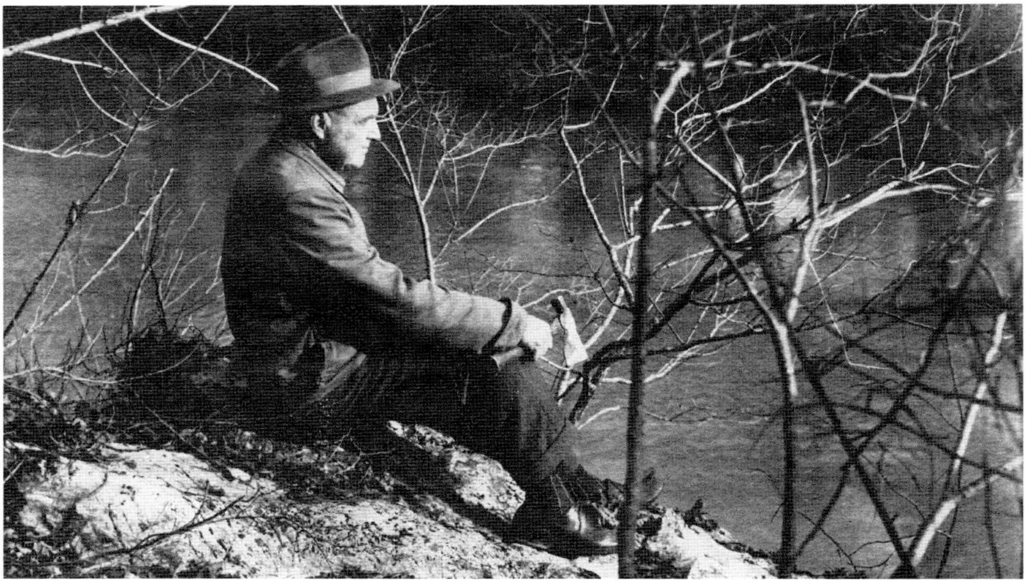

Robert S. Walker

Robert Sparks Walker made a living doing what he loved. And what he loved most was the natural world. He was best known as a nature columnist for the *Chattanooga Times*. But he also wrote poetry, had a radio show, was published in national magazines such as *Better Homes and Gardens*, and authored no less than 10 books. One of these books, *Torchlight to the Cherokees*, received a Pulitzer Prize nomination in 1931. As founder of the Chattanooga Audubon Society, he worked to protect historic sites in the area, identified and labeled more than 3,000 trees, and promoted the appreciation of the city's natural abundance. Born in 1978 in the Spring Frog Cabin—which still stands—he worked to preserve land in East Brainerd and build a nature preserve, the Elise Chapin Wildlife Sanctuary. Also known as Audubon Acres, this wooded lowland extends over 130 acres and contains four miles of quiet hiking trails and a section of the South Chickamauga Creek as well as the site where the Little Owl village once stood. Thankfully, it provides a quadrant of peace on the east side of town where commercial development around the Hamilton Place Mall has been intense in the last 25 years. (Courtesy Chattanooga Public Library.)

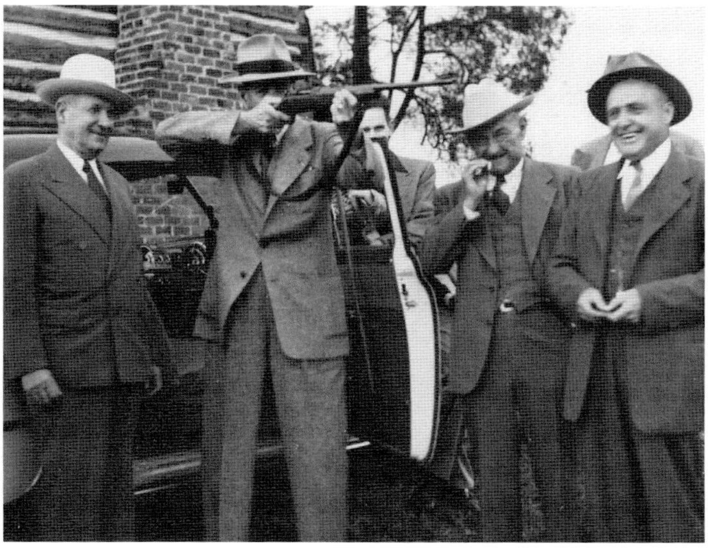

Robert S. Walker and Gang

Standing in front of Spring Frog Cabin, Mayor Hugh Wasson (left) watches as Gen. Jonathan M. Wainwright takes dead aim with his rifle. Col. O.J. Holman puffs on a cigarette while Robert S. Walker enjoys the banter. (Courtesy Chattanooga Public Library.)

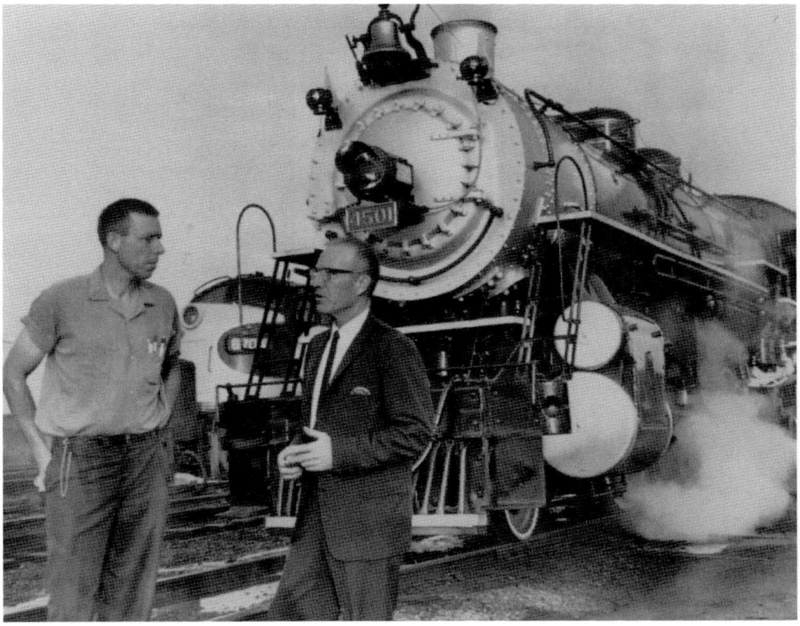

Tennessee Valley Railroad Museum

By the late 1950s, the steam engines that once ran across the country had become a thing of the past. But two friends decided that the era of the steam railroad was too embedded in Chattanooga's memory to let it slip away forever. The result was the Tennessee Valley Railroad Museum (TVRM), created by Bob Soule (left) and Paul Merriman (right) in 1961. Paul Merriman was an electrical engineer who specialized in aluminum welding and worked for DuPont in Chattanooga. He purchased Southern Railway Engine 4501 for $5,000 and refurbished it, giving it to the TVRM. Its many journeys throughout the Southern system were instrumental in revitalizing regional interest in steam locomotives. Robert Soule began drawing trains at the age of seven and eventually made a career working for the Southern Railway. As a train enthusiast, he worked tirelessly acquiring train cars and then extending the length of the operating rail line. His insistence that the goal of the museum was to be self-sustaining was key to its success. To that end, he felt it was critical that a working maintenance shop was part of the museum. When such a facility in East Chattanooga became part of the museum it was named in his honor—the "Soule Shops." Indeed, what began as a few rail cars 50 years ago is now a nationally known tourist destination. (Courtesy Tennessee Valley Railroad Museum.)

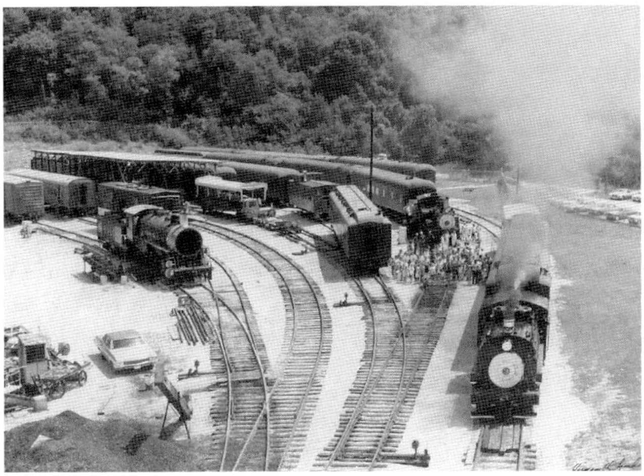

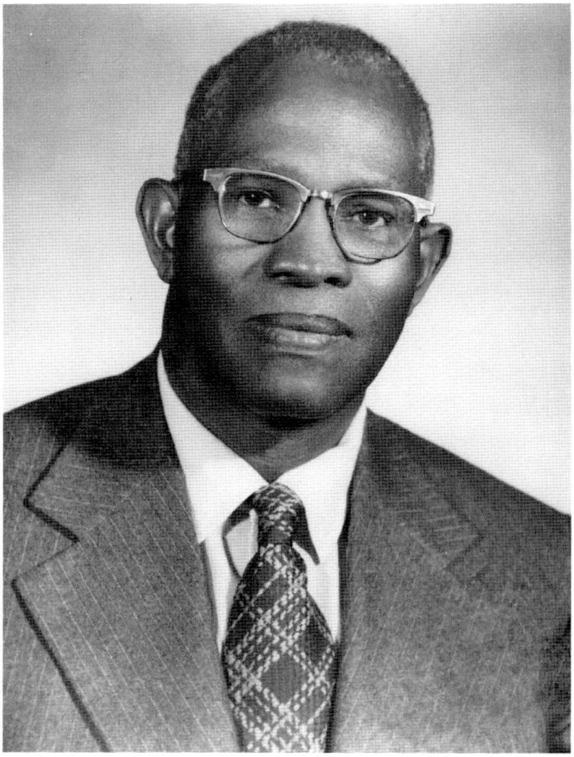

C.B. Robinson

Clarence B. Robinson began life in the community known as Hornesville in 1911 on the east side of town and made a living as an outstanding teacher and administrator in the Chattanooga public school system for 39 years. He came to prominence in 1941, when he served as a plaintiff against the same school system for equalization of teacher salaries and, eventually, was elected to the Tennessee statehouse for 18 years. During this time, he was elected chairman emeritus of the Black Caucus for the Tennessee General Assembly and played a role in the national Democratic platform in 1980. Known as a patient adjudicator and a bridge builder, he won numerous awards, including recognition from the NAACP and Tennessee State University. In 1981, the state of Tennessee named the bridge south of the Chickamauga Dam in his honor. (Courtesy Chattanooga Public Library.)

Roy Ketner McDonald

One might say that Roy Ketner McDonald got into the publishing business through the back door. He began by handing out a free advertising paper for his father's grocery, the Home Store, in 1933, going door-to-door on Thursdays. In three years, he turned it into a full-blown newspaper, the *Free Press*, and within four years, had a booming circulation of 33,000. After absorbing another paper, it became the *Chattanooga News—Free Press* and was the longtime evening conservative rival of the *Chattanooga Times*. "Mr. Roy," as he was known, was an active board member of Erlanger Hospital as well. He introduced the idea of prepaid hospital insurance locally that later evolved into Blue Cross Blue Shield of Tennessee, where he served as chairman of the board until 1990. (Courtesy Chattanooga Public Library.)

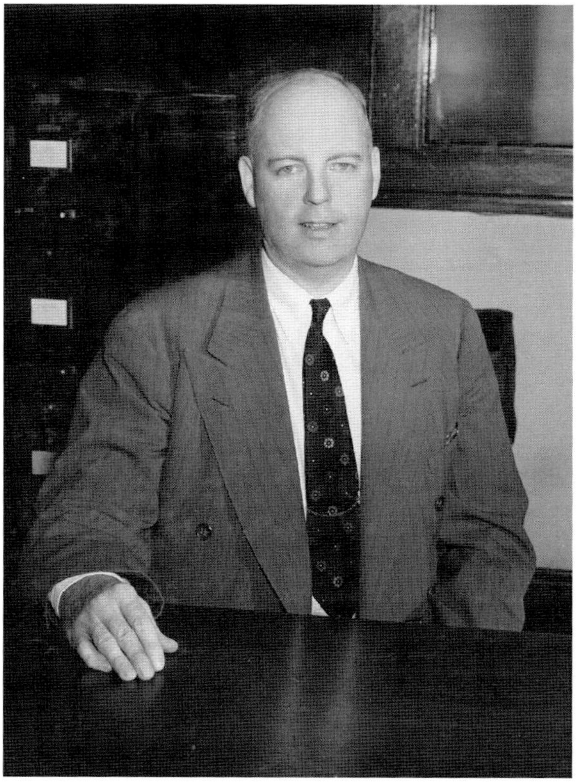

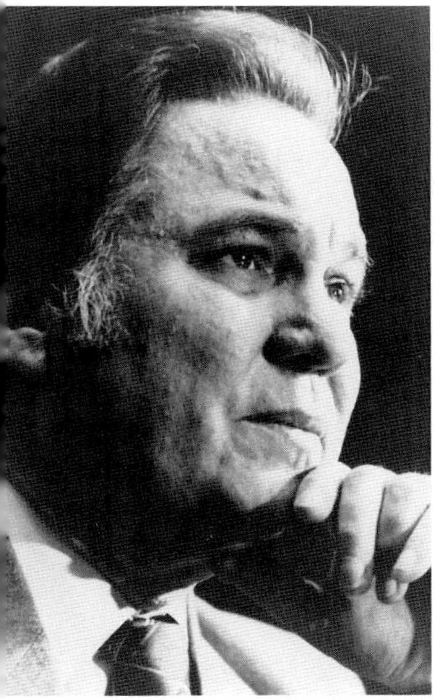

Dalton Roberts

Dalton Roberts was the first mayor of Hamilton County for 16 years in a trying time in Chattanooga's history, a new era of racial integration and economic struggle. Unusually outspoken for a public figure, Roberts was never one to shy away from saying what he meant and getting straight to the point. Nonetheless, he won the respect of foe and friend alike and was instrumental in making county government an agency of change and commitment that would lead to Chattanooga's celebrated urban revival. His time since he left office has presented him in a different light. As a columnist for the *Chattanooga Times Free Press*, he has written on social issues and mused on broader philosophical themes. He has a thoughtful, homespun approach, grounded in many years of problem-solving and leavened with a pungent sense of humor. It would be remiss not to add his renown as a lifelong singer, songwriter, and entertainer, one whom many Chattanoogans have heard and enjoyed with a smile. (Courtesy Chattanooga Public Library.)

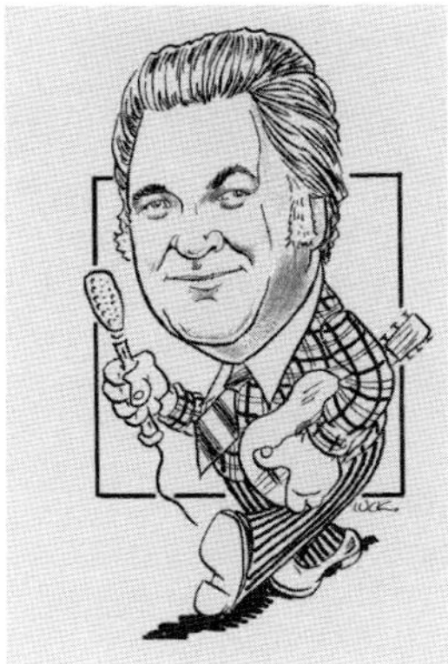

Roberts Cartoon

This cartoon by Willie King captures in a nutshell Roberts's persona. The microphone reflects his public voice, and the guitar shows his "down home" style of connecting with everyday folks to get his point across. (Courtesy Chattanooga Public Library.)

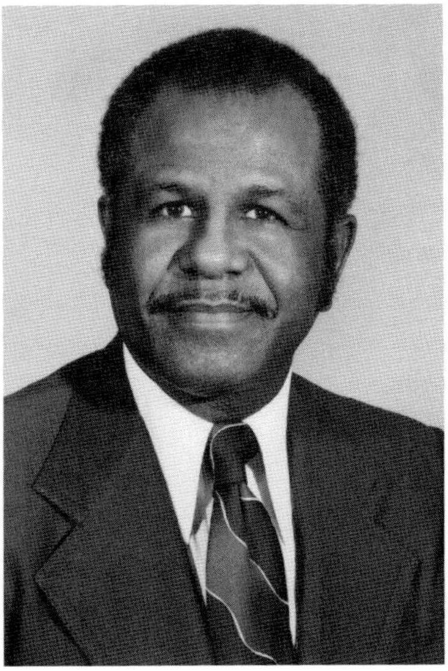

John Franklin

In 1971, John R. Franklin became the city's first African American city commissioner, a political feat that had not been equaled in close to a century. He would later serve four terms as vice mayor of the city. A solid candidate who was principal of Alton Park Junior High School and then chairman of the school board, his deep roots in the community as director of the Franklin-Strickland Funeral Home engendered respect and popularity at the ballot. His grandfather G.W. Franklin was the first black funeral director and embalmer in Chattanooga when, in 1894, he started the Franklin Funeral Home, a long-standing business that still operates today. (Courtesy Chattanooga Public Library.)

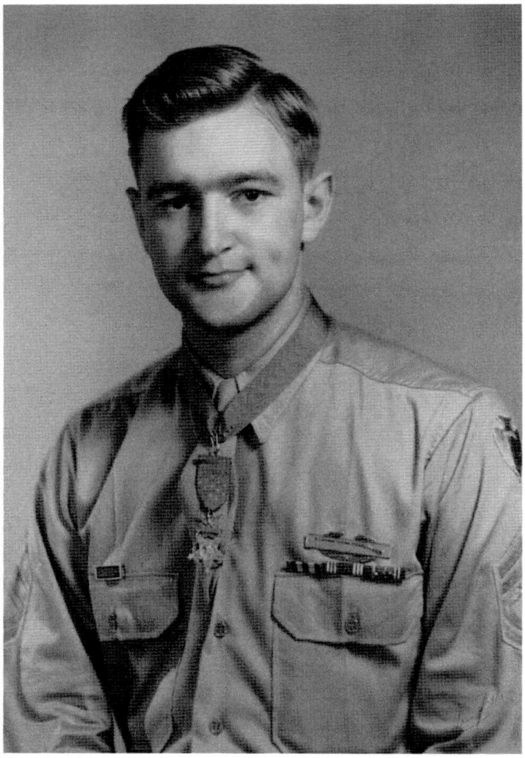

Charles Coolidge

Coolidge Park sits on the Tennessee River directly across from downtown Chattanooga and is widely viewed as a key part in the city's revival in the 1990s. The green space is named in honor of Signal Mountain native Charles Henry Coolidge who was awarded the Medal of Honor for action in France in October 1944 during World War II. In the rain and cold east of Belmont-sur-Buttant, he voluntarily took command of a unit of soldiers, many of them new to combat, and courageously fought a much larger German force in dense woods. Refusing to vacate their position at one point, the technical sergeant crawled to within 25 yards of enemy tanks armed with a bazooka; when that malfunctioned, he attacked the armored vehicle alone with a handful of grenades. His bravery and leadership over four days accomplished the mission. In September 2006, French officials came to Chattanooga to award him the Legion d'Honneur medal in recognition of his service in a ceremony at Coolidge Park. (Courtesy Chattanooga Public Library.)

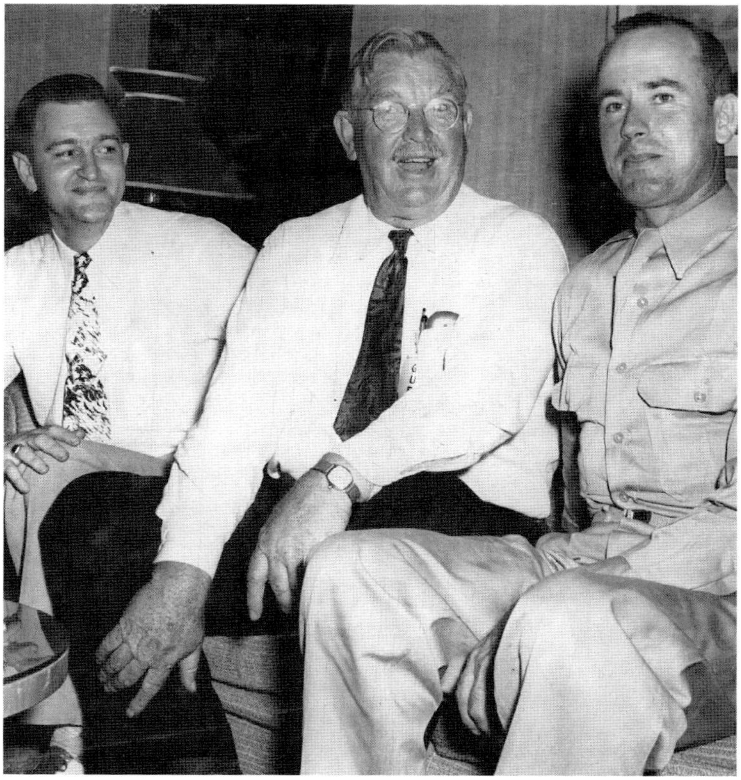

Coolidge with York

Sgt. Charles Coolidge (left) smiles as he listens to Sgt. Alvin York (center) tell a story to Sgt. Charles McGaha (right) in July 1949. York, the famous World War I hero, was serving as the grand marshal of the American Legion parade in Chattanooga. (Courtesy Chattanooga Public Library.)

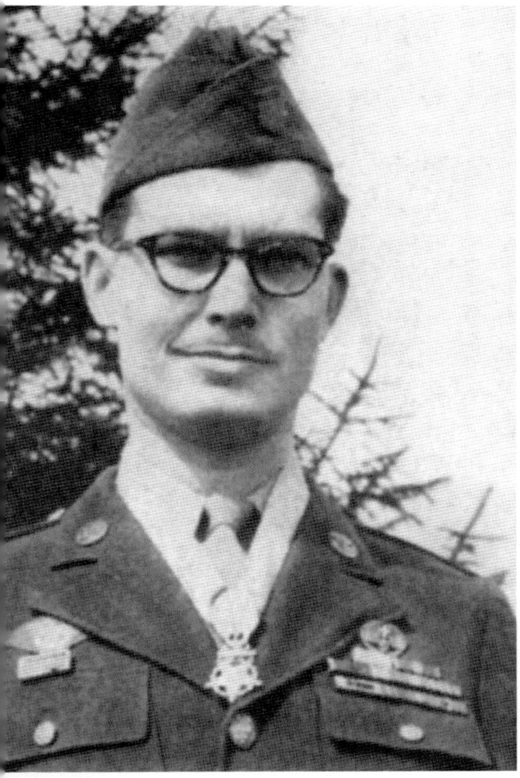

Desmond Doss

Desmond Doss was a true hero—one of the few conscientious objectors to receive the Medal of Honor. As a Seventh Day Adventist who did not believe in killing of any kind, he enlisted in the Army as a medic in the 77th Infantry Division so that he might save lives. Stationed on Okinawa in May 1945 and in a brutal fight with the Japanese, he rescued 75 American casualties from high ground and lowered them over a cliff on a rope-supported litter to safety—doing it one person at a time for 12 hours. Two days later, he crawled to within eight yards of an enemy cave, dressed the wounds of four different soldiers, and evacuated each of them separately under grenade attack. Later in the fighting, he gave aid to the wounded while he was suffering from grenade shrapnel. When he was picked up, he gave up the litter he was on for another hurt soldier; while waiting for help, he was shot in the arm, used a rifle stock to make a splint, and then dragged himself 300 yards to safety. The Desmond T. Doss Medal of Honor Highway in nearby Walker County, Georgia, keeps the memory of his bravery alive for future generations. (Courtesy Chattanooga Public Library.)

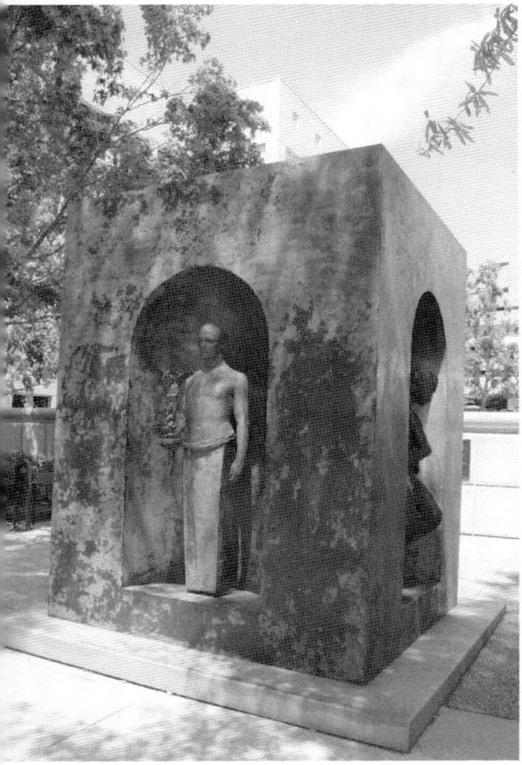

Law Enforcement Memorial

This monument stands as a tribute to peace officers who have lost their lives in the line of duty. In 2003, the dedication ceremony for the bronze sculptures was highlighted by the recent death of Julie Jacks. Jacks, who was the rookie of the year with the Chattanooga Police Department in 2001, lost her life on May 6, 2002, while trying to apprehend a suspect on foot. The sculpture by Cessna Decosimo stands on the 600 block of Market Street and is a silent testimonial to these officers' courage. (Author's collection.)

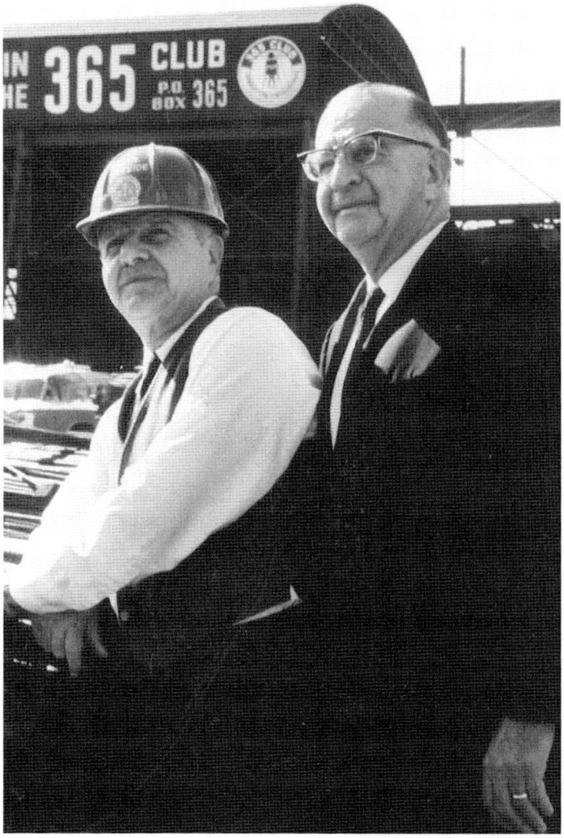

Mose and Garrison Siskin

Mose (left) and Garrison (right) Siskin were two brothers who walked side-by-side. When Garrison was threatened with losing his leg after a train accident in 1942, he prayed to God that if he could keep his leg, he would help others. His prayer was answered. His brother promised to fulfill the vow with him, and they diligently saved money from their scrap metal business to establish the Siskin Memorial Foundation dedicated to charitable purposes especially those involving physical rehabilitation. They began the Siskin School (later the Siskin Children's Institute) in the 1950s and the 365 Club, which asked for a penny-a-day to support the foundation's programs. Carefully shepherding their funds, the foundation grew along with their business, Siskin Steel and Supply, and in 1990, the Siskin Hospital for Physical Rehabilitation for adults became a reality, as did the Child and Family Research Center in 2008. What began as a prayer became a loving effort to assure that those among us with disabilities can have brighter days, better health, and a hope for a fuller life. (Courtesy Siskin Children's Institute.)

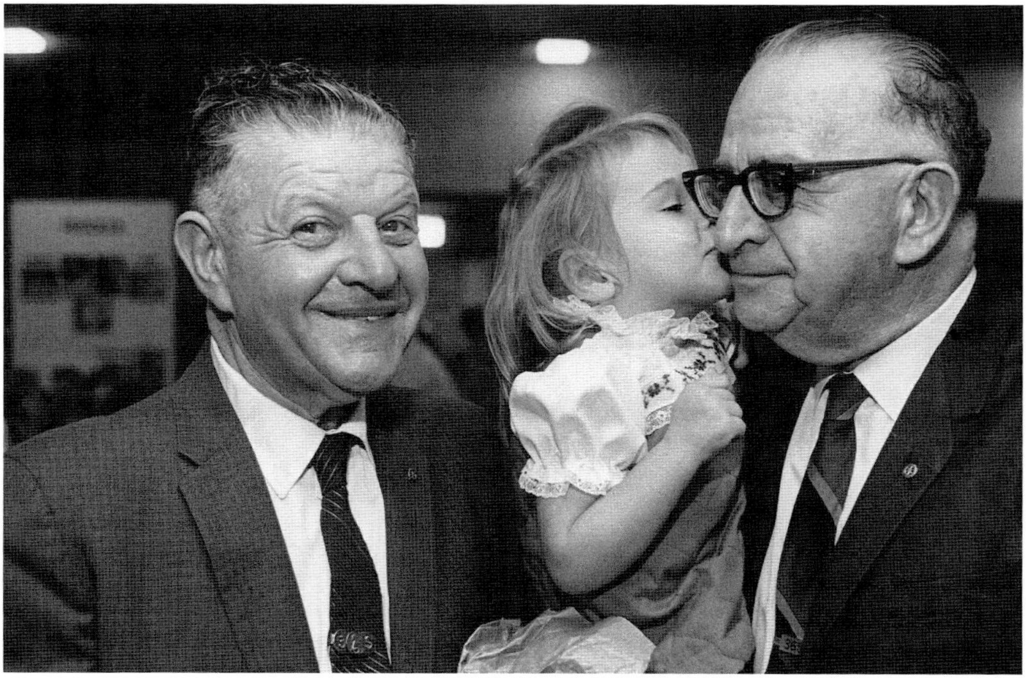

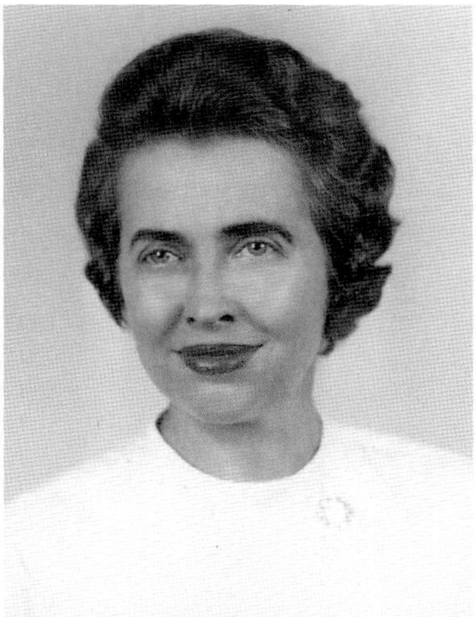

Jean Meacham
Jean Meacham was an English professor at the University of Chattanooga who gave an endowment grant to encourage creative writing. What resulted was the Meacham Writers' Workshop, which began in 1986 and is held twice a year. A lover of literature, Meacham stipulated that entry to the semiannual event was always free. Dedicated to her husband, Judge Ellis Meacham, who wrote three fiction novels, it is the only workshop in the country that welcomes writers of any ability at no cost. (Courtesy University of Tennessee at Chattanooga/Special Collections.)

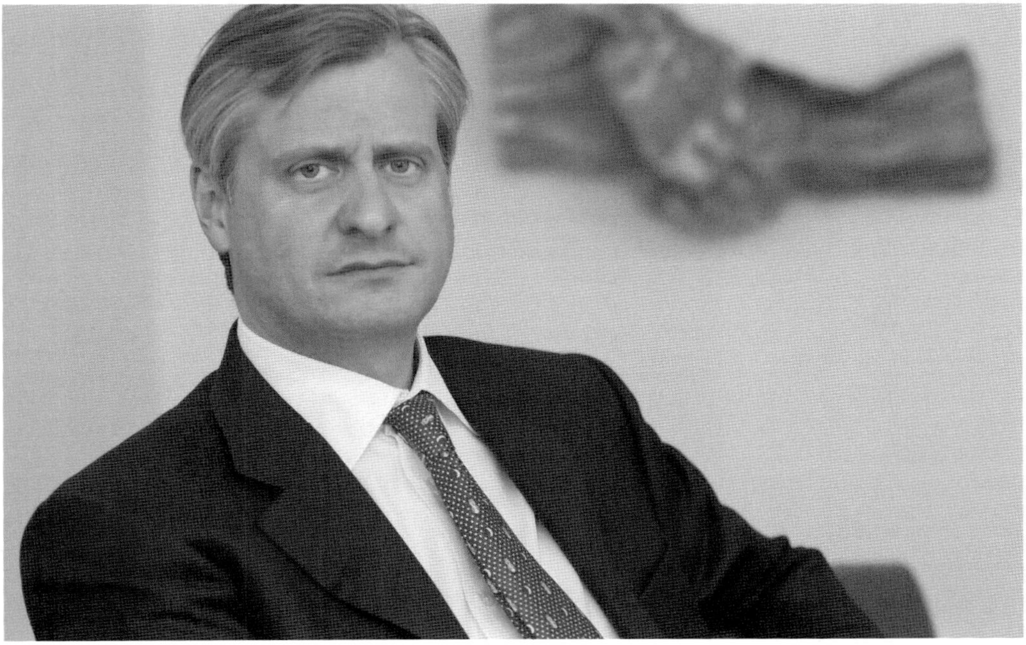

Jon Meacham
Some writers, such as journalists, work on a deadline, honing their skills in the daily grind. Others work in a longer time frame, thinking in more complicated, novelistic forms. Jon Meacham does both and does both well. A native Chattanoogan, he grew up on Missionary Ridge and attended McCallie School where he was a diligent student. In high school, he lived with his grandfather, Judge Ellis Meacham, a writer in his own right, whose love of history and politics influenced the young man. Meacham's hard work took him to the University of the South where he graduated Phi Beta Kappa and then to a job with the *Chattanooga Times*. But the South could not contain him, and by the young age of 29, he had become managing editor at the prestigious *Newsweek* magazine. During a career with the magazine, he also managed to write several works of nonfiction, the last of which, *American Lion*, a biography of Tennessean Andrew Jackson, won the Pulitzer Prize for biography. Always quick to acknowledge his Southern roots, it is fair to say that this perceptive and disciplined writer of American history truly sprung from his roots in Chattanooga and the Tennessee mountain land. (Courtesy McCallie School/Jon Meacham)

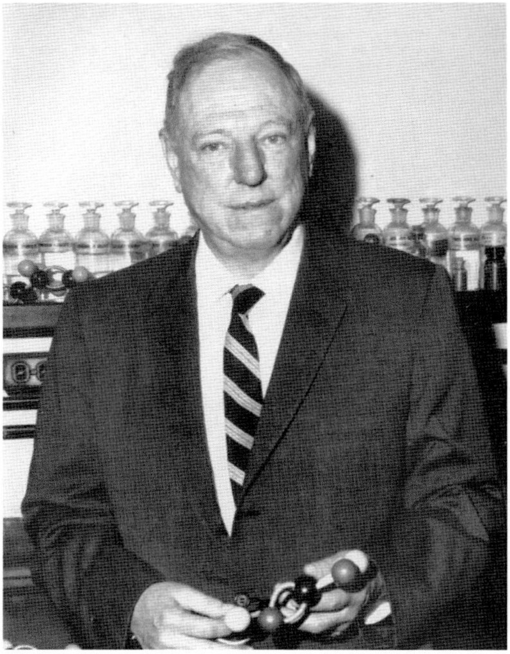

Dr. Irvine W. Grote

Dr. Irvine W. Grote made a lot of little pains go away. A Chattanooga native, he grew up in the Cameron Hill section of town and then became known as a first-rate chemist at the University of Chattanooga. He is credited with creating the active ingredients for the stomach reliever, Rolaids, and a headache soother, Bufferin. He also created Soltice for the Chattanooga Medicine Company, a deep-heating gel that this writer often used for aching muscles. (Courtesy University of Chattanooga at Tennessee/Special Collections.)

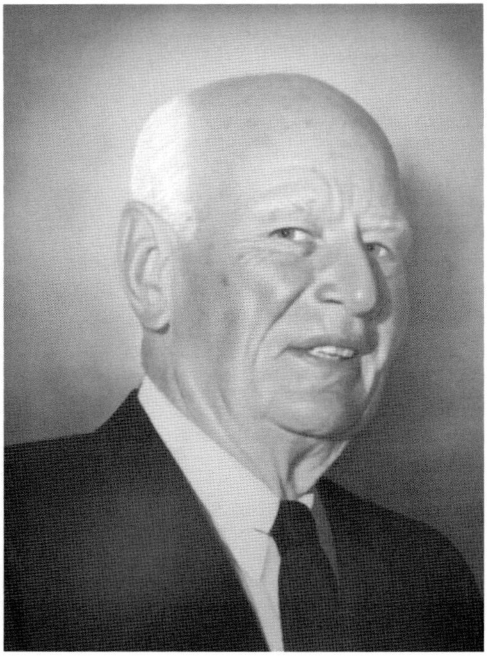

Burkett Miller

Burkett Miller thought long and hard about the public good. And to that end, he made an impact on life in Chattanooga for the better. The son of a judge and a Chattanooga native, he received his bachelor of laws degree from the University of Virginia. He set up the Burkett Miller scholarship for "needy and worthy students" at the University of Tennessee at Chattanooga in 1954. Similarly, he endowed the Burkett Miller Chair of Management and Technology at the same institution. Alongside that, a series of talks titled the "Burkett Miller Distinguished Lecture Series" brings renowned speakers to the campus for social and political speeches. Burkett studied history and sought to understand the "deep trends" in America, and he worried about the political and social divisions in the country during the Vietnam and Watergate years. For that reason, he founded the Miller Center of Public Affairs at the University of Virginia so that important issues of the day could be studied in a thoughtful and scholarly way. The institute is now headed by former governor of Virginia Gerald L. Baliles. For everyday Chattanoogans, he is best known for Miller Park, which stands across from the federal post office between Market and Cherry Streets with its sweeping lines and water fountains, a graceful memorial for a generous man. (Courtesy Miller and Martin.)

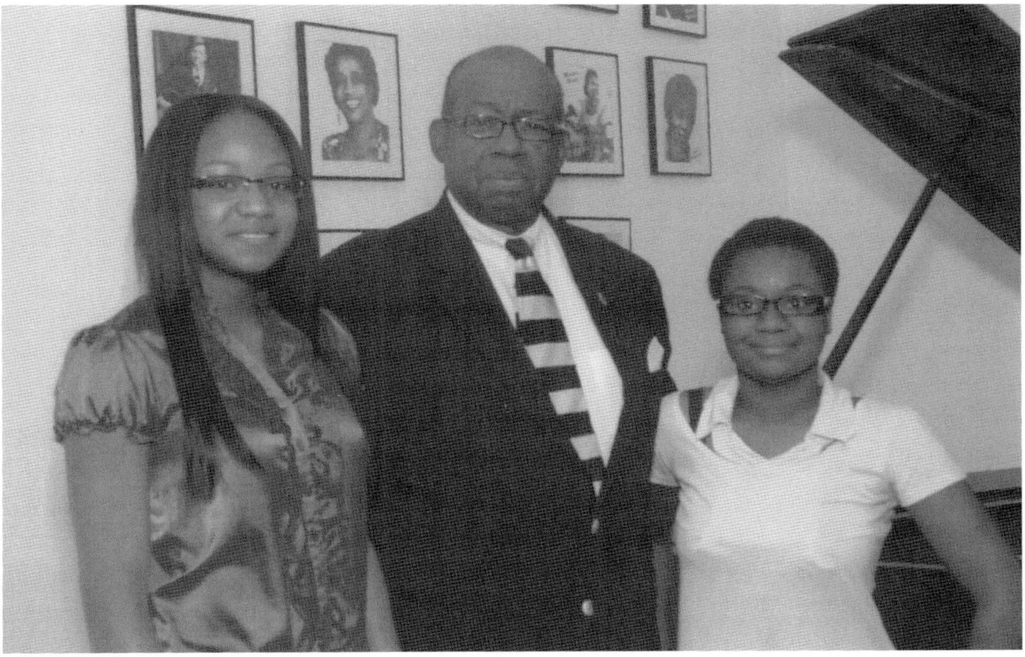

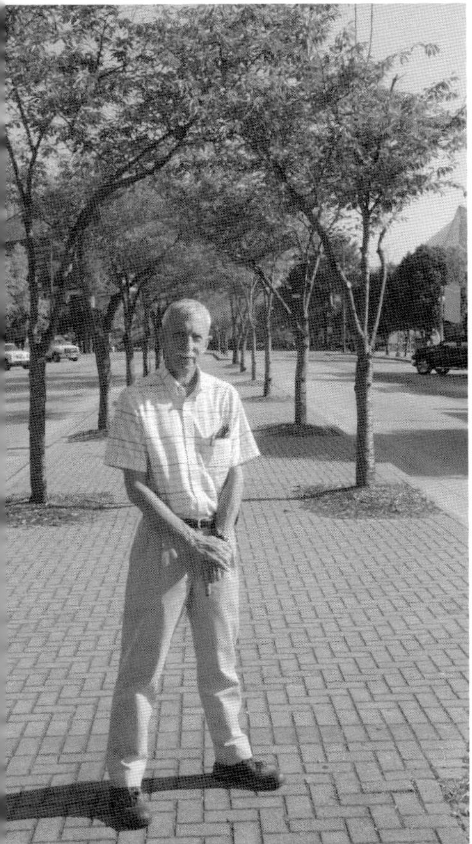

Napoleon Williams

Law enforcement appealed to Napoleon Williams at a young age. As a student, he loved the time he spent as a school crossing guard. When he went to Howard High School—which was only blocks from his south Chattanooga home—he was a stalwart lineman in football. It was here that coach Fred White gave him his nickname "Donut" because the opposing team was running over him like a hole in a doughnut. Williams joined the Chattanooga Police Department in 1964 and became the first black detective on the force in 1968. He left that job in 1993 and directed security at Chattanooga State Community College for 16 years. Well known throughout the community, he is involved with youth and is an active spokesman for current issues. His mellow voice is familiar to radio listeners as well, as he is especially known for humming along with the songs he plays. (Courtesy Napoleon Williams.)

Gene Hyde

Tennessee is known for beautiful forests, and Chattanooga keeps that vision alive through the effort of Gene Hyde. The town's first urban forester, Hyde has worked tirelessly to plant a thoughtful variety of hardwoods throughout our town for over 20 years. With an eye towards "spring blooms, summer shade, and fall color," Chattanooga has achieved one of the highest canopy covers of any city east of the Rocky Mountains. (Author's collection.)

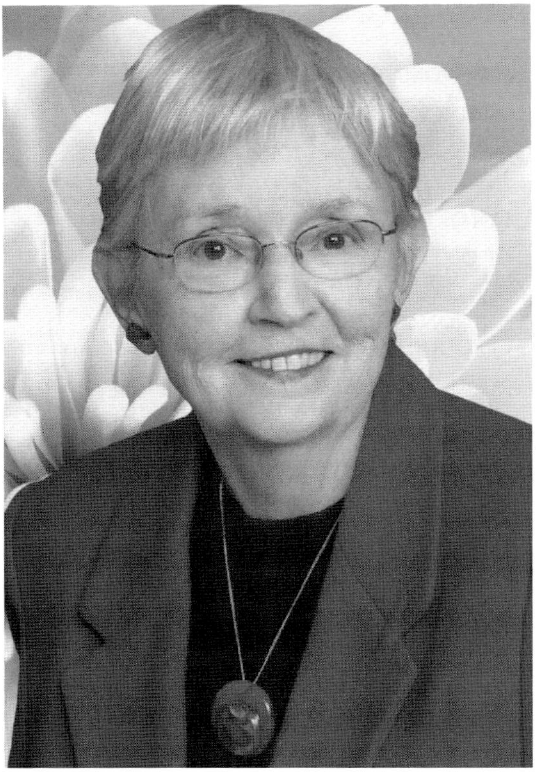

Mai Bell Hurley

Chattanooga native Mai Bell Hurley has seen great change in her city, and she has been in the middle of much of it. A University of Chattanooga graduate and a newspaper reporter, she was instrumental as the first chairperson of Chattanooga Venture, the citywide visioning process begun in 1983 that would set the goals and build the foundations for a renewed city. Her desire to broaden the power of the community decision-making process by the inclusion of many kinds of citizens was a major accomplishment during this process. Whether she is a member of the board of a bank or the library, Hurley believes in civic commitment in the finest democratic tradition. The first woman to serve on the city council and to head the United Way Board, she shows devotion to the possibility of a better life for all. (Courtesy Mai Bell Hurley.)

Garnet Chapin

If there is a visible symbol of Chattanooga's renaissance in the new century, it is the Walnut Street Bridge. And if there is one key person to connect to that blue bridge, it is Garnet Chapin. A fifth-generation citizen, Chapin and his friend archaeologist Jeffrey Brown set about to stave off the demolition of the structure after it was closed by the department of transportation in 1978. By having it registered as a historic site, he was able to persuade city hall to imagine a different use for it—that of a "linear park." With the endorsement of engineer and preservationist Al Lichtenstein, a strategy to refit the bridge was worked out through an ingenious method of wrapping steel cable throughout the structure. With some Washington money, city contributions, and local donations, the old bridge came to life again. For the final touch, Chapin picked a shade of blue—somewhere "between the color blue of the river and the blue of the sky"—to give the old span some panache. Reopened in 1993, it has been an unqualified success as well as a wonderful platform for local activities. It is such a part of the fabric of Chattanooga that it would be hard to imagine today's city without it. (Author's collection.)

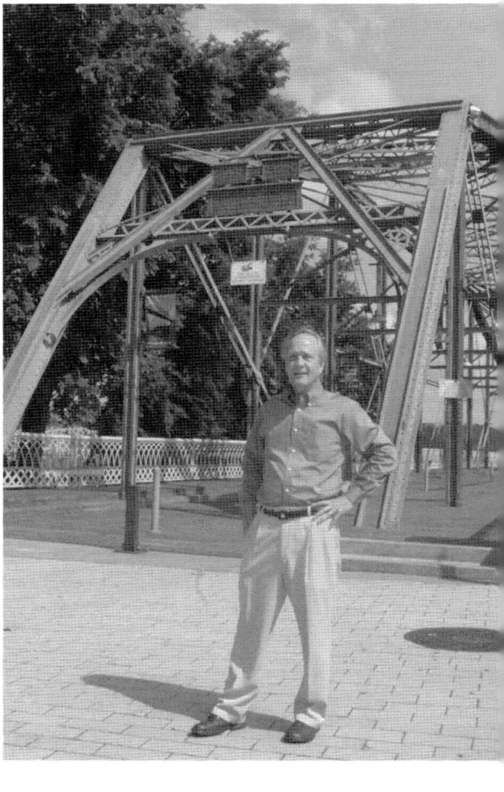

Sonia Young
Sonia Young has a passion for the color purple. Not only does she dress in purple and lavender shades, her home is also appointed in colors from this spectrum of the rainbow. When she was five, she danced as an orchid in a recital. While working at Siskin Hospital, Dr. Tepper coined the term "Purple Lady," and the title stuck. Not only has she used her style to promote her own life, but she has also used her local celebrity to promote Chattanooga theater, advocate for the arts, and instruct students in the art of public speaking at the university level. Her love affair with the violet hue has even landed her a spot on the *Dr. Phil* show. An individual in every sense of the word, Sonia Young is a Chattanooga original. (Courtesy Sonia Young.)

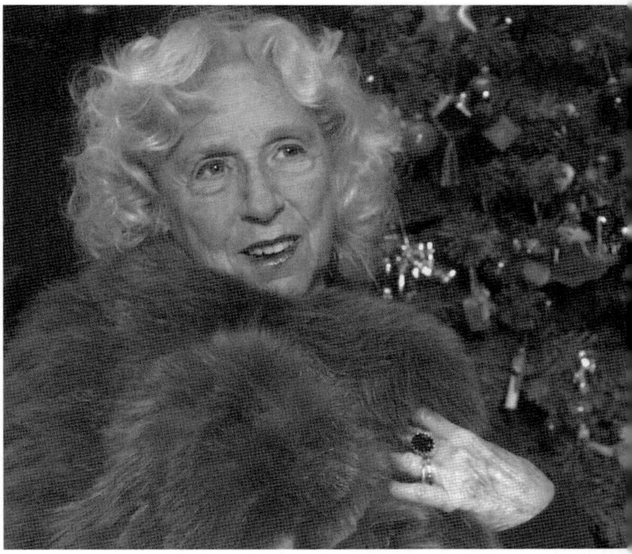

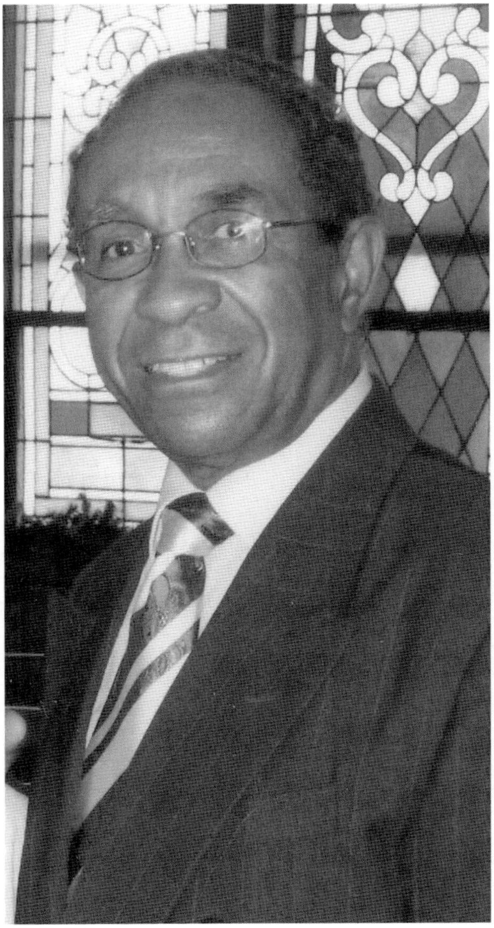

Booker Scruggs II
If you had to pin down the one thing that Booker T. Scruggs does well, you would be hard pressed to come up with an answer. That is because he excels at a number of activities. He served as director of the Upward Bound program for 36 years, directing low-income high school youth to become first-generation college graduates. Today, he is an adjunct professor of sociology at the University of Chattanooga at Tennessee, work that keeps him continually involved with the rising generation of college students—a task he relishes. Scruggs grew up on the west side and attended Howard High School and then Clark College in Atlanta. It was at Howard that he first studied woodwinds seriously, leading him to a lifelong devotion to music. As a clarinet player, he fronts the Booker T. Scruggs Ensemble. His band has made two CDs and in 2005, produced a tribute to the music of Duke Ellington. Sales from that CD totaled over $10,000, and the proceeds went to students from low-income families to further their education. His legacy may be his long-running television program *Point of View,* a production that he moderates and produces. Begun in 1970, it has been broadcast continuously on WDEF-TV, making it what Scruggs called the "world's longest-running, locally produced television show." With a community-oriented focus, the interview format allows him to talk with a wide variety of people who are making an impact in Chattanooga. (Courtesy Booker T. Scruggs II.)

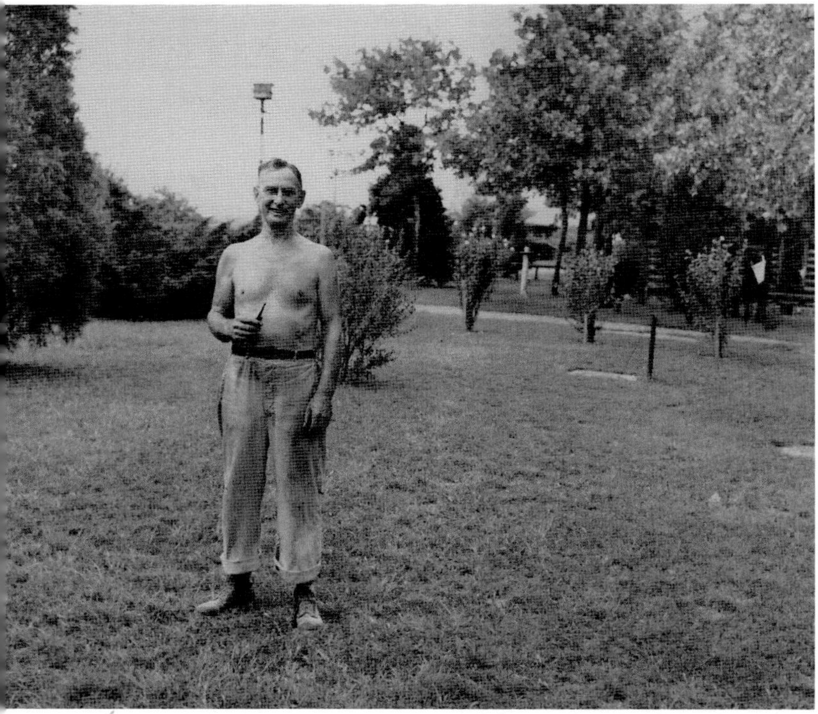

Claude Fuller
Claude Fuller was a true collector of local memorabilia, whether it was currency or bottles. But his great passion was building his enormous collection of more than 350 firearms, spanning three centuries and about which he wrote five books. Though he designed factories for a living, the real fruits of his labor may be seen at the Chickamauga and Chattanooga National Military Park in the detailed display of these weapons, which he left to the park in his will. (Courtesy Chattanooga Public Library.)

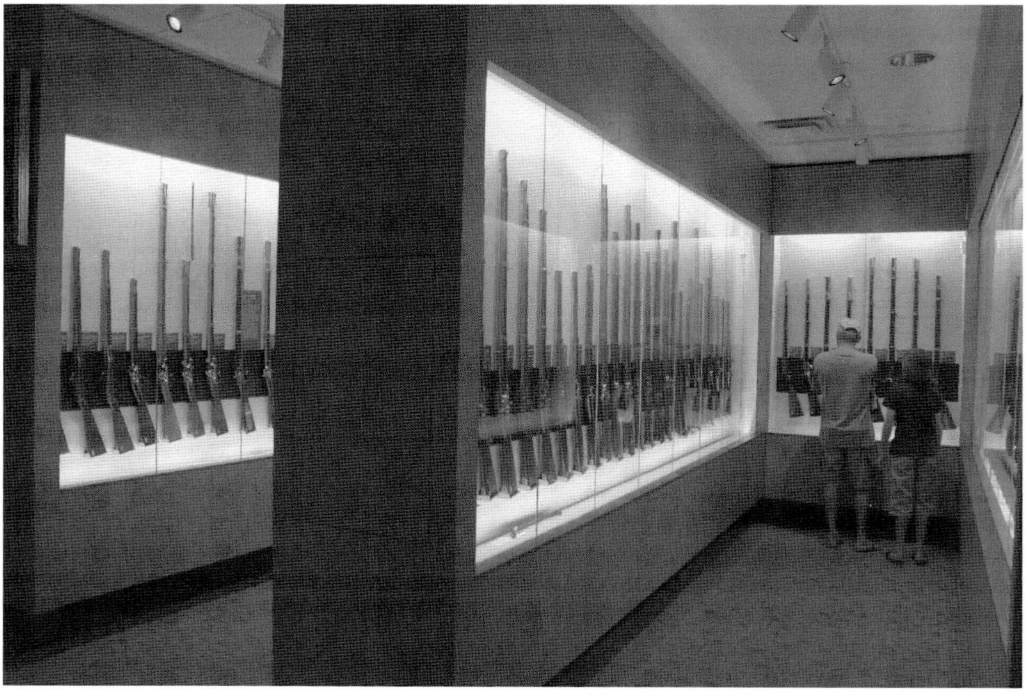

Fuller Collection
The Fuller gun collection is displayed in a dedicated space at the park south of Chattanooga. Broad in scope and unique because of its rare items, the collection is considered one of the finest of its kind in North America. (Author's collection.)

CHAPTER FOUR

Sporting Life

The earliest records of sporting events of any substance begin in the early 1900s and center on baseball, both professional and amateur, and nascent college football. Some automobile racing and pugilism events made their mark, but they were sporadic in nature. And, of course, fishing and hunting are an East Tennessee tradition practiced by many families. Certainly, the town team for decades was the Chattanooga Lookouts baseball club that, under the leadership of the magnetic and creative Joe Engel, entertained fans for decades. Engel's stunts and promotions kept fans coming out to the ballpark for years. The University of Chattanooga Moccasins, led by Scrappy Moore, had a loyal following from football fans regardless whether they had attended college or not. Hard-nosed, "three yards and a cloud of dust" gridiron gamesmanship, plus a willingness to play some powerhouse teams in the Southeastern Conference gained Moore's squads' respect.

Most recently, Chattanooga has taken a different tack and seen the growth of outdoor sports gaining in popularity. The Lookout Mountain flight park provides first-rate hang-gliding, and the Tennessee River hosts rowing competitions. Strenuous bicycle races over rough mountain paths, bouldering on rocky faces, and spelunking in mountain caves have captured a new generation's fancy in the Scenic City of the South.

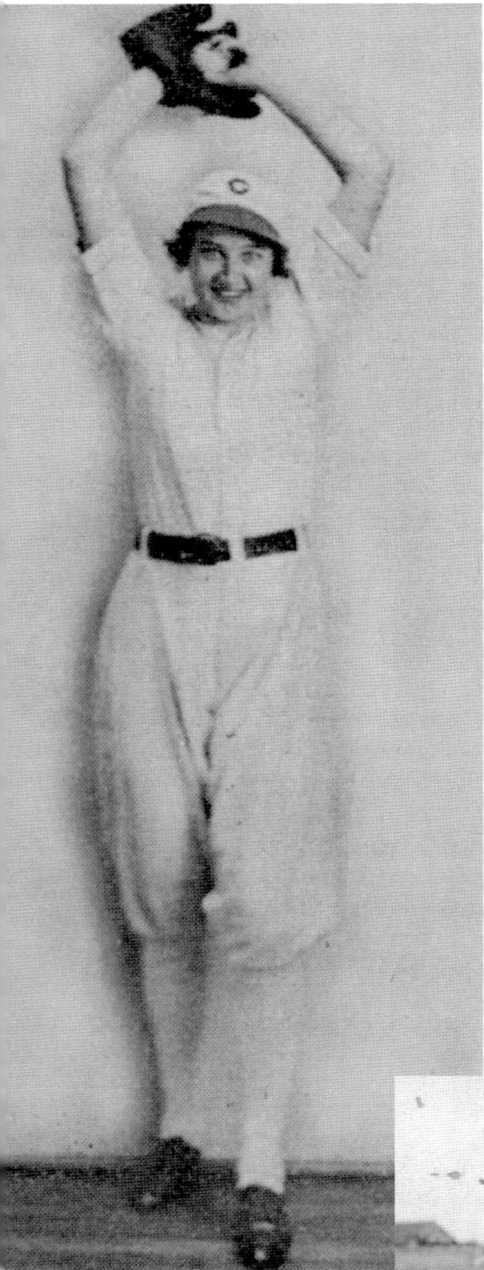

Jackie Mitchell

Jackie Mitchell was a 17-year-old girl who loved baseball and got the chance of a lifetime in 1931. In the days when all baseball spring training was in Florida, the New York Yankees would ride the train north to start the season in April. On April 1, they stopped in Chattanooga to play an exhibition game against Joe Engel's Chattanooga Lookouts. A big crowd came out to see the famous Yankees and legends Babe Ruth and Lou Gehrig. Brought out to pitch in the first inning, she faced the Sultan of Swat. The mighty Ruth swung at the southpaw's first two offerings and then was called out looking on the third strike addressing the umpire with a growl. Gehrig likewise fanned. The crowd was wild with excitement and the news was carried over the wires to New York and other major cities. Jackie Mitchell was instantly famous only to be insulted a few days later when baseball commissioner Kennesaw Mountain Landis canceled her contract declaring the game "too strenuous" for women. The next few years, she kicked around minor league baseball as something of an extra attraction but soon went to work for a living with the memory of a flash of greatness forever associated with her name. She lived in Fort Oglethorpe and was buried in Forest Hills Cemetery. (Courtesy Chattanooga Public Library.)

Kid Elberfeld

Kid Elberfeld (left) was a tough competitor in Major League Baseball in the early 1900s. Called "the Tabasco Kid" because of his fiery disposition, he was known to yell at umpires and challenge other players. Opponents frequently spiked him; he was one of the most hit-by-pitch batters of all time. When the shortstop retired, he coached the Lookouts for two years and raised a family on Signal Mountain where his five girls were known as the "Elberfeld Girls basketball team." A road on the mountain still bears his name. (Courtesy Chattanooga History Center.)

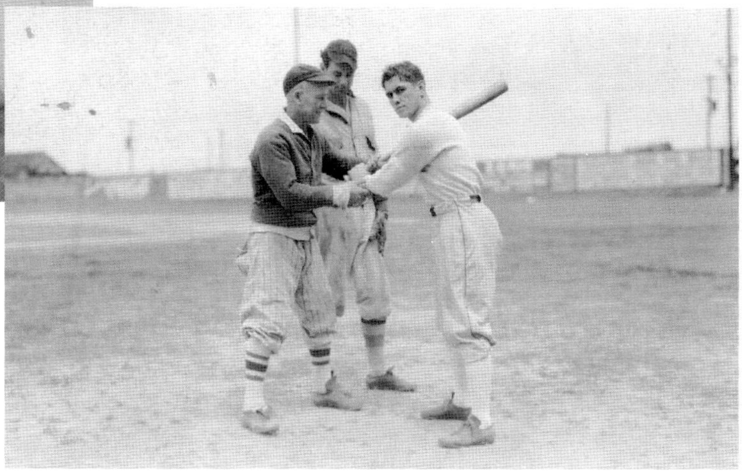

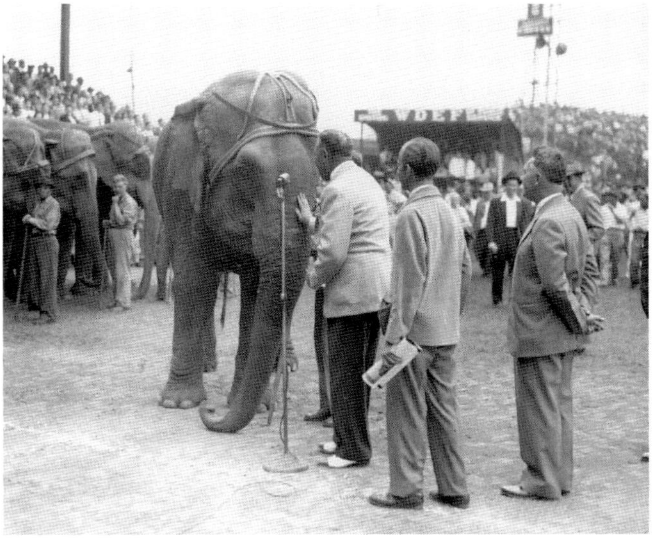

Joe Engel

Joe Engel was a vivacious, colorful, shrewd man who ran the Chattanooga Lookouts, the town's AA professional baseball team. The son of a German immigrant, he played big league baseball for eight years for the Washington Senators. He arrived in Chattanooga in 1929 and immediately built a ballpark, Engel Stadium, which stands today on East Third Street. His reputation revolved around his zany promotions. He once traded a player for a turkey. Drawings were held for cars, and during the Depression, he even had a raffle for a new house that was won by one lucky fan. Always the showman, he had his players enter astride elephants during one Opening Day. Engel (pictured touching the elephant) became known as the "Barnum of the Bushes" for his minor league stunts. A vital part of the city's life for 34 years, the Lookouts won the Southern Association pennant in 1932 and 1952 and along the way, groomed the talents of hall-of-famers slugger Harmon Killebrew and pitcher Ferguson Jenkins. A bigger-than-life character involved in many civic activities, he helped feed hungry people at the park during the Depression; he showed a quieter side by raising birds at his home on Missionary Ridge. (Courtesy Chattanooga History Center.)

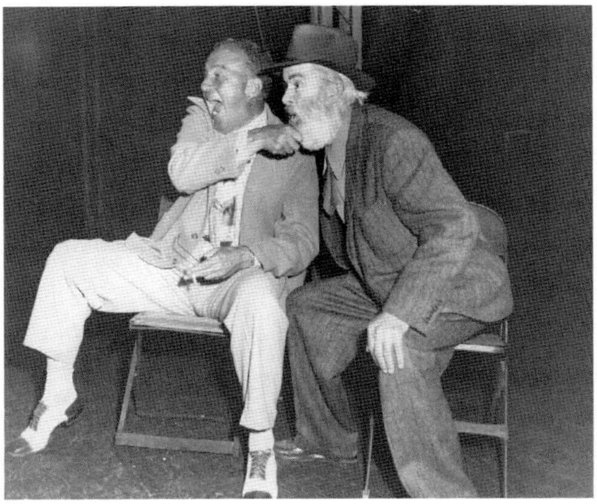

Joe and Gabby Yuck It Up

Known around the country not only in baseball circles but also by a number of entertainers and public figures, Engel would often work well-known people into game-day events or for fundraisers. He was a charitable man who believed in using his celebrity for good causes. Here, Engel (left) cuts up with Gabby Hayes, legendary movie cowboy. (Courtesy Chattanooga History Center.)

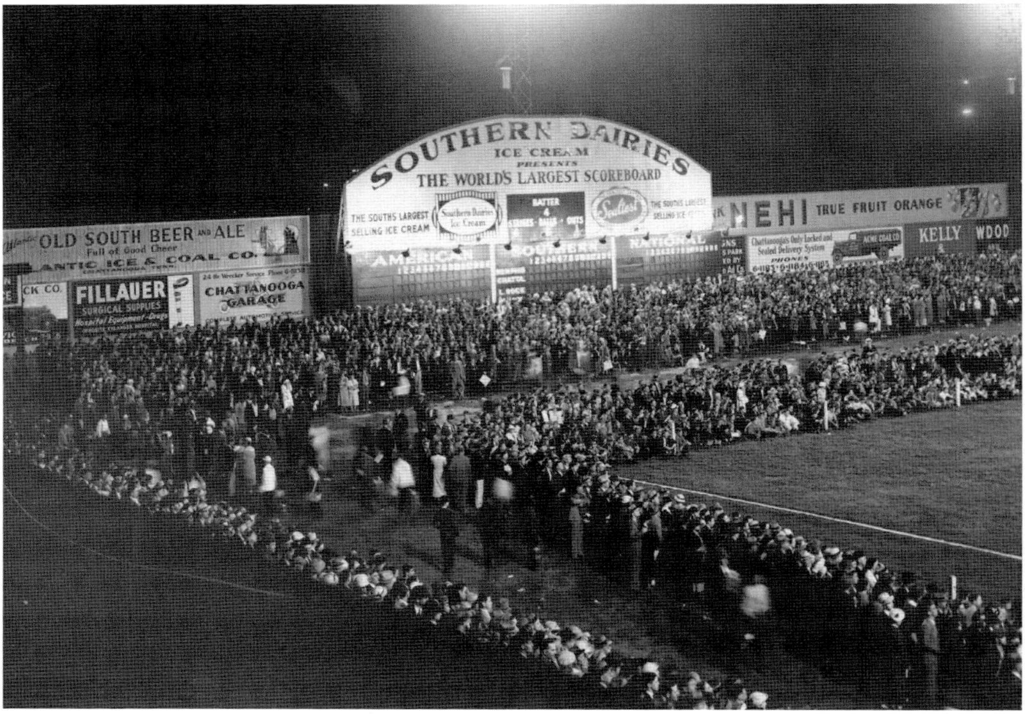

Engel Stadium

In May 1936, Joe Engel offered a brand-new house to the holder of the lucky ticket stub for this game. The largest crowd to see baseball in Chattanooga—and some say the entire minor leagues ever—attended

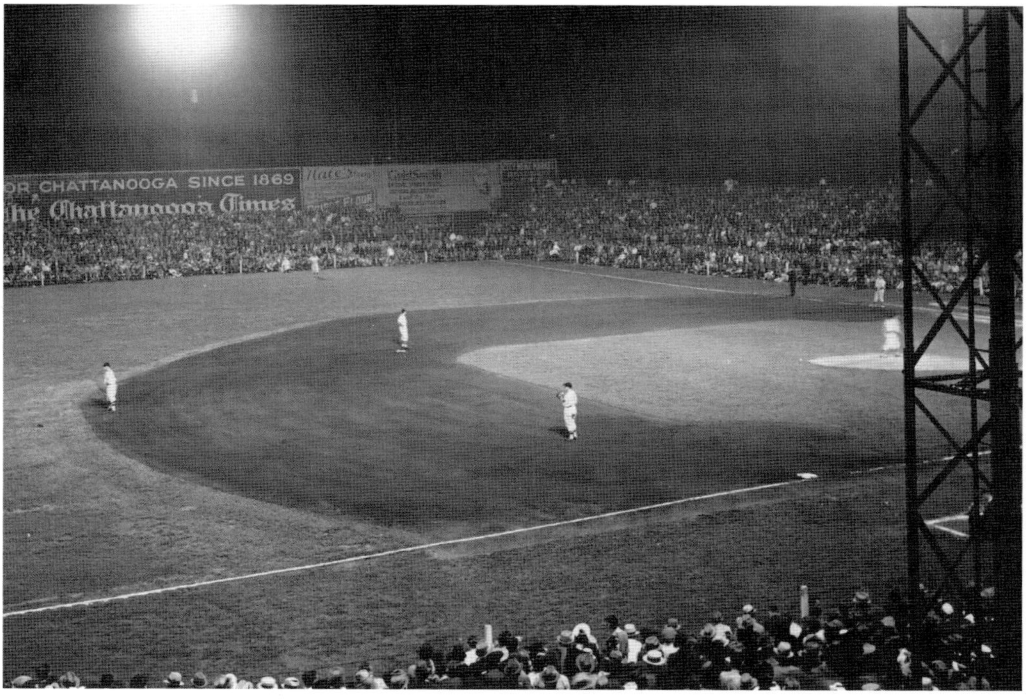

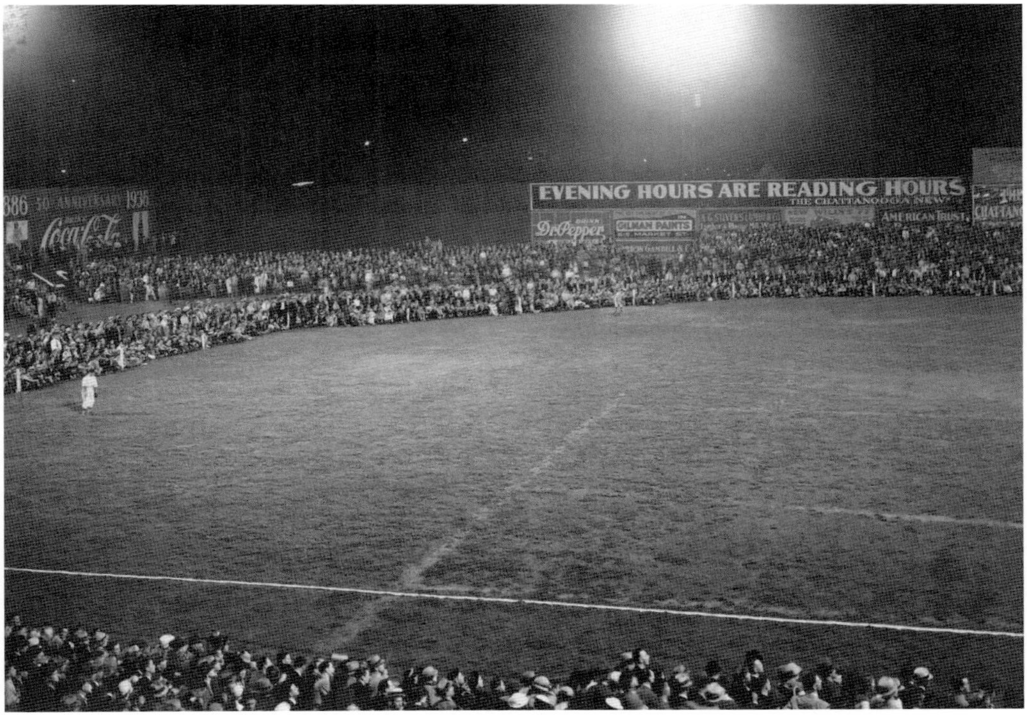

that night: 26,639 people. To make sure no one in the outfield was hit with a batted ball, Engel had the balls frozen before the game to make them heavy. (Courtesy Chattanooga History Center.)

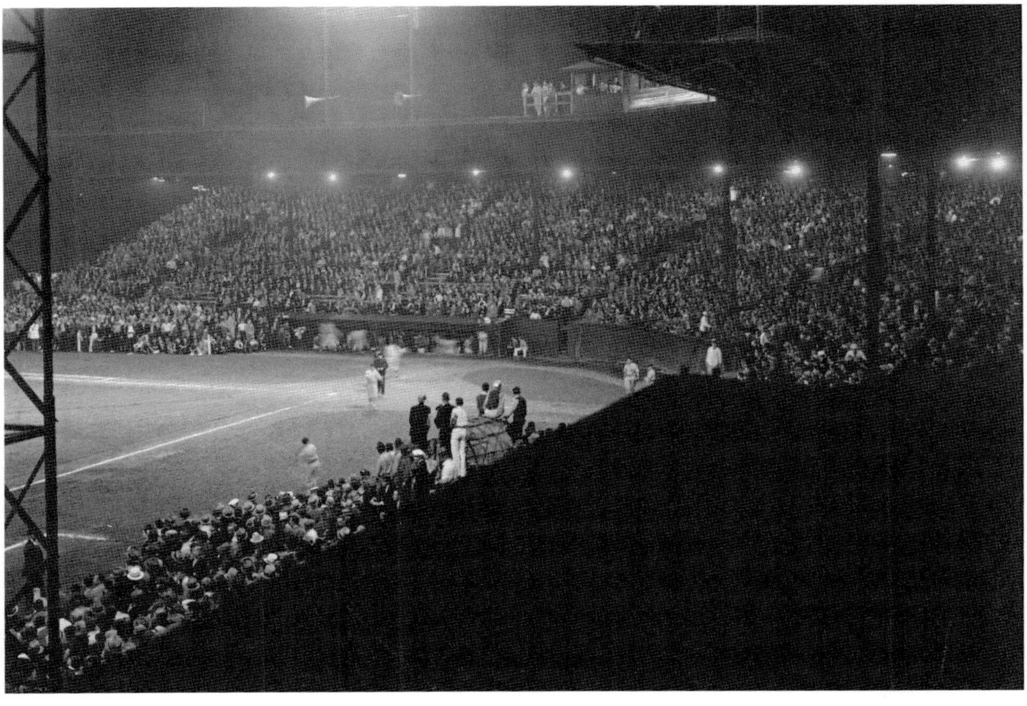

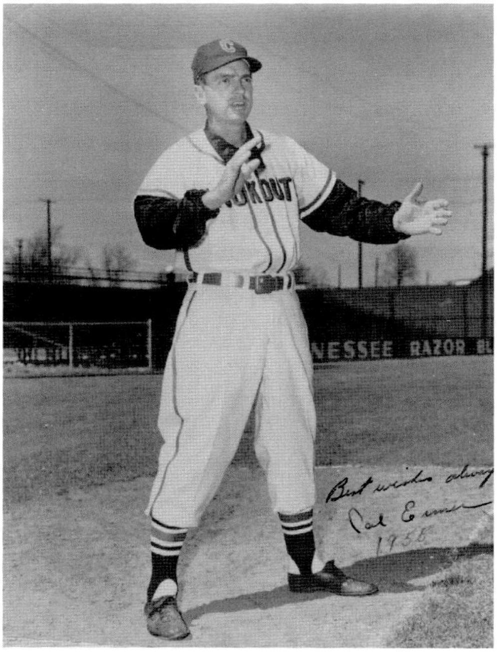

Cal Ermer

Calvin Coolidge "Cal" Ermer's career in professional baseball lasted 60 years and involved playing and scouting, but most of all, managing. Working for the Minnesota Twins (formerly the Washington Senators), he managed farm teams for five decades and captained the Chattanooga Lookouts from 1952 to 1957, winning the 1952 Southern Association title. Ermer was named the *Sporting News* Minor League Manager of the Year (1958), a tough award to garner. He had a brief, brilliant stint in 1967 as captain of the Twins, bringing his team to within a game of going to the World Series. During the off-season, Cal lived in Chattanooga for 57 years with his wife, Gloria Williams, a former Miss Chattanooga and Miss Tennessee of 1952. A popular figure around town, The Chattanooga Lookouts dedicated their press box to him in 2008, a year before he died. (Courtesy Chattanooga History Center.)

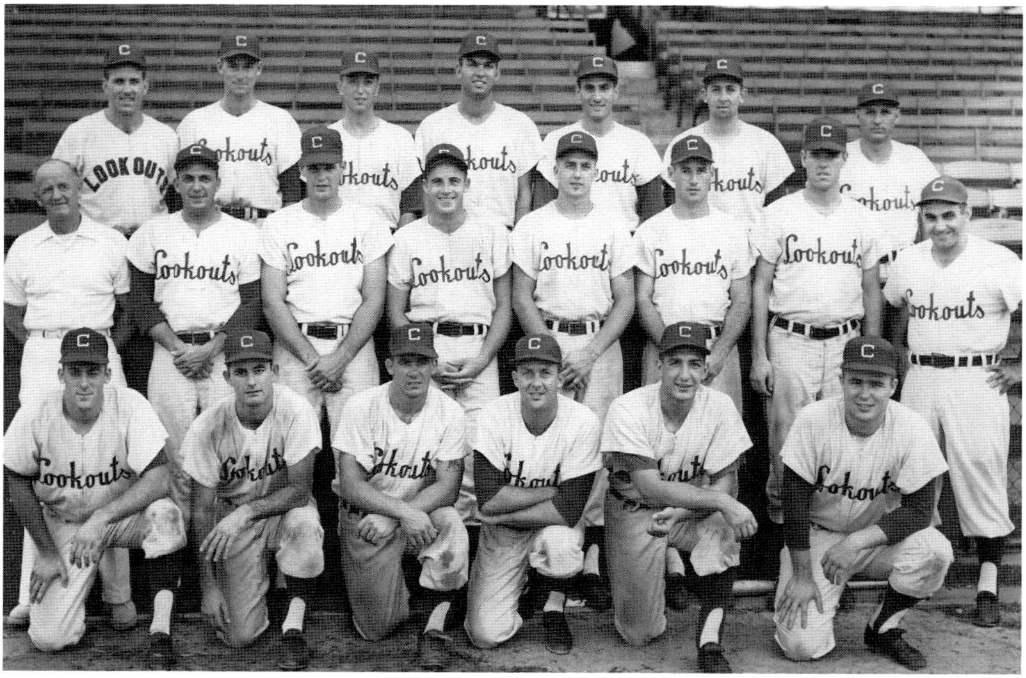

Lookouts Team

The Chattanooga Lookouts are pictured in 1961 when the team won the Southern League championship with Frank Lucchesi at the helm. Lucchesi went on to manage in the big leagues with the Philadelphia Phillies and the Texas Rangers. At left with a plain white shirt is the Lookouts' long-time, beloved trainer, Sandy Sandlin, who also served as athletic trainer at the University of Chattanooga for 37 years. (Courtesy Chattanooga Public Library.)

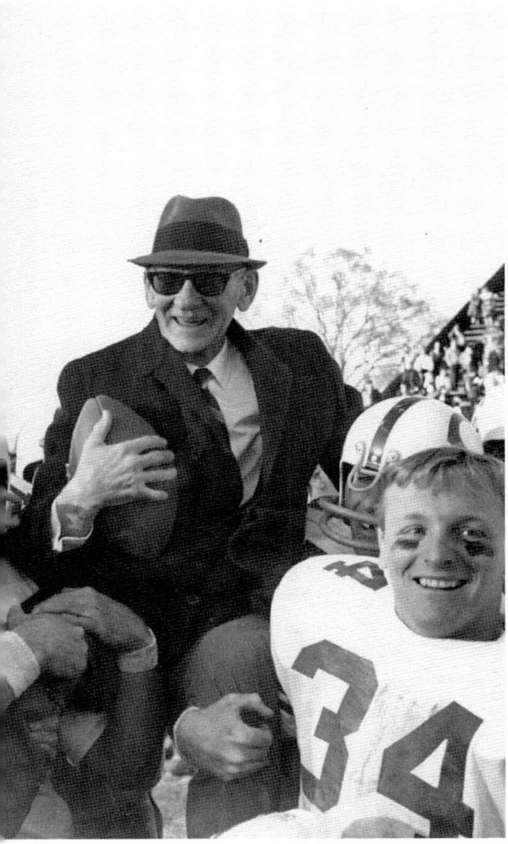

Scrappy Moore

Football coach Andrew "Scrappy" Moore was a fixture at the University of Chattanooga for decades. He joined the team in 1927 as assistant coach and became head coach in 1931. He held that spot until his retirement in 1967, when he was named coach of the year by the American Football Coaches Association. Given the nickname "Scrappy" from his football playing days as a quarterback at the University of Georgia, Moore was known as a spirited coach who regularly played big name, powerhouse Southern teams, usually with little hope of winning. One exception came in 1958, when the UC Mocs (Moccasins) stunned the mighty Volunteers of Tennessee—on their home turf—by the score of 14-6. UC students tore down the goal posts and began celebrating downtown, starting a riot that brought out police with tear gas. The students were arrested that night. It was a David versus Goliath upset and a game long remembered by Chattanoogans of that era. Moore finished his long tenure with a 170-147-14 record and the respect of people all over Tennessee. He was especially loved because he had been offered coaching jobs at major colleges and in the professional game but had elected to stay at the school in the town he called home. (Courtesy University of Chattanooga at Tennessee/ Special Collections.)

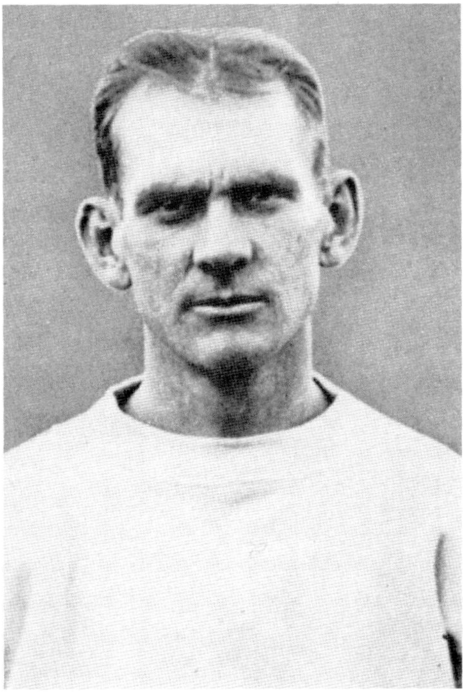

Young Scrappy

Moore is pictured here in his younger days around 1923 at the University of Georgia where his tenacious play at quarterback for the Bulldogs earned him the name "Scrappy." (Courtesy University of Tennessee at Chattanooga/Special Collections.)

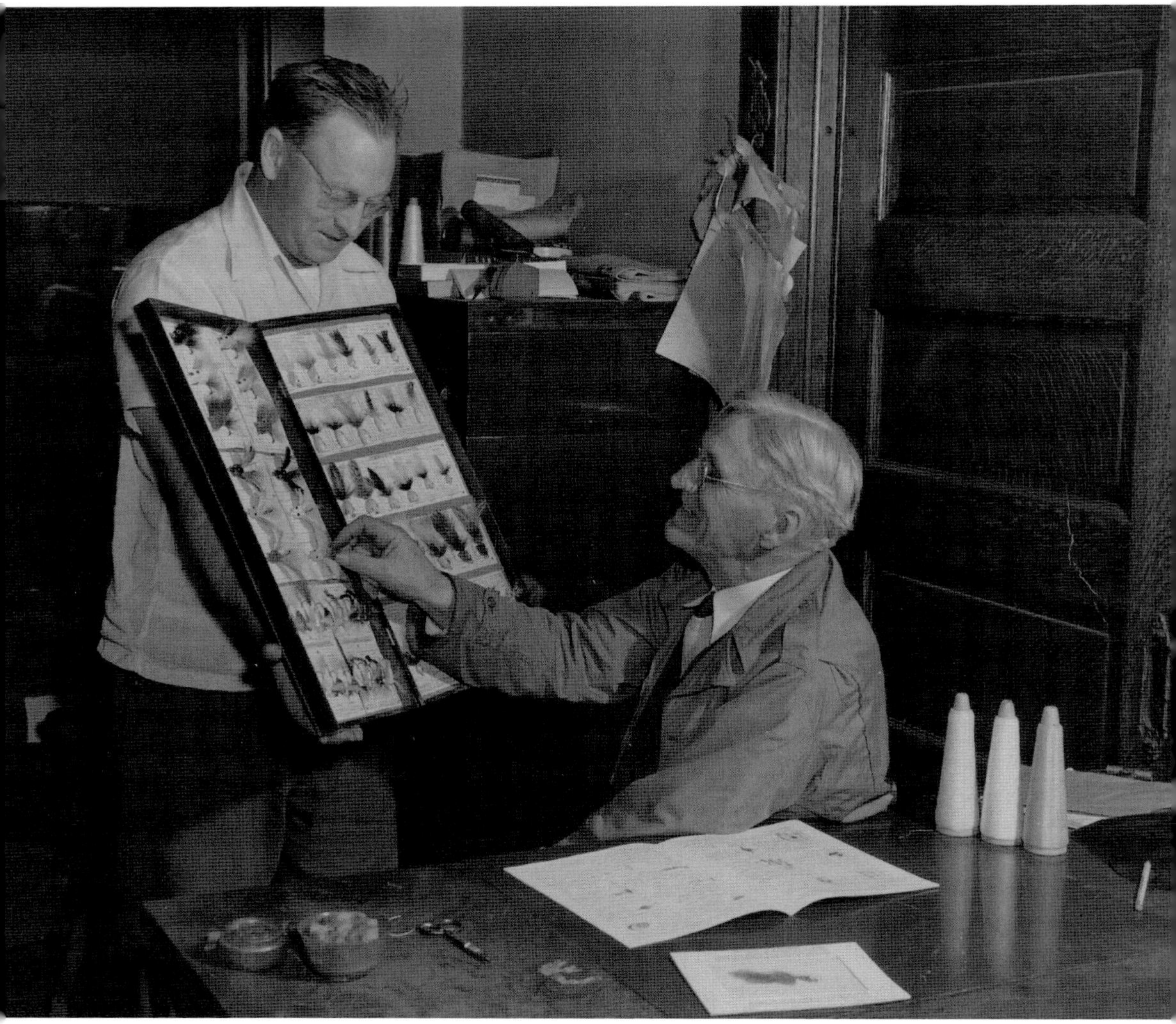

Earnest Peckinpaugh

The Tennessee Valley is fertile ground for great fishing, and for a young man named Earnest Peckinpaugh, it would become a way of life. Around 1907, while waiting for a fish to strike his line, he conceived of the modern bass bug by splitting his cork. Eventually, he added some wings and a tail, and what became known as Peckinpaugh's "night bug" was born, the first of what would be many cork-bodied bugs to come from the hand of the man known as "Peck." He began spending as much free time as he could talking to older fisherman and making variations on his "poppers," and soon, Peck's Popping Bug and the Floating Feathered Minnow were part of fishermen's kits around the South. By 1920, the lures were so popular that he created the E.H. Peckinpaugh Company to manufacture his poppers, and his renown with fly rod fisherman around the country was on the rise. Soon, his factory was churning out thousands of quality bass flies and bugs in a myriad of color combinations with enticing names such as the "Snake Doctor" and the "Flash Skitter Bug." With a catalog full of advice, lore, and tricks of the trade, he regularly sold out of his inventory each year. Though he passed away in 1952, his night bugs are still treasured today and collected as prize pieces of work in the world of angling. (Courtesy Tennessee State Library and Archives.)

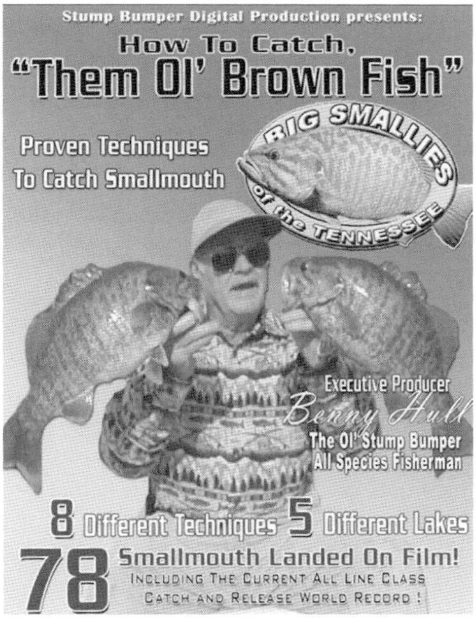

Benny Hull

Benny Hull has a passion for fishing that began as a child. Born in Rossville, Hull's dad took him out on the Tennessee River to fish in a rowboat at the age of eight. He was hooked on fishing from then on, and by the time he was able to travel on his own, he discovered the Florida Keys and took to saltwater fishing. There, he became a guide for sportsmen looking for the big strike. When he came back home, he started his own service station and even a car wash, but the lure of the water was too great. Hull began to make a name for himself in local television beginning in 1986 when cable was just beginning to catch on, and soon, he was being shown on the Outdoor Channel and Comcast Sport South's *American Outdoors*. His show has been on the air for 25 years with Hull often acting as cameraman, editor, and producer. He also did a stint on Chattanooga talk radio and, of course, has been working as a fishing guide also, becoming especially well known for his smallmouth bass catches. Known as the "Ol' Stump Bumper" his prowess with a hook and sinker has landed him in the Fishing Hall of Fame; he and his wife together hold 10 records. Hull currently holds the record for a freshwater drum fish at a hefty 54.5 pounds. (Courtesy Benny Hull.)

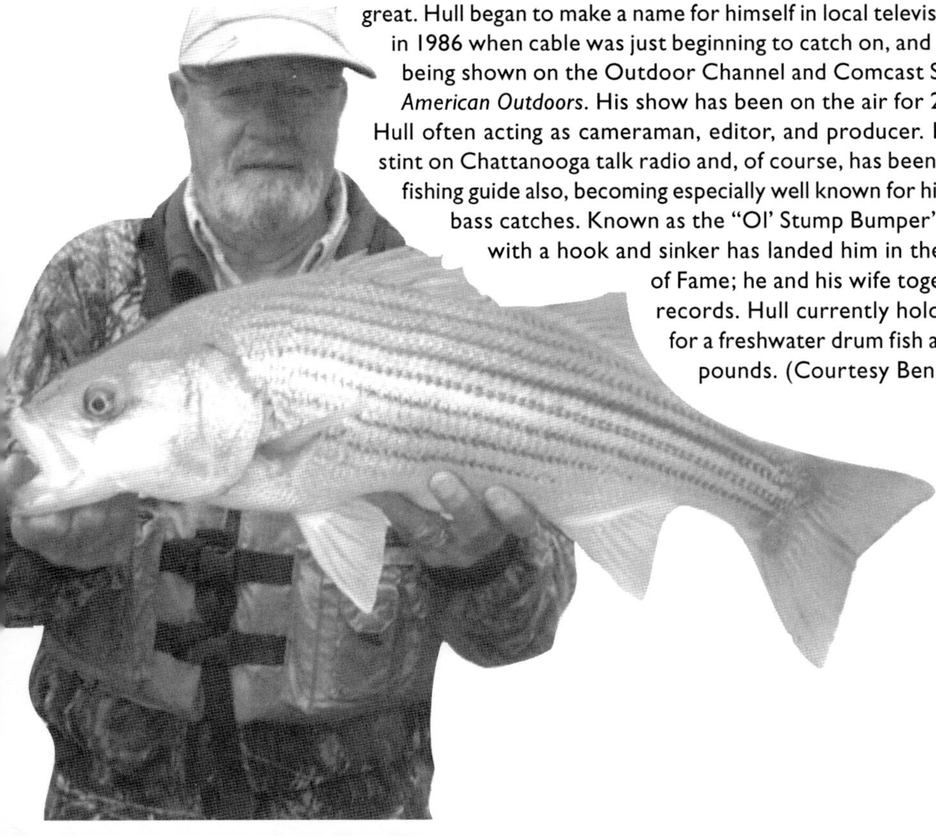

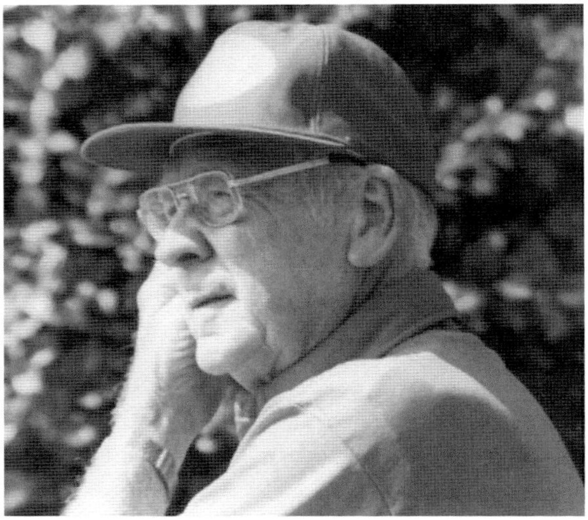

Red Etter

In the 1950s and 1960s, there was one team no high school football team wanted to face: the Central High School Purple Pounders. Coached by the legendary E.B. "Red" Etter, the team won an astonishing seven state championships in football from 1943 to 1964, including a run from 1951 to 1954. The team was so dominant that it had to go out of state to find competitive teams, playing regular season games with opponents from Louisville, Little Rock, Memphis, and even Miami, Florida. Etter was wooed from Central High School to skipper rival Baylor in 1970 and brought home a state championship and national championship in 1973. Known as a genteel conversationalist with a keen mind, he retired in 1983 as the most winning coach in Tennessee secondary football history. (Courtesy Baylor School.)

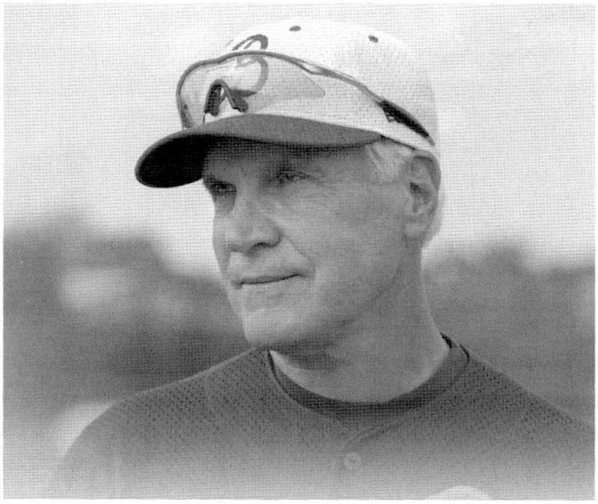

Gene Etter

One of the players Red Etter coached at Central was his own son Gene Etter who won 10 letters in football and baseball in high school and went on to play tailback at the University of Tennessee. He also starred in baseball and was signed by the Chicago Cubs to a professional contract and played in their minor league system for nine years. As a teacher at Baylor, he was the defensive coach for his dad's winning teams in the 1970s but really excelled as the varsity baseball coach for Baylor, a position he has held since 1975. Some people say talent skips a generation but not in this instance. Gene Etter's teams have won over 700 ball games, several regional trophies, and snagged the state championships in 2003 and 2006. Surely, both of these men personify the Baylor motto, "Amat Victoria Curam." (Courtesy Tracy Knauss.)

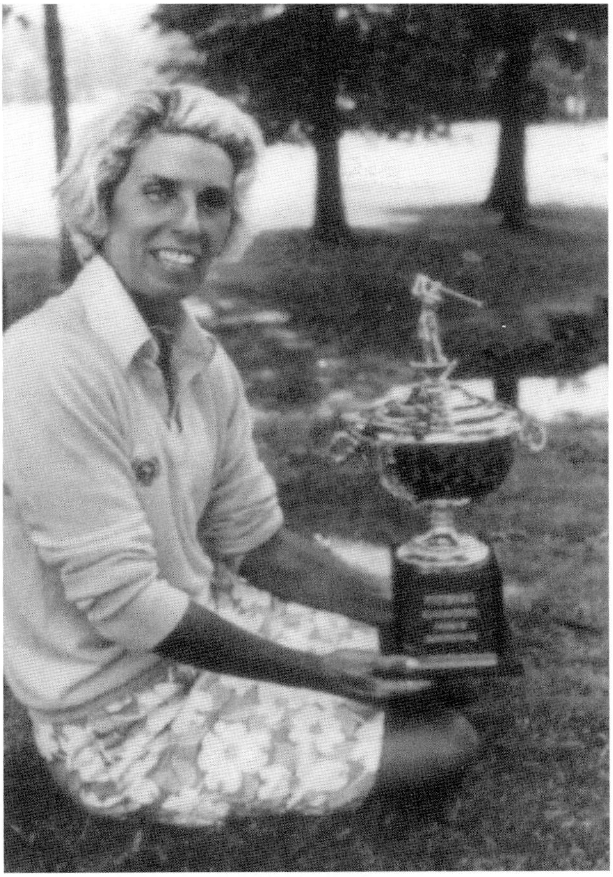

Betty Probasco
Betty Probasco has excelled at golf since a young age. With a natural love of competition on the links and an unusually even game, she has captured the Women's Tennessee State Amateur title eight times in four different decades. She also snagged the Kentucky State Amateur title four times. Her biggest personal thrill was winning the NCAA championship in 1950. Probasco was crowned the Women's Southern Amateur top golfer in 1955 and has served as captain of the Curtis Cup as well. The first woman to be inducted into the Tennessee Golf Hall of Fame, she still plays and can break 80 on a good day. (Courtesy Betty Probasco.)

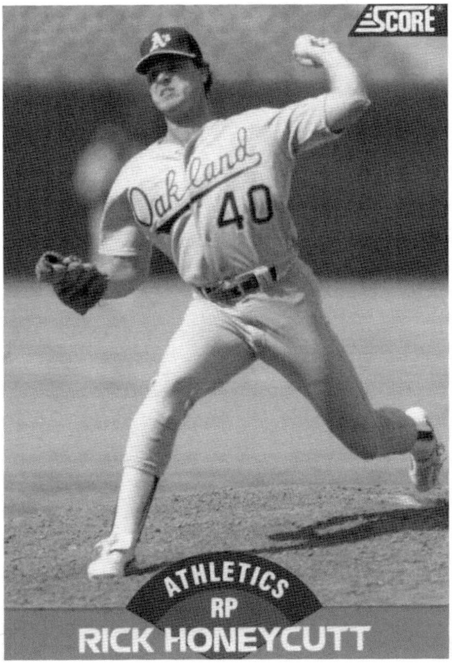

Rick Honeycutt
Making it to the big league is tough, but pitching for 21 years is something few players in the history of the game can claim. Rick Honeycutt was born in 1954 in Fort Oglethorpe, south of town, and played at Lakeview High where his baseball team won a state championship. Like many boys in the South at that time—before the Braves moved to Atlanta—he followed the New York Yankees and idolized Mickey Mantle. He attended the University of Tennessee where he was a baseball All-American, playing first and pitching while winning the SEC batting title with an impressive .404 average. His early career was as a starter, but in 1988, he became a relief pitcher. Honeycutt gained a World Series ring with the Oakland Athletics in 1989. He finished his career with a quite respectable 3.42 career ERA and is presently a pitching coach with the Los Angeles Dodgers. Locally, his annual Rick Honeycutt Youth Benefit Golf Tournament, now in its 28th year, benefits the horseback-riding program for special needs children at his family's Heartland Ranch as well as other projects of the Kiwanis Club of Fort Oglethorpe. (Author's collection.)

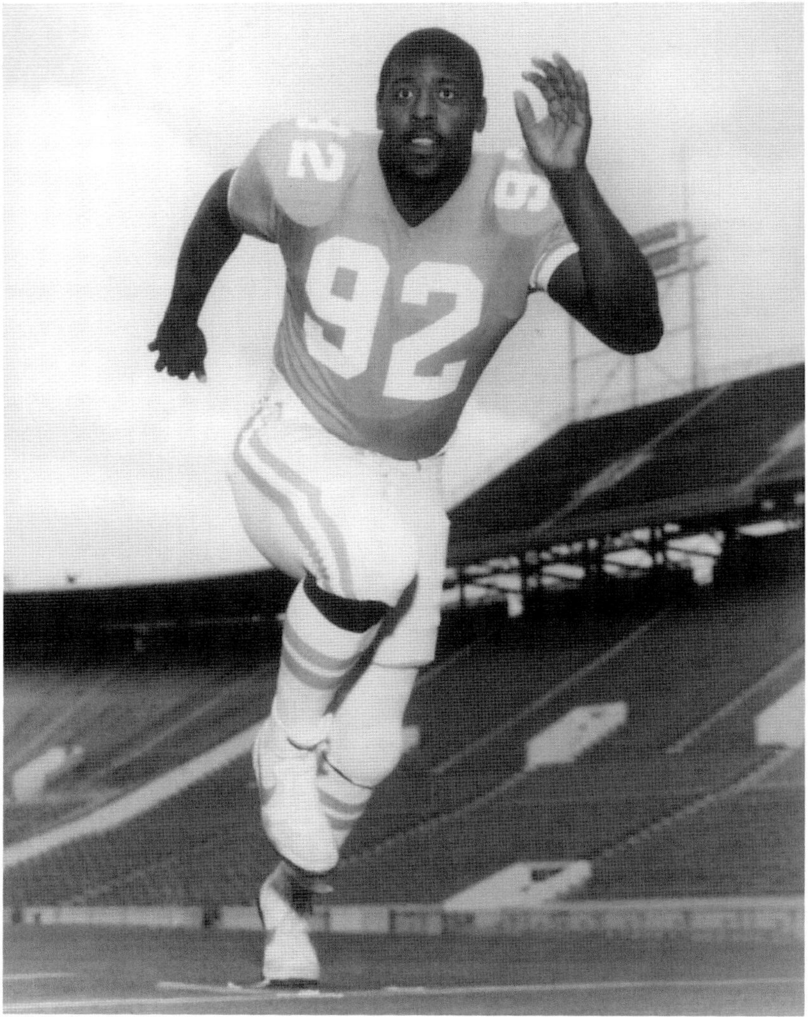

Reggie White

The Howard Hustlin' Tigers have been winning football games for decades and along the way, have produced some great athletes. Certainly, the finest player of all was Reggie White. At Howard, he was an All-State basketball player and an All-American football player. Raised by his mother and grandparents, he grew up in the Baptist Church where his faith grew steadily, guiding him throughout his career. When his career blossomed at the University of Tennessee—where he became an All-American—he often prayed with his teammates. White continued to preach on Sundays at the invitation of different churches and soon gained the moniker, "the Minister of Defense." White started in the NFL with the Philadelphia Eagles in 1985 but came to real fame with the Green Bay Packers from 1993 to 1998 with his celebrated teammate Brett Favre, winning the Super Bowl in 1997. He was selected to the Pro Bowl 13 consecutive times. His relentless rush as a defensive end was legendary, and at six feet, five inches and 300 pounds, he was tons of trouble for quarterbacks. At the height of his powers, he was double- and triple-teamed (blocked) to keep him at bay. When he retired from football, White held the all-time record for sacks (198) and was named to the NFL's 75th anniversary all-star team. He was an associate pastor at a church in Knoxville and put up $1 million of his own money to start a bank for inner city residents that had difficulty qualifying for loans. A leader on and off the field, he was considered one of the greatest NFL players ever when he died unexpectedly at the age of 43 in 2004. (Courtesy University of Tennessee.)

CHAPTER FIVE

The Arts

When looking at Chattanooga's life in the arts, James Cameron's colorful tableau of the Whiteside family must be considered. One of the few pieces remaining from the antebellum period, this large family portrait—on display at the Hunter Museum of American Art—is a classic of 19th-century American portraiture. Since that time, the visual arts here have long leaned toward the representative, the landscape in particular, as shown in the work of Hubert Shuptrine or Gordon Wetmore. Barry Moser's wonderful use of line has gained him national acclaim. Jim Collins's wry sense of humor is notable in his public sculpture. In the world of drama, the Chattanooga Theater Center (originally the Little Theater) claims to be the longest-running community theater in the country since its founding in 1923. Native son Coleman Barks has made his mark not only as a poet but also as an interpreter of poetry, especially that of the Sufi poet Rumi. He has almost single-handedly introduced and popularized him in North America. And Chattanooga has sent some voices into the world as well. Bessie Smith is easily one of America's great singers, a blues belter supreme with that lowdown feeling. The Impressions, one of the 1960s great soul groups, took their gentle gospel harmonies and moving rhythms to the national charts numerous times. Neo-soul singer Usher grew up here and formed his first vocal groups in junior high school. Others, like Ann Patton, a celebrated harpist, or Dan Landrum, a hammer dulcimer player, have called Chattanooga home. Donald Pippin, the Broadway impresario, and Clyde Stubblefield, the great funk drummer, all have sprung from the Scenic City's sounds and pulse.

Roland Hayes

Roland Hayes, born in 1887, is considered to be the first internationally recognized African American singer. He grew up in Chattanooga having moved here as a boy from Gordon County, Georgia, with his mother. To earn money for the family, he found work in an iron factory doing dangerous work handling molten pig iron, eventually becoming a core maker. His early singing was formed in the Baptist church choir where he studied with Arthur Calhoun, who had attended Oberlin College as a music student. Sources say that Calhoun introduced him to a white man who played recordings of Caruso and Sembrich on what would have been an early Victrola. Hayes said of that evening, "I was born again. It was as if a bell had been struck, that rang in my heart." His talent was recognized when he sang with the Fisk Jubilee Singers in 1911 in Boston, setting the stage for his career that took him all over the United States and Europe. Among his many triumphs, he is credited with being the first black singer to perform at Carnegie Hall in New York City. (Author's collection.)

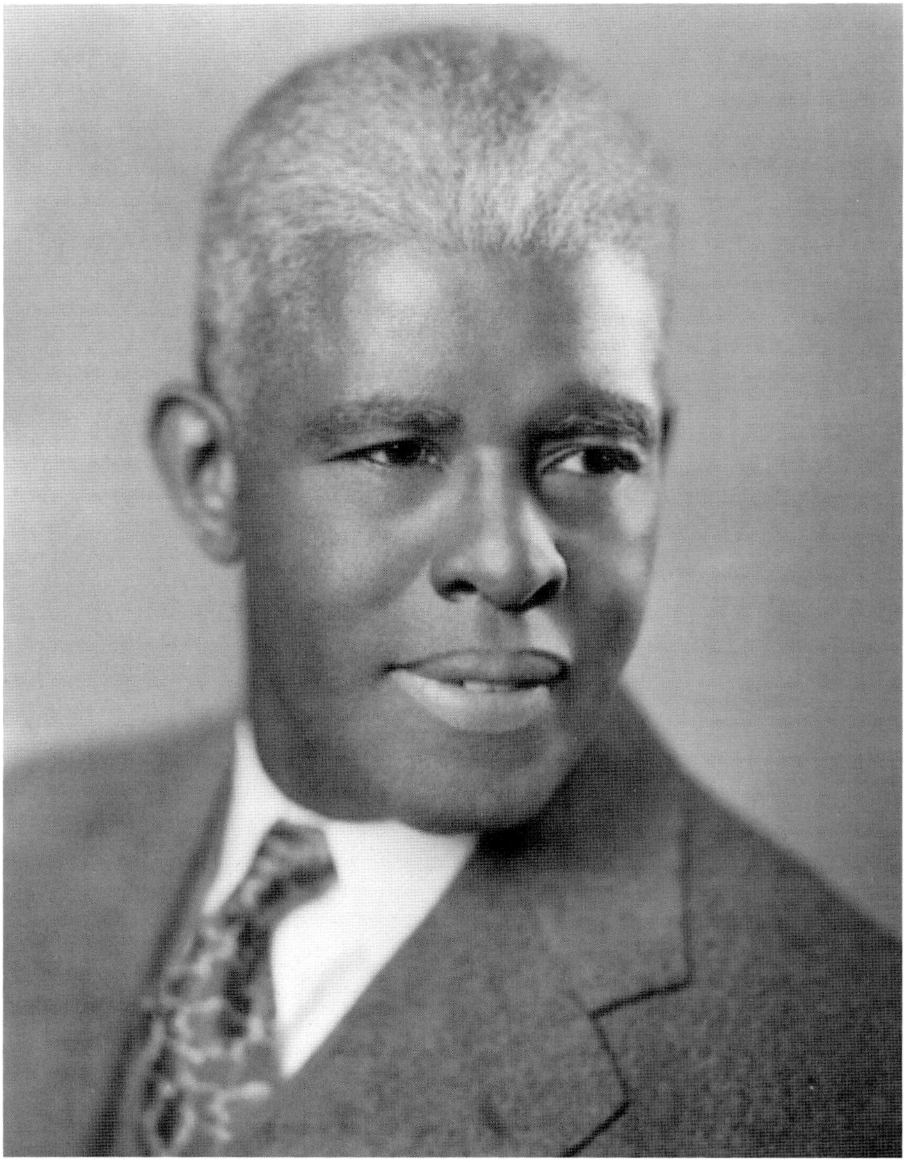

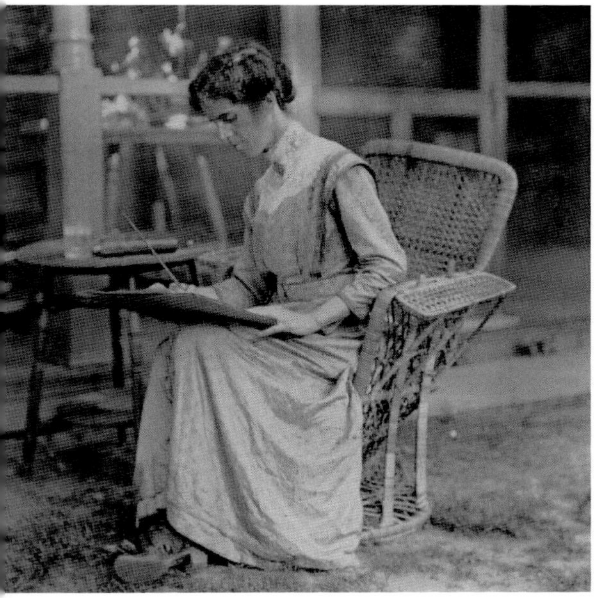

Emma Bell Miles

Writers are often inspired by the bounty of nature, something Chattanooga has in abundance. Emma Bell Miles found inspiration in her world on Walden's Ridge as a writer who lived and loved the life of the southern Appalachians. She cautioned her fellow mountain dwellers to conserve their land and its resources. Though much of her life was a real struggle, she worked diligently and became adept at prose, writing a newspaper column and gaining entry to literary magazines such as *Harper's Weekly.* Her great success, published in 1905, was *The Spirit of the Mountains.* In this book, she was able to combine poetic elements, personal musings, and narratives about local life into thoughtful literary substance. (Courtesy University of Tennessee at Chattanooga/Special Collections.)

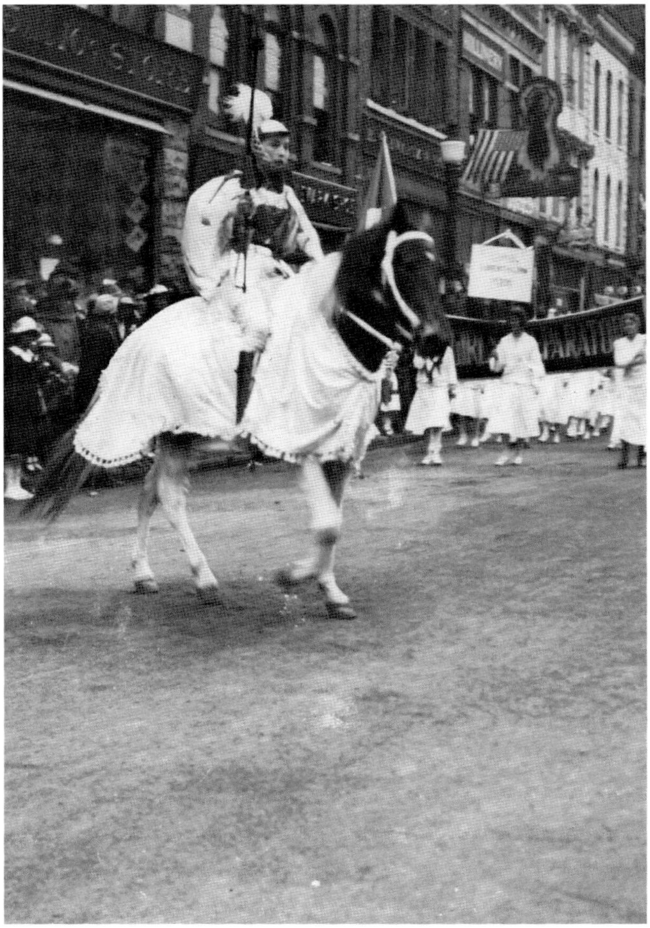

Dorothy Patten

Born in 1905, Dorothy Patten showed a theatrical flair from an early age as this photograph of her in a parade dressed as Joan of Arc demonstrates. Her life on Broadway began in 1929 in the play *Subway Express.* Steady work through the 1930s and into the 1940s made her well known in New York circles. One of her most famous movie roles was in the 1953 hit *Botany Bay.* She is remembered today as the namesake of the Dorothy Patten Performance series in Chattanooga, known for bringing excellent national and international performers to Chattanooga. Wynton Marsalis, Dave Brubeck, and the Vienna Boys Choir are a few of the names that have performed under its auspices. (Courtesy Chattanooga Public Library.)

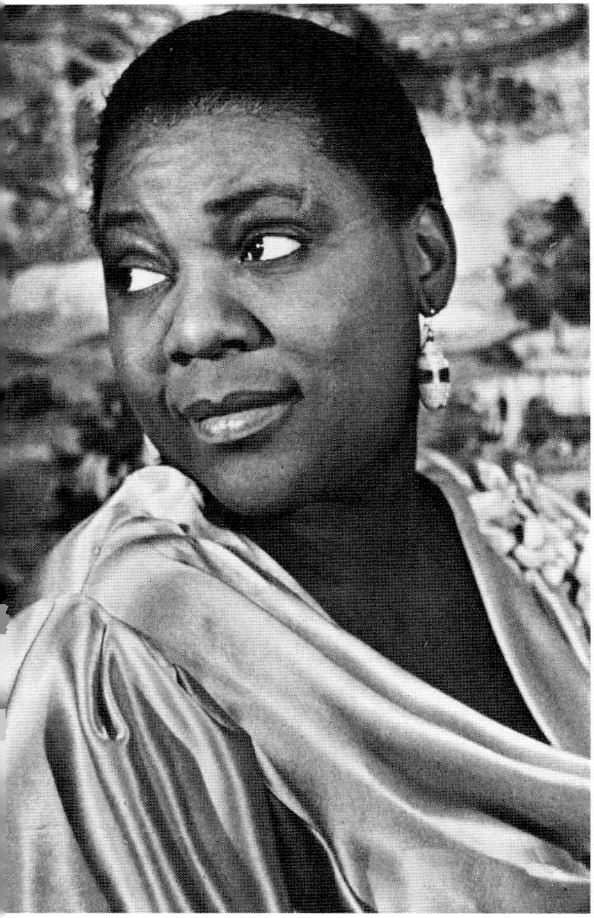

Bessie Smith
The great blues singer Bessie Smith was born in either 1892 or 1894 and grew up in the area around Cameron Hill near present-day Fourth and Chestnut Streets, the daughter of a man who was a laborer and part-time preacher. Both her mother and father had died by the time she was nine, and the family lived in poverty. Bessie was raised by her older sister, and the two took to dancing and singing in public to make money, often performing outside the White Elephant Saloon on Thirteenth Street. An opportunity to join a traveling troupe of entertainers with her older brother was all she needed to begin her career, hired first as a dancer and then a singer. Eventually moving to Atlanta, and then to Philadelphia, she made her first record when she was 30. Even though these were "race records," she became wildly famous with songs like "Down Hearted Blues" and "Gimme a Pigfoot (And a Bottle of Beer)." Her emotional, full-throated singing helped stamp her blues songs as some of the greatest ever put down on wax. Smith became the highest paid black singer of her time, touring incessantly as the headliner of her own shows. She even owned her own railroad car and claimed the title "the Empress of the Blues," playing with Louis Armstrong and Fletcher Henderson, to name a few. Her sudden death in 1937 left her Philadelphia community in shock, and as many as 10,000 people attended her funeral. (Courtesy Chattanooga Public Library.)

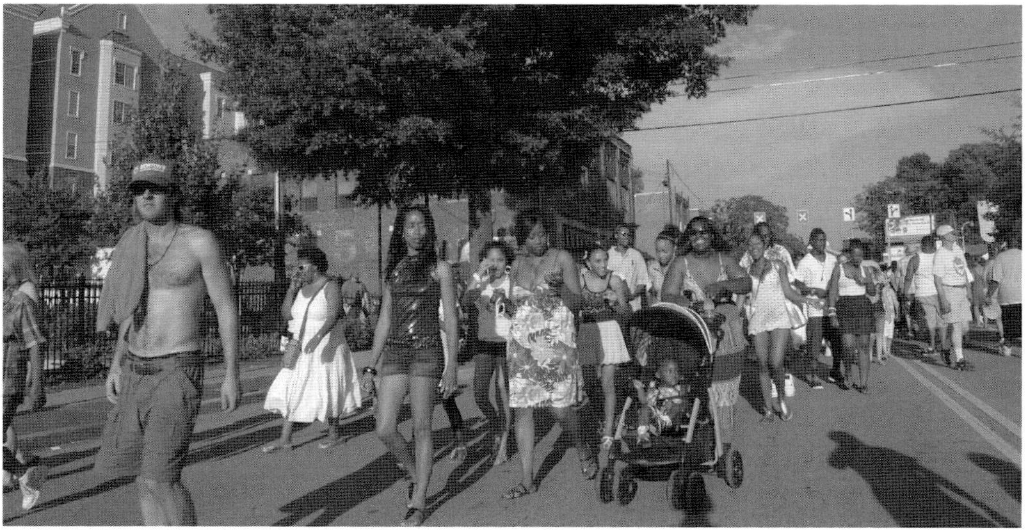

Bessie Smith Strut
The Bessie Smith Strut is held annually in June on Martin Luther King Boulevard.

Grace Moore

Mary Willie Grace Moore possessed a strong, mellifluous voice that garnered her the moniker "the Tennessee Nightingale." In 1920, she made her first appearance on Broadway at the age of 21 in Jerome Kern's Hitchy-Koo and after training in France, debuted at the Metropolitan Opera in February 1928 in La Boheme. Moore spent 16 years with the Met while developing a career in the "talkies," where she made numerous films such as *One Night in Love*. She is widely credited for popularizing operatic singing through her film appearances. In this photograph, she receives the key to the city after a Chattanooga performance. Her death in a plane crash in 1947 in Denmark shocked the musical world. She is buried at Forest Hills Cemetery at the foot of Lookout Mountain. (Courtesy Chattanooga Public Library.)

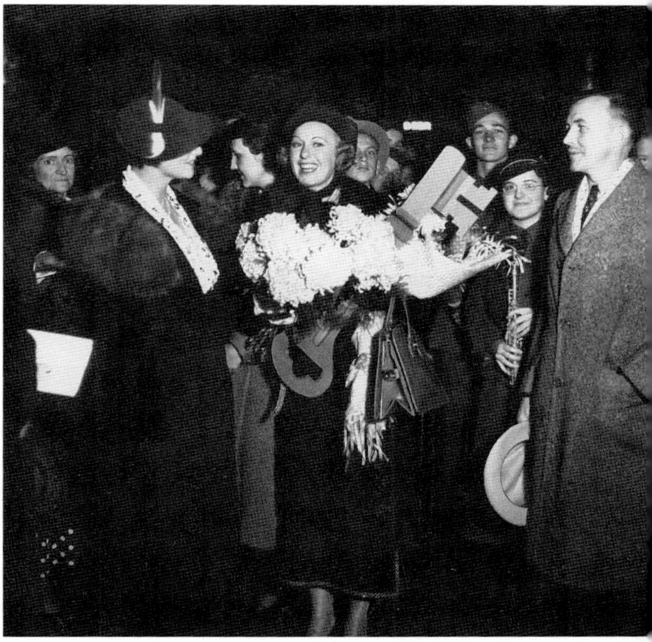

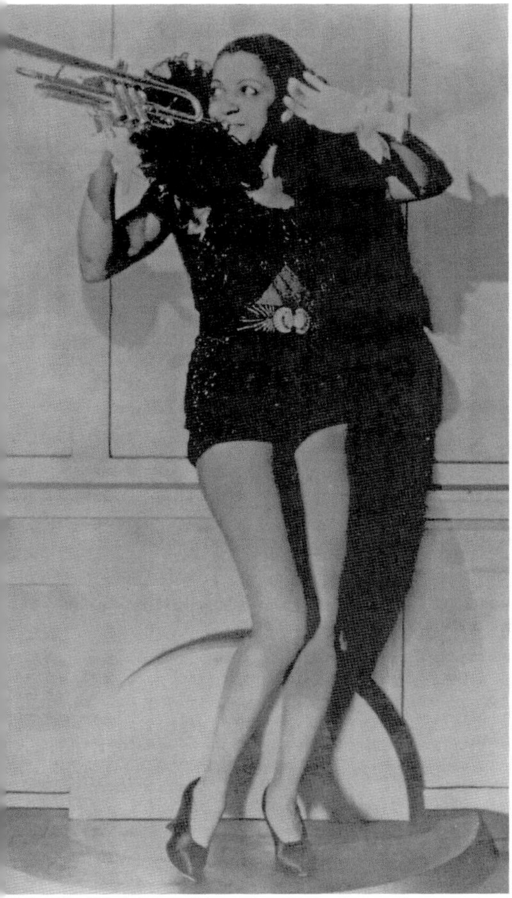

Valaida Snow

Valaida Snow grew up in Chattanooga in a musical family. Performance was part of living, and in that tradition, she was able to play mandolin, banjo, bass, clarinet, accordion, and saxophone, and sing and dance as well by 1920 when she was 16. But her strong suit was the trumpet. So good was her tone that no one less than Louis Armstrong called her the second-best jazz trumpet player in the world (next to him, of course) earning her the nickname " Little Louis." Her hit song, "High Hat, Trumpet, and Rhythm," became her signature piece on tours of the United States, Europe, and even Russia and China. She toured with the Noble Sissle-Eubie Blake musical review, The Chocolate Dandies, in the 1920s and made films in the 1930s, actively recording all the time. Known in London and Paris, she was presented with a golden trumpet by Queen Wilhelmina of the Netherlands; at one point in her career, she traveled in a chauffeur-driven Mercedes-Benz with a lavender-dressed monkey. Tragically, while performing in Denmark in 1941 with an all-women orchestra, she was taken prisoner by the Nazi army and sent to a concentration camp. Released after 18 months, she struggled to regain her sense of self and gradually returned to performing and recording which she did successfully until the night she died in 1956 during a show at the Palace Theater in New York City. (Author's collection.)

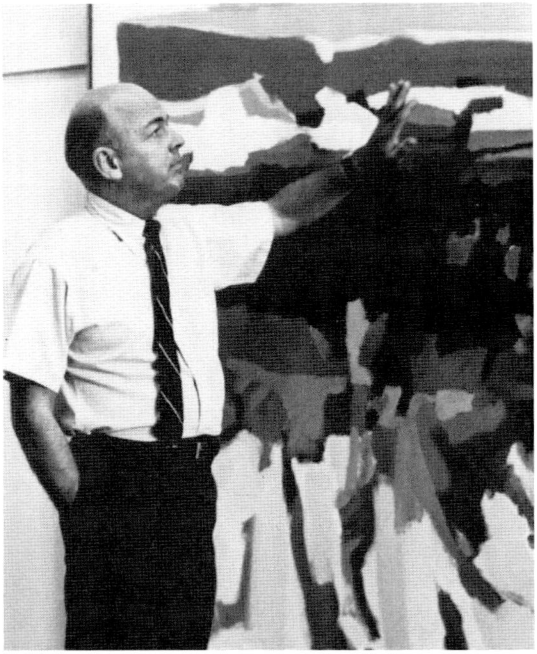

George Cress

George Ayers Cress was a blessing to all that knew him. He was a gifted and prolific painter who worked in an abstract, colorful style, especially in the realm of the landscape. Educated at Emory University and with a master's degree in fine art from the University of Georgia, where he became friends with Lamar Dodd, Cress joined the University of Chattanooga in 1951 and taught there for 56 years. He was an inspiration to his students, who spoke fondly of him. A believer in living and painting life outside the studio and constantly working, he became chairman of the department of art and later a Guerry Professor Emeritus of Art. A founder and central figure in Chattanooga's art community, his death in early January 2008 was noted with great sadness. (Courtesy University of Tennessee at Chattanooga/Special Collections.)

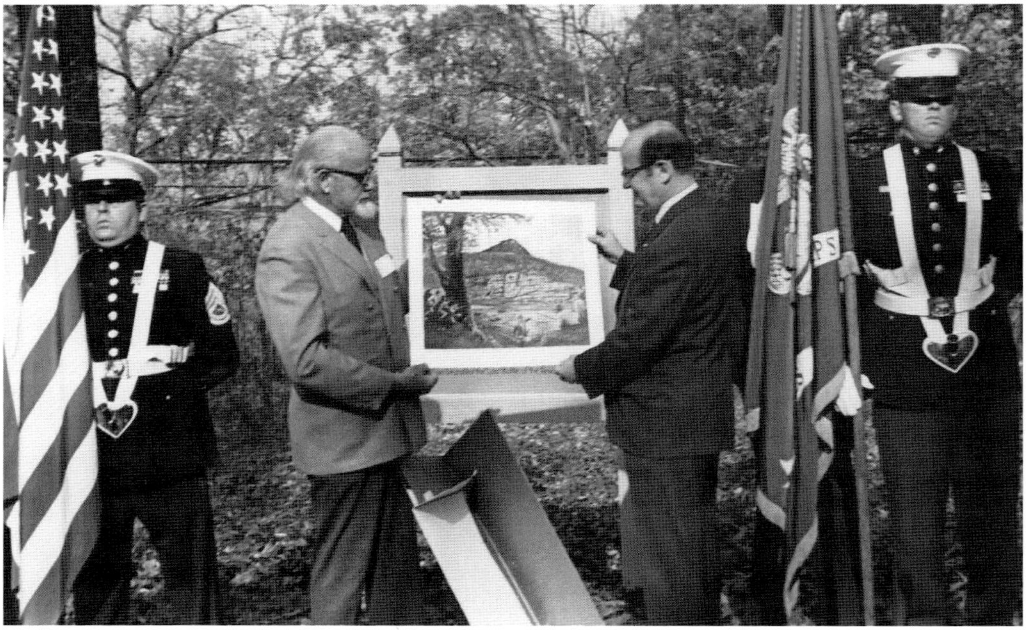

George Little

For a generation, the Little Art Shop stood on the corner of Frazier Avenue across from the Walnut Street Bridge in one of Hill City's (North Chattanooga) oldest buildings. Begun by George Little (left, holding painting) in 1960, the store sold fine art supplies and supported the painting life of George Little. Little's paintings were a frequent sight in stores and businesses around town. He painted numerous landscapes of the Chattanooga of his own time and historic events—notably the Civil War—as well. Here, he presents a painting to congressman Lamar Baker. The shop was in business until 1983 when he sold it to family members. It continues to operate as an art supply store today. (Courtesy Chattanooga Public Library.)

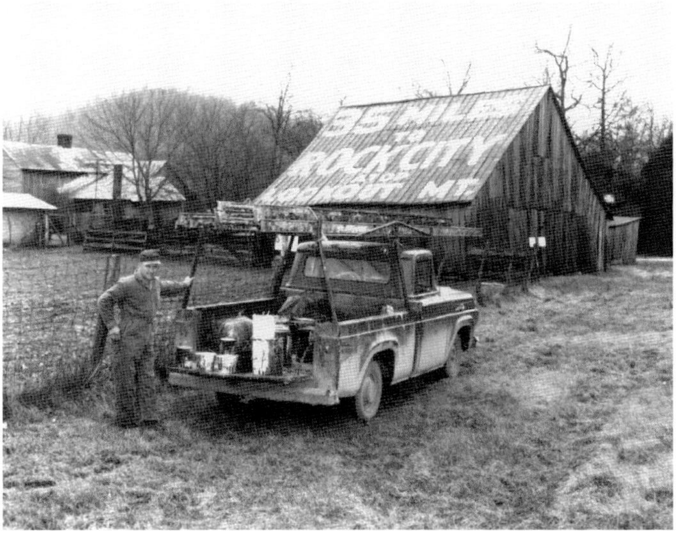

Clark Byers

Clark Byers was a painter who had a gigantic canvas, namely the barn roofs that flanked America's highways from Michigan to Florida. Hired by Rock City to paint slogans like "Beautiful Beyond Belief" or "To Miss Rock City Would Be a Pity," Byers painted some 900 barns over 30 years. A native of Trenton, Georgia, near Lookout Mountain, Byers painted the large letters freehand and relied on a four-inch brush to make his bold marks. (Courtesy Chattanooga Public Library.)

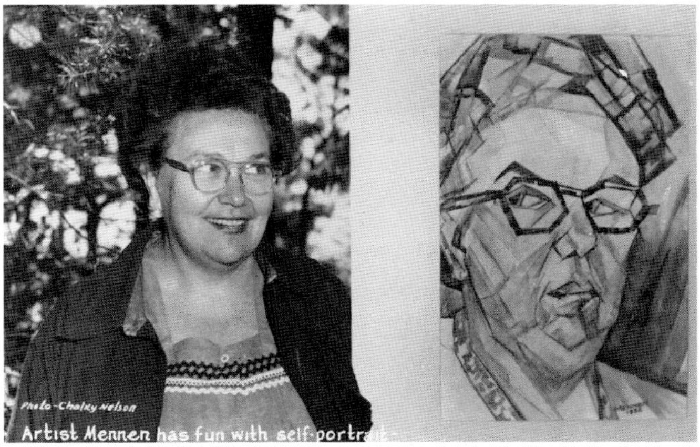

Fannie Mennen

October in the southern Appalachians is a beautiful month full of color and deep blue skies, and for years, it brought a weekend when thousands of Chattanoogans trekked up Lookout Mountain to Fannie Mennen's house in the community of New Salem to see local artists display their wares. The outdoor display of art that began in 1947 became known as the Plum Nelly Clothesline Show. The name "Plum Nelly" came to be because one of Fanny's relatives described her place as "plum out of Tennessee and nearly out of Georgia," which it was. The moniker stuck, and the show became a colorful, annual tradition. But by the early 1970s, the enormous traffic congestion on the little, two-lane mountain road near her place led Fannie Mennen to call off the annual affair for good. An art teacher by trade with a love of painting and the solitary beauty of the mountains, her namesake lives on through Plum Nelly, a local arts and crafts shop that has been open in North Chattanooga since 1972, the final year of the outdoor art exhibit. (Courtesy Chattanooga Public Library.)

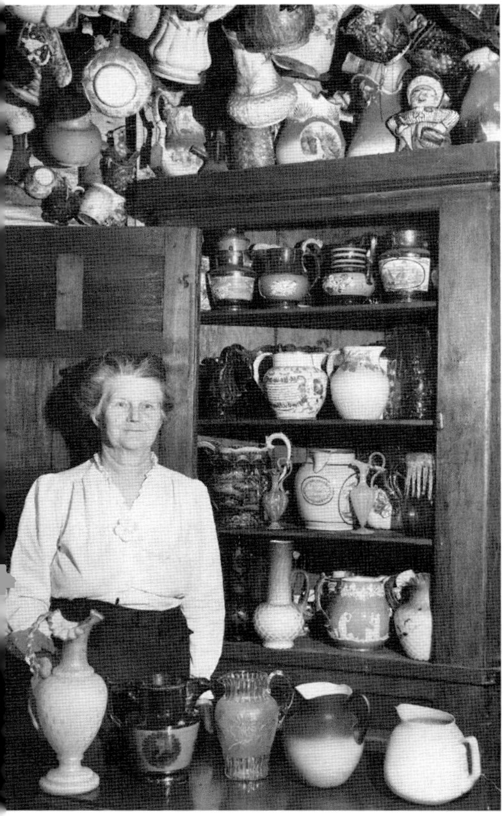

Anna Safely Houston

The antique business tends to attract curious, obsessive, and fascinating people to its world, and Anna Safely Houston was no exception. Born in Arkansas in 1876, this energetic woman helped raise her own brothers and sisters after her mother died. As a teenager, she left home, apparently living by her wits and eventually coming to Chattanooga with her second husband. No stranger to romance, she would marry nine times. But her greatest love was beautiful ceramics in the shape of colorful pitchers, embellished plates, eye-catching glassware, or decorative bowls. She spent a lifetime collecting an enormous variety of domestic wares that were housed in a barn, hanging from every nook and nail. Successful in real estate and business enterprises, she was a keenly intelligent woman years ahead of her time. But the Great Depression ruined her financially like so many people around the South, and her income dried up, leaving her in dire economic straits. Nevertheless, so dedicated to her vast collection was "Antique Annie" that in her final years, she lived in poverty refusing to part with any of her precious pieces. She had a house of sorts built with her own hands near Missionary Ridge where she lived with her objets d'art, hanging many of the pitchers from the roof beams by rope. In her will, she left all she had to the city of Chattanooga, and today, the Houston Museum of Decorative Arts displays her wares and stands as a testament to her vital and singular life. (Courtesy Chattanooga Public Library.)

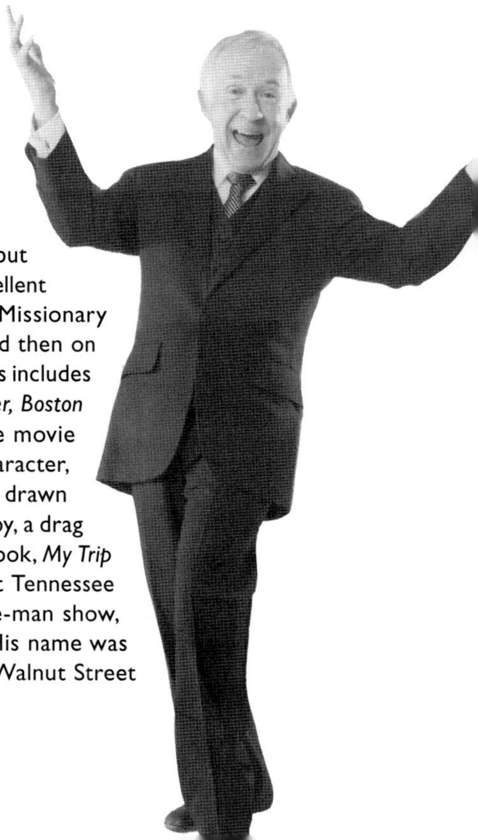

Leslie Jordan

Some actors become well known through a starring role, but some, like Leslie Jordan, seep into consciousness through excellent performances as many different characters. Raised near Missionary Ridge, the affable Jordan went to Brainerd High School and then on the University of Tennessee. His list of television appearances includes roles in *Murphy Brown*, *Pee-wee's Playhouse*, *Star Trek: Voyager, Boston Legal*, and *Desperate Housewives*. He also appeared in the movie *The Help*. In *Will and Grace,* he received an Emmy for his character, Beverly Leslie, in 2006. Not limited to television, Jordan has drawn raves on stage, notably in *Sordid Lives* as the character Big Boy, a drag queen. Most recently, he has released an autobiographical book, *My Trip Down the Pink Carpet*, which recounts his childhood in east Tennessee as a short, funny, effeminate youngster. The resulting one-man show, produced by Lily Tomlin, opened off-Broadway in 2010. His name was recently placed on the inaugural Walk of Honor on the Walnut Street Bridge. (Author's collection.)

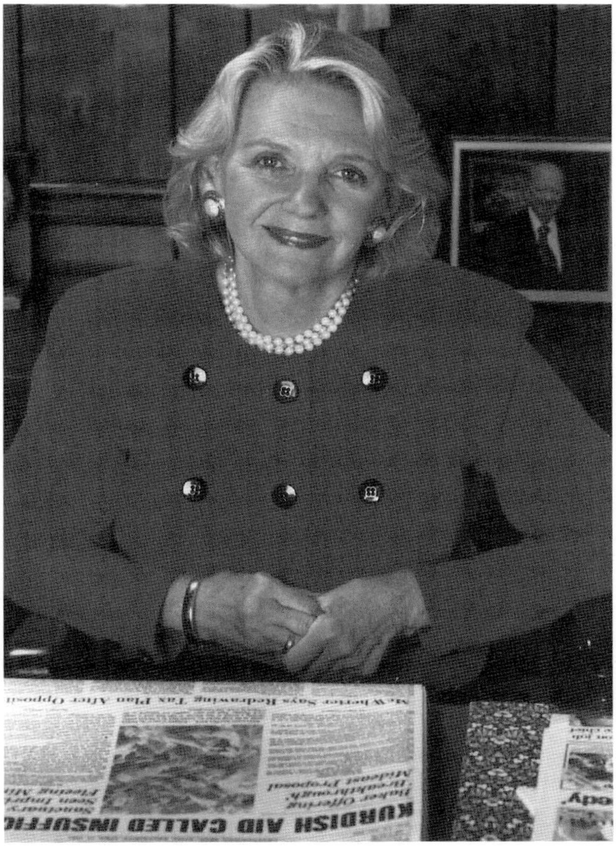

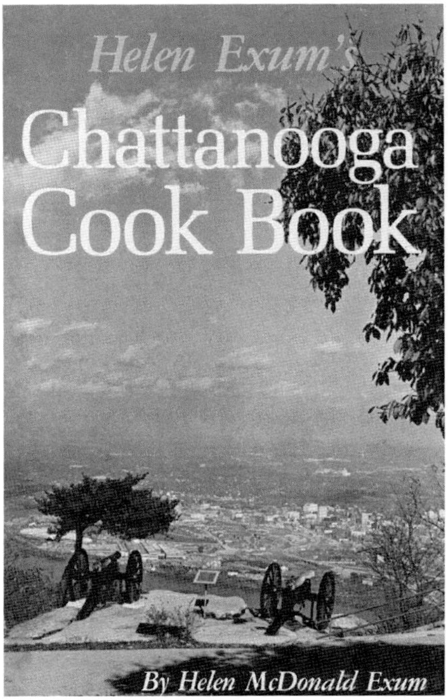

Helen Exum
Recipe books are a dime-a-dozen, but in every burg and hamlet, there are usually one or two cookbooks that are kept, used, and reused until the pages begin to fray. Helen McDonald Exum's *Chattanooga Cook Book* was certainly that culinary go-to book for decades. Her interest in cooking took flight when she lived in California with her husband and began taking pies to neighbors to introduce herself. The enjoyment and conversation that came from preparing food for her family and friends gave real meaning to the "joy of cooking." In order to raise money to pay for her children's schooling, she decided to put together a cookbook and was soon writing the food column for the *Chattanooga Times Free Press*. Her love of food and friendship has made her friends all over the world. She has traveled through Europe on canals—fixing breakfast for the crews on one trip—and once spent a week cooking with Julia Child. A believer in the importance of people sitting down to eat and talk together, her books are filled with stories of local life and the kinship that culinary fellowship can bring. (Courtesy Helen Exum.)

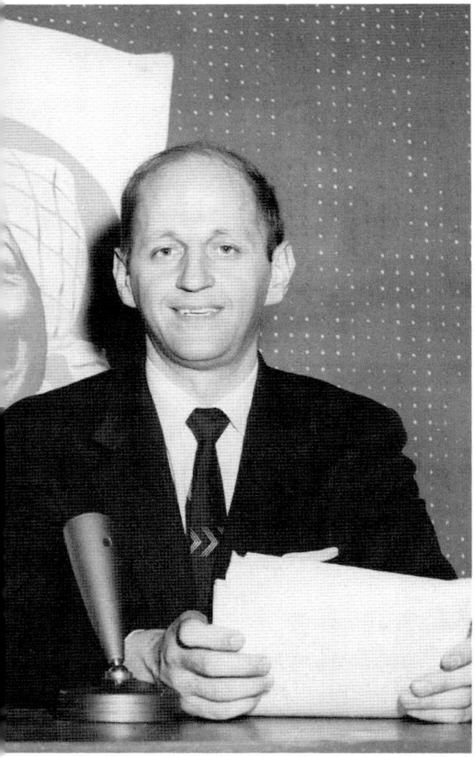

Luther Masingill

Luther Masingill is a true legend. Known simply as "Luther," he was discovered by Joe Engel, who heard him talking at a gas station and asked him to take a job as a telephone receptionist on WDEF radio. His voice was so rich that he was immediately put on the air beginning on New Year's Eve in 1940. Except for a stint during World War II in the Pacific, he has been on the air for an astonishing 70 years. A native of the city, he grew up in the Avondale community and attended Central High School. When television came along in 1954, he naturally made the transition as a show host. But his first love was always radio, and his reputation for reuniting people with their lost pets via his radio show is well known. During his prime years as a broadcaster, he often drew ratings with a 60-percent share. Winner of the honored Marconi Award from the National Association of Broadcasters as well as a proclamation from the Tennessee State Legislature, a section of Broad Street now bears his name. According to local broadcaster David Carroll, "he is the longest running broadcaster in the history of the world" and probably the only one that reported both Pearl Harbor and the attacks of 9/11. Astoundingly, he never called into work sick from 1947 to 2001. Still a voice on the air for morning drive time and still working for the same station he first signed on with, he and his wife, Mary, live in the same house they moved into when they were married in 1954. (Courtesy Chattanooga Public Library.)

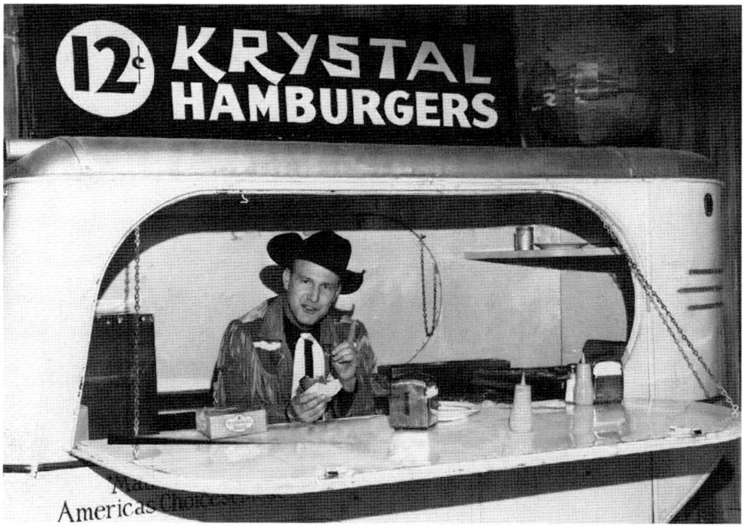

Bob Brandy

In the early days of television, local, live broadcasting was a key ingredient and when it came to children's programs, none did it better than Bob Brandy, seen here extolling the virtues of Chattanooga-made Krystal hamburgers. Dressed as a 1950s Western cowboy, Brandy teamed with his wife, Inga, who oddly enough spoke with a German accent, and his trusty horse, Rebel, on weekday afternoons. Showcasing students each day from a different school, the show was an afternoon delight to kids at home after classes. Milk, cookies, and cartoons on the *Bob Brandy Show* were all a youngster needed to end a good day at school before mom made supper for the family. (Courtesy Chattanooga Public Library.)

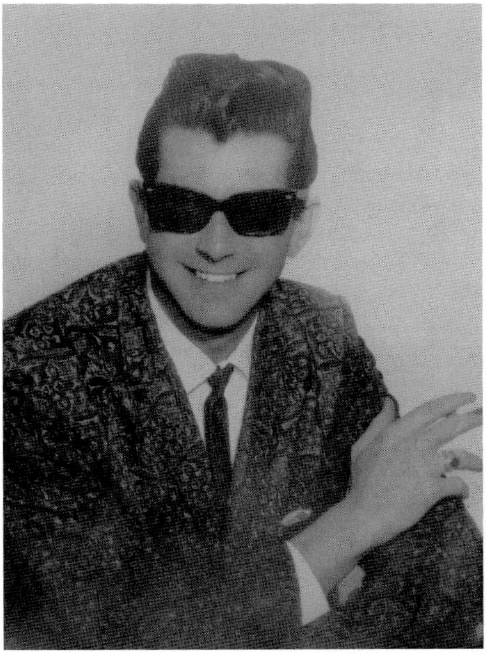

Tommy Jett

In the 1960s, "the fastest jet in the air" was Tommy Jett, the foremost rock 'n' roll disc jockey in town on "Jet Fly" WFLI, a station that played Top 40 rock. The station hired Jett in 1961 as an afternoon drive-time disc jockey. Its ratings soared; at one point, he received a phenomenal 80-percent share. With a tag line of "Hey now," he started an evening show, *Night Train*, named for the James Brown song, and his popularity soared. He created an onstage presence as well, hosting the Jet Fly Spectaculars, live rock concerts with a panoply of stars. The first one in 1965 cost a whopping $2.50 to see. In 1970, he moved to WDOD and was behind the microphone for 16 years, spinning country music platters and interviewing singers like Conway Twitty and Loretta Lynn. His career continued as an oldies DJ until 2009. Today, his voice can still be heard on his online broadcasts when he signs off with: "Shoot for the moon. Even if you miss, you will be among the stars." (Courtesy Tommy Jett.)

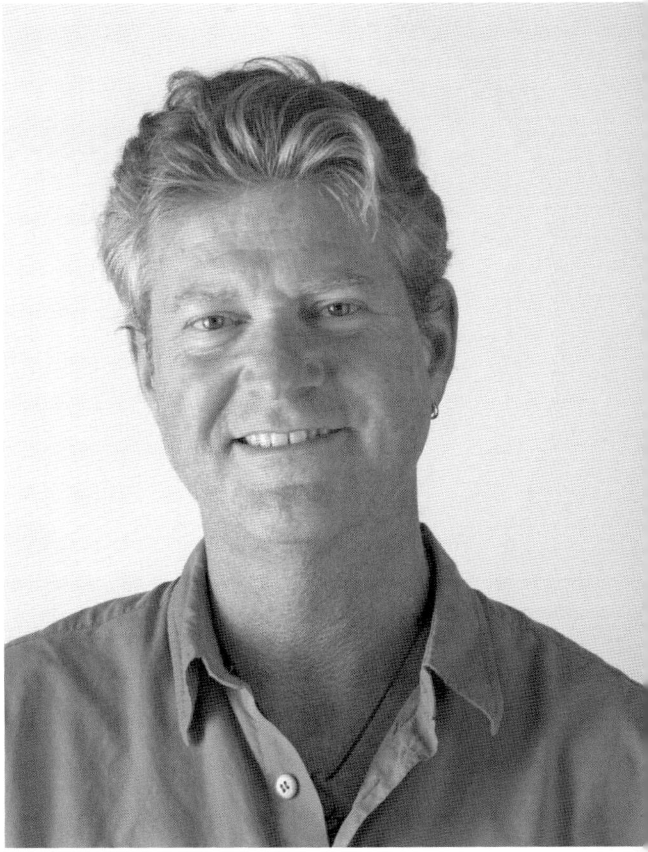

Jeff Styles

Jeff Styles came to Chattanooga to learn to hang glide through the air high off Lookout Mountain; today, his voice travels through the airwaves of the city on talk radio. His show is titled *FRED*—letters standing for Free Radio Every Day—and his listeners are Fred Heads. His topics spring from personal interviews, community concerns, talks with movers-and-shakers as well as ordinary folks, and, of course, the vagaries of local politics. Coupled with his own musings about life in the Tennessee Valley and beyond, the show is always changing, something of a daily work in progress, which always makes for interesting listening. A free-spirited liberal in a conservative city, Styles is not shy about stepping in the hornets' nest of controversy when he feels an issue needs to be addressed. Contrary to the garden-variety talk show host, his manner and intention is honest and never sensational or mean. A devoted kayaker and hiker, he coined the phrase "The Boulder of the South" before Chattanooga's rise in acclaim in the natural sporting world and has been a booster of Chattanooga's outdoor possibilities for decades. (Courtesy North Light Imaging.)

Dr. Roland Carter

Dr. Roland Carter is a man of many accomplishments. A graduate of Howard High School, he dedicated his life to music, specifically the choral arts. As a youngster growing up in the Bushtown community, he loved singing in the church and by 15, was the director of the adult choir. In high school, he found great inspiration in the teaching and guidance of music teacher Edmonia Simmons, who helped him to matriculate at Hampton Institute in Virginia. It was here that he studied Nathaniel Dett, the choral composer and arranger of spirituals, and worked with Charles Flax, the director of church music at Hampton during Carter's years. Even today, he still recalls the profoundly moving sound of the student body's resonant mass singings. Presently, he serves as the Ruth S. Holmberg professor of music at the University of Tennessee at Chattanooga. His talents have landed him an honorary membership in the Morehouse Glee Club, an award only given previously to the former Atlanta Symphony Orchestra choral director Robert Shaw and Leonard DePaur. An honorary membership was also bestowed on him by Phi Mu Alpha Sinfonia, America's largest music fraternity, for the mark he has made in American music. For instance, his arrangement of the classic "Lift Every Voice and Sing" is a standard in choral presentations around the country. And his quietly beautiful version of "Bright Mansions" is a touching piece of vocal mastery. It is no surprise that he is a respected authority on the preservation of African American spiritual music and as such, has been director (and founder) of the Chattanooga Choral Society for the Preservation of African American Song for 19 years. Besides sitting on numerous boards over time—such as the Tennessee Arts Commission and Allied Arts of Chattanooga—he was recently honored to have the UTC Chamber Choir, under the direction of Dr. Kevin Ford, record and release volume one of *The Choral Music of Roland Carter.* Known as an exacting and vibrant teacher, Dr. Carter continues to write, direct, and perform music that lifts the spirit and enriches the community. (Courtesy Dr. Roland Carter.)

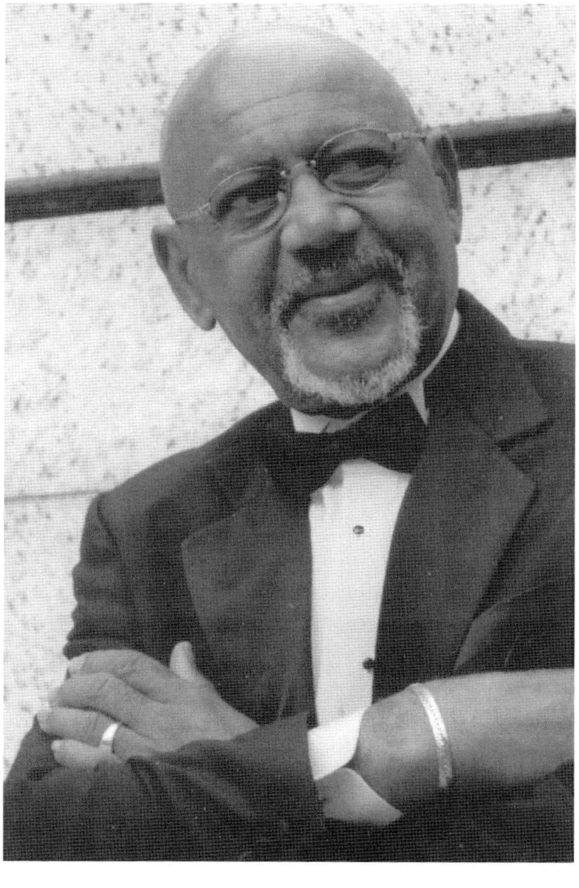

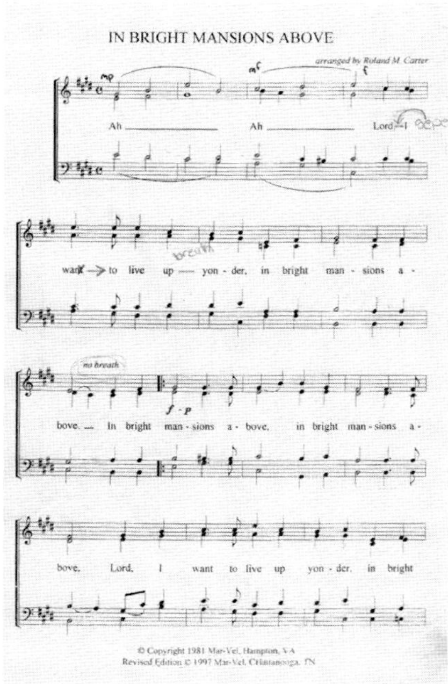

Roland Carter Music

This is a copy of the sheet music to "Bright Mansions," one of Dr. Carter's signature pieces.

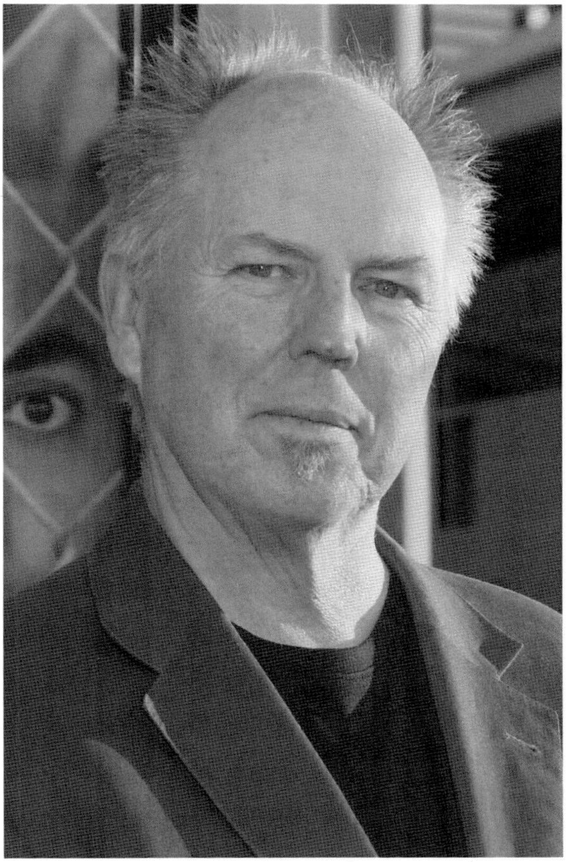

George Clinton
George Clinton absorbed the musical stew of the South and turned it into some wonderful orchestral music that has earned him a reputation as one of today's leading film composers. His mother was the organist at Ridgeview Baptist Church on Moore Road; music was in his blood from a young age. At Brainerd High School, he sang in the choir and played trombone in the marching band, but more importantly began writing arrangements under the tutelage of teacher Bill Henson. His first rock band, The Velveteen Rabbits, played around town at clubs like the Coat of Arms (near the Missionary Ridge tunnel) and his folk duo, George and Kipper, won the Jaycees Hootenanny contest, garnering them a recording date at Peanuts Faircloth's studio. With call-ins from their friends, they actually had the No. 1 record in the city for one night. For extra cash, Clinton delivered pianos for the long-lived Al Miller Music Store. A new Music Studies Department at Middle Tennessee State University was Clinton's home for four years, where Paul Britt was especially instrumental in his work. A trip to the Atlanta Pop Festival in 1969 opened his eyes to the possibilities of a musical life, and he decided to try professional songwriting in Nashville, where he landed a job with Tree Music, publishing company of the legendary Buddy Killen. But he realized rock 'n' roll was in his blood, and he relocated to Los Angeles to play and write for Warner Bros. music. One night, when his band was winding down its show (and getting ready to call it quits permanently), Clinton was approached by Cheech Martin of Cheech & Chong and asked to write a film score for *Still Smokin'*. Since that time, he has written music for the television series *Red Shoe Diaries* and many movies, such as *Mortal Kombat* and *Big Momma's House* 2. But his best-known score is surely *Austin Powers: International Man of Mystery* and its sequels with its wide musical range of suave moods, catchy rhythms, and snappy wind motifs. As such, Clinton is a great supporter of orchestral music and is an adviser to the Chattanooga Symphony Orchestra with whom he has appeared at the Tivoli Theater, where he first heard symphonic music as a boy. (Courtesy George Clinton.)

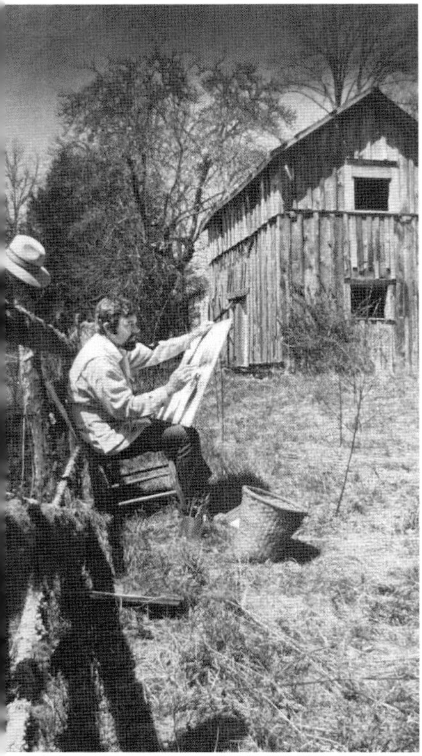

Hubert Shuptrine

Hubert Shuptrine was a master of watercolor, a man who could create landscapes and portraits with beautiful washes of color and exquisitely rendered lines. He grew up in Brainerd and went to Chattanooga High School before entering the University of Chattanooga with the idea of becoming a veterinarian. But when he took an art class, he became enthralled with painting in oils. Under the tutelage of George Cress, he graduated in 1959 with a bachelor's degree in science and fine arts painting and steadily honed his craft in work and leisure before making the leap to become a full-time painter in 1967. A trip to Maine in 1970 became the catalyst for his conversion to watercolor, more particularly the dry brush technique. *Southern Living* magazine brought Shuptrine together with the southern novelist James Dickey and the result was the book *Jericho: The South Beheld,* published in 1974. The landmark art book searched for the Old South on the back roads and among the folk of the deep country. His carefully drawn faces and gentle, atmospheric renderings of the southland struck a nerve for its reverent nature and the true character it revealed. The large volume was a stunning success for an art book selling over 150,000 copies in the first edition alone. The work received the Carey-Thomas Award and was nominated for a Pulitzer Prize. In 1987, Oxmoor House published *Home to Jericho,* which further cemented his artistic reputation. Today, his work is held in both private and museum collections around the nation. He passed away in Chattanooga in 2006.

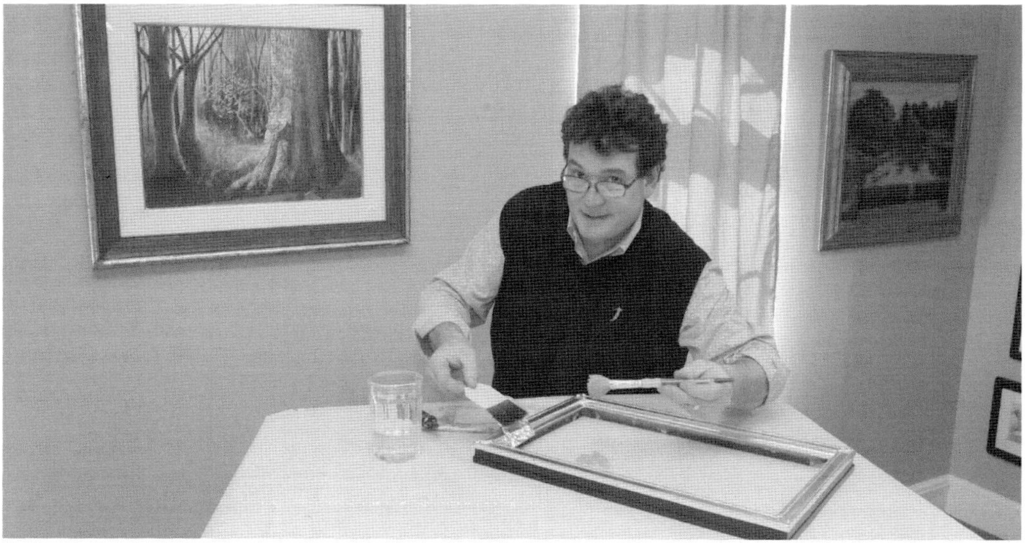

Alan Shuptrine

As a child, Alan Shuptrine loved the sound of his father's brush as it tapped the glass and brushed the canvas. Today, he creates his own beauty with paint as a watercolor realist in the American tradition of Andrew Wyeth with a unique touch. As a gallery owner, he is constantly offering a variety of services, such as workshops, exhibits, or consultations to private collectors. In the studio, he is especially known for his rare talent for gold leafing, notably water gilding, and his careful, detailed restorations of frames and mirrors that has brought him clients from around the country. Always painting and exhibiting, he is now at work on a book about trees with bestselling Virginia author Sharyn McCrumb. (Author's collection.)

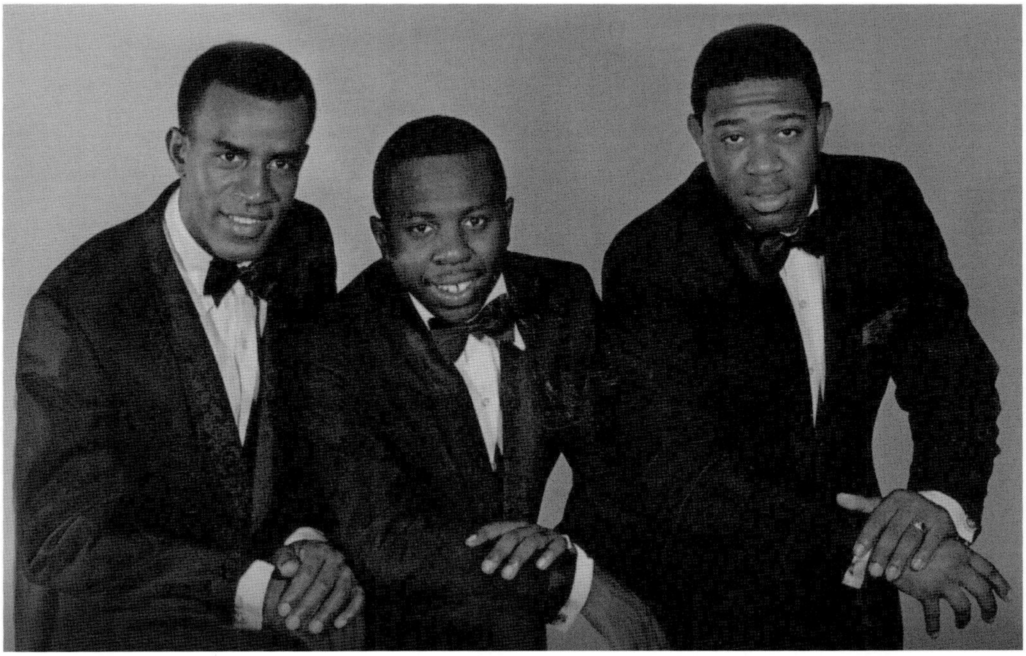

The Impressions
Sam Gooden and Richard Brooks were born singers who loved harmony and music with "that gospel feeling." They joined The Roosters, an early soul group in Chattanooga. The group then went north to Chicago and eventually became The Impressions adding the talented Curtis Mayfield and Fred Cash. "For Your Precious Love" was their first success followed by the mysterious "Gypsy Woman" in 1961. With its optimistic lyrics, "It's All Right" went gold in 1963. The next year, the Civil Rights song "Keep on Pushin'" hit the charts followed by the beautiful and moving "People Get Ready," a song considered by many musicians to be one of the finest soul songs of all time. Songs like "Amen" continued their spiritual message. Members of the Rock and Roll Hall of Fame and the Grammy Hall of Fame, the Impressions remain in good voice and still do some performing today. (Author's collection.).

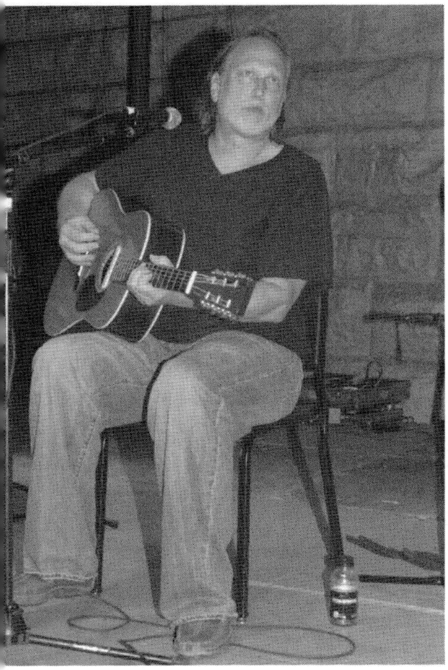

Roger Alan Wade
The sounds of singing in the mountain air of Beckley, West Virginia, still ring through Roger Alan Wade's memories of summer, when as a boy, he first felt the real power of music at his family reunions. After graduating from Brainerd High, he took a job at the Happy Valley Dairy "busting my knuckles" on the cold milk containers for three years. But it was one night when he went downtown to see the great Waylon Jennings that he knew he wanted to sing country music. He bought a guitar the next day and played in Gatlinburg then moved to Nashville, where he worked as a songwriter for Curb Records. His songs were picked up by Waylon, George Jones, and Johnny Cash. When Hank Williams Jr. recorded his song "Country State of Mind" and it went to No. 1, Wade's career was established. Since that time, he has continued to make music that goes from traditional honky-tonk country with a dash of humor to more reflective pieces like "The Light Outlives the Star." Now back in Chattanooga, Wade hosts a weekly show on Sirius XM radio's Outlaw Channel called *Big Ass Happy Family Jubilee* with his cousin, television personality Johnny Knoxville. (Author's collection.)

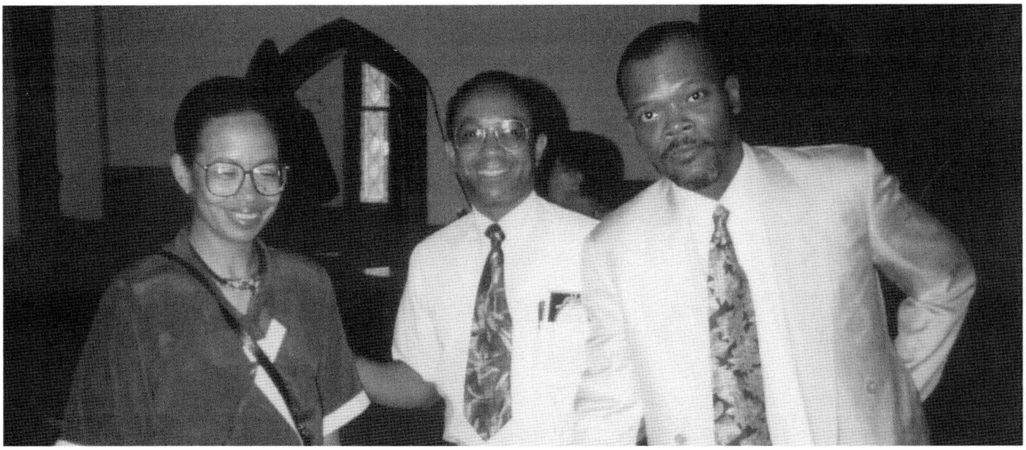

Samuel L. Jackson on Lookout Street
Samuel L. Jackson grew up on Lookout Street in Chattanooga. As a youngster, he attended East Fifth Street School, a segregated school on the west side of town during a time when much of that residential neighborhood was being destroyed by urban renewal. He attended Riverside High School—now known as Chattanooga School for Arts and Sciences—on Third Street near Erlanger Hospital. There, he played French horn and trumpet in the school orchestra. Jackson was accepted at Morehouse College, the prestigious black college in Atlanta, during the late 1960s and was much affected by the tumult of the civil rights movement. He served as an usher at the funeral of Dr. Martin Luther King Jr. It was there that he gave himself over to acting, though it was many years, after many trials, before his star finally rose with performances in *Jungle Fever*, *Pulp Fiction*, and *Jurassic Park*. An iconic figure on the screen around the world, he still visits Chattanooga from time to time to see relatives and old friends. Here, Jackson (right) is pictured with his long-time friend Booker Scruggs II and his niece Deborah Walton at the Bethlehem Wiley Methodist Church on Lookout Street. (Courtesy Booker T. Scruggs II.)

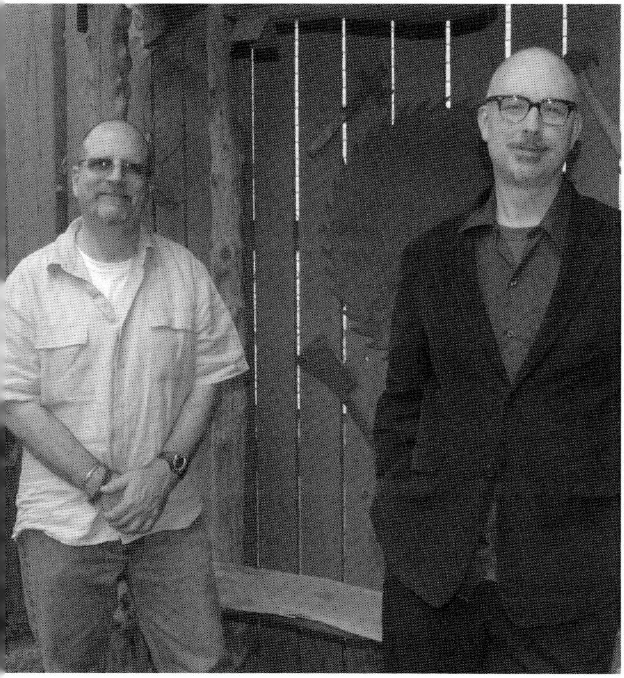

Shaking Ray Levi Society
Dennis Palmer and Bob Stagner "go back a ways" as they say down South. Friends since they were six, they formed the Shaking Ray Levi Society to bring nontraditional music to town—people like Derek Bailey, John Zorn, and David Greenberger. Focused on improvisational music, they seek to tap into the moment of creation as heard in the free play of sound and rhythm in their performances. As such, the two were the first American group signed to Incus Records, a respected European free-jazz label and are included in the *Penguin Guide to Jazz*. Palmer, a keyboardist and Moog synthesizer devotee, and Stagner, a drummer/percussionist, make community outreach a part of their mission as well. Their sessions in schools and in hospitals with healing work are well known in Chattanooga for the joy and the learning that they bring. What's a "Shaking Ray Levi?" It can be understood as another iteration of Johnny Appleseed, sprinkling seeds of "sonic goodness" to all those with ears to hear. (Author's collection.)

INDEX